STANFORD UNIVERSITY PUBLICATIONS
UNIVERSITY SERIES

HISTORY, ECONOMICS AND
POLITICAL SCIENCE
VOLUME I   NUMBER 1

THE
GERMAN REVOLUTION
1918-1919

RALPH HASWELL LUTZ

AMS PRESS
NEW YORK

CONTENTS

CHAPTER I.
THE COLLAPSE OF THE GERMAN EMPIRE

CHAPTER II.
BEGINNINGS OF THE REVOLUTION

CHAPTER III.
THE NINTH OF NOVEMBER

CHAPTER IV.
SOCIALISM AND SOCIALIZATION

CHAPTER V.
THE STRUGGLE OF PARTIES FOR POWER

CHAPTER VI.

The Convocation of the National Assembly

CHAPTER VII.

Revolutionary Problems

CHAPTER VIII.

Consolidation of the Republic

CHAPTER IX.

The Acceptance of the Treaty of Peace

CHAPTER X.

The Adoption of the Republican Constitution

After the Revolution.

PREFACE

The German revolutionary movement of 1918 and 1919 not only destroyed the Bismarckian Empire but fundamentally altered the life and institutions of the German people. Although it has as yet received little attention from historians, a knowledge of the revolution is essential to an understanding of contemporary Germany and of those economic and political problems resulting from the defeat of the German Empire in the World War.

This monograph is a study of the origins, events, tendencies, and results of the German Revolution based upon personal observations and an examination of the documentary and other printed materials available. As a member of the American Military Mission in Berlin under the command of General George H. Harries, from March to August, 1919, the author had opportunities to observe the revolutionary struggles in the capital as well as in the several states.

The principal sources of authority for this work are, however, the materials in the German section of the Hoover War Library, and include the collection of German Government Documents and Delegation Propaganda secured from the Berlin Foreign Office in August, 1919, by Professor E. D. Adams. In addition this collection contains books, pamphlets, newspapers, periodicals, posters, and manuscripts all of exceptional value for a study of the German Revolution.

R. H. L.

I.

THE COLLAPSE OF THE GERMAN EMPIRE

The Military Defeat

The belief in her imperialistic mission was the fundamental error which caused the tragic fate of modern Germany. After three years of successful but indecisive warfare, the German empire at the close of the campaigns of 1917 was confronted with a new enemy, America, which hastened to the aid of England, France, Italy, and Belgium. The sudden collapse of Russia appeared, however, to give Germany the means of ending the war in the west before the arrival of large American forces. The disastrous defeat of the Italian army by the central powers in the autumn of 1917 seemed the prelude to the final military tragedy.[1]

Throughout the winter of 1917-18 every preparation was made by the German General Staff to bring the war on the western front to a victorious conclusion. Veteran German divisions were brought from Russia to re-enforce the imperial armies in France and Belgium. Tactical and strategical plans for the German troops were perfected in the training areas behind the front. Field Marshal von Hindenburg and General Ludendorff were at the head of the German forces. Covered by the authority of the Kaiser as Supreme War Lord of Germany, they were the absolute masters of the army and nation, exercising a military dictatorship which was unparalleled in the course of modern history. They were confident of the success of their military plans and believed in a decisive victory which would end the war. Nevertheless they realized the seriousness of the military and political situation of Germany, and they neglected no opportunity to raise the morale of the troops and the home population. Propaganda against defeatists, profiteers, and agitators was carried on in the interior of Germany, while morale officers and civilian speakers and workers, all organized under the Fatherland Instruction System, were used to strengthen the morale of the army and the will to victory.[2] In a confidential order of July 29, 1917, General Ludendorff wrote: "The German army is, through the spirit which inflames it, superior to its enemies and a strong support for its allies."[3]

The decisive blow to the Entente, which was to give Germany victory, commenced the twenty-first of March. General Pershing has stated that

---

[1] Freytag-Loringhoven, "Politik und Kriegführung," 251.

[2] Nicolai, "Nachrichtendienst Presse und Volkstimmung im Weltkrieg," 113–136.

[3] Ludendorff, "Urkunden der Obersten Heeresleitung," 271.

the German army which began this series of attacks on the Allies was the mightiest force which the world had ever seen.[4] As the first offensive drove the British back upon Amiens, a wave of enthusiasm swept over Germany. The morale of the advancing army was at its height, and the ranks, stiffened by the veteran eastern troops, were confident of ultimate success. The second offensive west of Lille on April 9 brought the Germans to the heights dominating the channel ports. In May the army group of the German Crown Prince advanced over the Chemin des Dames, and on June 9 an attack on the Compiegne front widened the sector there. On June 15 the Germans commenced their decisive offensive on the western front by striking at Rheims and the Marne. In the second battle of the Marne the German empire put forth its utmost strength. The allied line, despite local reverses, held while Marshal Foch swiftly and secretly prepared for a counter offensive, which, opening on the eighteenth of July, marked the turning of the tide. After four years of war the German empire was confronted with inevitable military defeat.[5]

As early as May, 1918, General Ludendorff must have known that a victorious peace was impossible. The failure to reach a decision in the first offensive made a definitive victory problematical.[6] By the first of June the Bavarian Crown Prince was convinced of the seriousness of the military situation and wrote to the imperial chancellor urging immediate action to save the empire.[7] Possessing supreme military power and exercising at the same time a virtual dictatorship over the empire, Ludendorff nevertheless continued the struggle with the Allies. He trusted to the fortunes of war, to the help of a *Deus ex machina,* and to his ability to weaken the allied will to victory. Ludendorff also underestimated the ever-increasing strength of the American Expeditionary Forces.[8] On June 11 the Prussian Minister of War declared in the Reichstag that the Foch reserve army did not exist any more.[9]

The failure of the Germans in the second battle of the Marne is the first cause of the German revolution. The reports of the success of Marshal Foch in July, 1918, reacted upon Germany with telling force.[10] On July 21

---

[4] *Ibid.,* 492–496, contains excerpts from the report of General Pershing.

[5] Helfferich, "Der Weltkrieg," 3: 522–526. Von Moser, "Kurzer Strategischer Uberblick über den Weltkrieg, 1914–1918." 110–120. Stegemann, "Geschichte des Krieges," 4: 634–637. Valentin, "Deutschlands Aussenpolitik, 1900–1918," 374.

[6] Von Lerch, "Kritische Betrachtungen über die letzten Kaempfe an der Deutschen Westfront," 4.

[7] Hertling, "Ein Jahr in der Reichskanzlei," 139.

[8] Ludendorff, *op. cit.,* 360–367, contains Ludendorff's defense of his intelligence reports.

[9] Menke-Glückert, "Die November Revolution," 6.

[10] Von Zwehl, "Die Schlachten im Sommer 1918 an der Westfront." Erzberger, "Erlebnisse im Weltkrieg," 313–326. August Failures. Immanuel, "Siege und Niederlagen im Weltkriege," 133–134.

Ludendorff announced that the German offensives had not been successful, but that the high command was confident. On the first of August the Kaiser declared: "We know that the hardest part lies behind us." But the continued successes of the Allies left no doubt in the minds of the German General Staff that the tide had turned. On the thirteenth of August the Emperor of Austria appeared at German General Headquarters and discussed the terrible situation of the dual monarchy, which was unable to continue the war.[11]

Ludendorff states in his memoirs that after the successful English offensive on the eighth of August, he realized that the front of his armies might be broken at any time. From this day he traces the beginning of the final collapse. Yet the attack of August 8 was but a single phase of the general allied advance. It was at the Marne rather than before the Hindenburg line that the German General Staff and armies first began to waver. Not only did the German intelligence section fail in the second Marne battle to locate the reserve army of Foch in the Villers Cotteret Forest, but the Fatherland Instruction Service also failed to maintain the spirits of the troops. After the eighteenth of July the morale of the German armies slowly but surely declined, because the promised German peace now seemed impossible.[12] Field Marshal von Hindenburg had declared: "The army will do its duty and conquer for the German people and Fatherland a foundation for a strong and lasting peace. Hard are the times, but sure is the victory."[13] Neither the army nor the people could, however, see even one possibility of success, and consequently gradually lost the power to continue the unequal struggle. General von Freytag-Loringhoven states: "Against their superiority more in technical means of warfare, rather than in man power, our west army was unable to maintain the gains of the spring of 1918."[14] Certain German writers have maintained since the armistice, that the March offensive should never have been undertaken and that the German armies should have stood on the defensive behind the line Antwerp-Metz.[15] Colonel Bauer stated definitely in his attempt to explain the German defeat that this line could have been held throughout

[11] *Auswaertiges Amt. Nachrichten-Abteilung Wochenberichte der Auslandslektorate*, 1918, Vom 24 bis 30 Juli, Nr. 30, 3753–3754, 3810, contains excellent summaries of conditions in the entente states.

[12] *Vorwaerts*, March 23, 1919. Scheidemann, in "Der Zusammenbruch," 185, cites a Division Order of the Forty-first Infantry Division, August 14, 1918, as evidence of declining morale. Foerster, in "Zur Beurteilung der deutschen Kriegsfuehrung," vehemently attacks the army and the Prussian propaganda.

[13] Stählin, "Hindenburg," 32.

[14] Freytag-Loringhoven, "Politik und Kriegführung," 251.

[15] Runkel, "Deutsche Revolution," 4.

the winter.[16] Ludendorff, however, was prepared on September 28, 1918, to retreat to the German borders and if necessary recommence hostilities there.[17] Freytag-Loringhoven asserts clearly that a continuation of the war was impossible.[18]

The fundamental miscalculation of the German General Staff was concerning the value of American aid to the Allies.[19] Unrestricted submarine warfare was decided upon by the high command only after careful and deliberate calculations of all eventualities. The success of submarine warfare was exaggerated and the German leaders asserted that only a few American volunteer corps would appear on the western front.[20] Hindenburg stated that the war would be over before American aid could arrive, while Ludendorff pinned his faith to submarine warfare. "The American military aid," the General Staff announced, "still stands in the hazy distance and if it should really come some time, it will not then be in a position to alter anything in the situation upon the European battleground." Admiral von Tirpitz exclaimed in January, 1918: "America's military help is and remains a phantom." [21] In 1917 the German General Staff regarded all American preparations as unimportant. Ludendorff said: "The American danger is not great. We will conquer, if the people stand in close unity behind our army." On July 2, 1918, the German General Staff reported that there were eight American divisions on the western front and a total of eighteen in Europe. Ludendorff admitted at last: "It cannot be doubted that the will of America is to place its entire strength in the service of the war." [22]

Another factor in the military collapse of the empire was the weakening of the morale of the army by internal and foreign propaganda. Both the Germans and the Allies had since 1914 sought to destroy the fighting value of their antagonists by clever propaganda. As the German offensives failed to reach a decision in the spring of 1918, the enemy propaganda lowered their morale. In May, 1918, 84,000 pamphlets were turned in by German soldiers to their officers, while by July the number had risen to 300,000. These pamphlets, gradually improved in tone, encouraged desertion. Among them were printed letters of German prisoners in allied prison camps describing their good food and others stating that the fight was hopeless. Often the Allies deluged the German lines with

[16] Bäuer, "Konnten wir den Krieg vermeiden, gewinnen, abbrechen?" 53.

[17] Ludendorff, "Das Friedens-und Waffenstillstandsangebot," 11.

[18] Freytag-Loringhoven, "Politik und Kriegführung," 252.

[19] Bernstorff, "Deutschland und Amerika," 11.

[20] Ludendorff, "Urkunden der Obersten Heeresleitung," 323. Binder, "Was wir als Kriegsberichterstatter nicht sagen durften," 29–30.

[21] Gumbel, "Vier Jahre Luege," 29.

[22] Ludendorff, *Supra*, 365, 414.

reprints of German and Swiss papers and pamphlets attacking the German emperor and the Junkers. The Kaiser was accused in French pamphlets of having instigated the war, and the Germans were therefore encouraged to form a republic. Propaganda pamphlets stated that whoever surrendered and gave the word "republic" would not be treated by the French as a prisoner of war.[23]

More important than the enemy propaganda was the attempt of certain groups of Independent Socialists to undermine the fighting power of the army. Since the failure of the general strike in Germany in January, 1918, these groups worked systematically for the overthrow of German militarism. Thousands of strikers who were sent to the fighting lines helped to spread this propaganda among the troops. Deserters organized with false papers worked among the front-line troops.[24] The divisions which were brought from the eastern front had seen the Russian army robbed of its leaders almost over night, and had been consequently profoundly impressed with the methods of the Bolsheviki. These troops as well as the few Bolshevist agitators set a bad example in the west army. Ludendorff exclaims: "The revolution from above and below dealt the German army the death blow, while it fought with the foe."[25] The grievances of the German soldiers against their officers were of course heightened both by enemy and Socialist propaganda until the hatred of their leaders became by November, 1918, one of the characteristic features of the German army. All national armies are of course incapable of fighting long wars. The mere presence in the ranks of older classes of soldiers ultimately causes general discontent.

Primarily, because of the continued allied victories, the declining morale of the imperial army, the collapse of Bulgaria, and the imminent destruction of Germany's other allies, the General Staff by September 28, 1918, came to regard the struggle as hopeless.[26] Ludendorff, fearing that his front would be broken at any moment and the entire army involved in the disaster, suddenly dispatched an ultimatum to Berlin demanding

---

[23] *War Information Library, British Ministry of Information,* contains an excellent collection of allied propaganda literature printed in the German language for distribution among German troops.

[24] Freytag-Loringhoven, "Was danken wir unserem Offizierkorps?," 86.

[25] Ludendorff, "Urkunden der Obersten Heeresleitung," 581. General von Wrisberg in "Der Weg zur Revolution" agrees with this view and attacks Edward Bernstein for stating in "Die deutsche Revolution" that the imperial army was not affected by the revolutionary movement. Kantorowicz in "Der Offiziershass im deutschen Heer" states that the so-called revolution was a general mutiny of the army. "We call," states Rathenau in "Kritik der dreifachen Revolution," 9, "the German revolution the general strike of a defeated army."

[26] Hindenburg, "Aus Meinem Leben," 392. Ludendorff, "Das Friedens-und Waffenstillstandsangebot," 10–11.

that the civil government of Germany request an immediate armistice of the Allies.[27] This demand arrived in Berlin in the midst of a chancellor crisis. Was it the result of a nervous collapse of Ludendorff? Since the revolution a controversy has developed in Germany over the significance of this move of Ludendorff. The facts are that before Prince Max had actually assumed office, Ludendorff dispatched this demand for an armistice to Berlin, and that on the afternoon of October 3 Hindenburg and a major of the General Staff appeared before Prince Max and explained the precarious condition of the front.[28] Ludendorff demanded peace because he no longer trusted the powers of resistance of his armies. Frantically the ministers asked for time, but the emphatic answer of the military party was: "No." Under the pressure of the army solely, the German civil government began the armistice negotiations. The dictatorship of Ludendorff was powerful enough to force his will upon the civil government.[29]

Now the General Staff had been since August 29, 1916, not only the supreme military but the supreme political power as well.[30] It had directed the war on all the fronts and time after time made important political decisions. In the last analysis, the successors of Moltke had waged a war of conquest. Colonel Bauer, the confidential man of Ludendorff, states that the supreme command rejected the idea of a defensive war and changed its character to one of conquest.[31] Admiral von Hintze has testified that even in August, 1918, the General Staff could not agree to the giving up of its annexionist plans, as well as to the complete restoration of Belgium! Just before the breakdown of the German General Staff, Hindenburg said: "The peace in the west shall not also be a weak peace."[32] Thus the policy of might abroad, coupled with unrest at home, hurled the empire into the abyss. As late as October 17 Ludendorff demanded that unrestricted submarine warfare should be maintained in full force.[33]

After the armistice a great controversy arose in Germany over the causes of the imperial military collapse and the outbreak of the revolu-

[27] Von Stein, "Erlebnisse und Betrachtungen aus der Zeit des Weltkrieges," 192. Immanuel, *op. cit.*, 138–139, 173–174.

[28] Nowak, "Der Sturz der Mittelmaechte," 252–254.

[29] Scheidemann, "Der Zusammenbruch," 184. Steinhausen, "Die Grundfehler des Krieges und der Generalstab," 27. Wrisberg, "Heer und Heimat 1914–1918."

[30] *Berlin Press Review,* issued daily by American Military Mission, Berlin. Letter of Hindenburg assuming responsibility, July 5, 1919.

[31] *Preussische Jahrbücher,* August, 1919.

[32] *Freiheit,* May 16, 1919.

[33] *Vossische Zeitung,* March 16, 1919, Ludendorff's letter of March 12, 1919, to Scheidemann.

tion.[34] Ludendorff and many militarists, as well as a great group of
Pan-Germans, attempted to explain away the military débâcle. It is a
remarkable characteristic of German militarism, that, in the very hour of
its final defeat, it raised the cry that the army had been betrayed in the rear
and stabbed in the back.[35] The Pan-Germans audaciously informed the
nation that the demand of Ludendorff for negotiations with President
Wilson was made because of the terrible political situation of Germany.[36]
They scoffed at the story of the nervous collapse of Ludendorff. General
von Boehn, commander of the Seventh Army, published a declaration that
the collapse was due to the conspiracies among the people and the home
front and not to the defeat of the front-line troops.[37] Colonel Bauer
naïvely states that it was necessary to make the peace offer in order to
explain to the people that the Allies would not grant a just peace.[38] Ludendorff also makes this astounding assertion. Even Freytag-Loringhoven
stated of the German army: "It really did not succumb to the superiority
and to the armed blows of its enemies, but, as is well known, to other
attacks." He admits, however, that the German people curse militarism
as the cause of the loss of the war.[39]

After the armistice Scheidemann publicly attacked Ludendorff for
prolonging the war, for failing to agree to a peace of justice, and for
leading the army like a gambler to final defeat. Ludendorff's expression,
"I regard myself as a *Hasardspieler*", was hurled against himself.[40] The
German revolutionary government proved to the satisfaction of all but
the parties of the right that Ludendorff had demanded, on the afternoon
of October 1, the commencement of peace negotiations, that he had admitted the front might collapse at any hour, and that he had told Minister
Solf that he could not hold the front three months longer.[41] Hugo Haase,
leader of the Independent Socialists, stated that Vice Chancellor von
Payer surprised the party leaders in a confidential meeting with the news
that the German army stood on the verge of collapse and that the army
leaders, Hindenburg and Ludendorff, had requested the government to

---

[34] Schwarte, "Die Militaerischen Lehren des Grossen Krieges," 459–477, contains a
bibliography of this literature.

[35] Balck, "Entwickelung der Taktik im Weltkrieg," 319. Bauer, "Der Grosse Krieg
in Feld und Heimat," 285–294. "Kritik des Weltkrieges," von Einem Generalstaebler,
245. Von Zwehl, "Der Dolchstoss in den Ruecken des Siegreichen Heeres."

[36] *Deutsche Tageszeitung*, August 2, 1919.

[37] Von Hoensbroech. "Zurueck zur Monarchie," 14.

[38] Bauer, "Konnten wir den Krieg Vermeiden, Gewinnen, Abbrechen?" 54.

[39] Freytag-Loringhoven, "Was danken wir unserem Offizierskorps?" 1.

[40] *Berlin Press Review*, March 26, 1919.

[41] *Berliner Tageblatt*, August 2, 1919.

bring about an armistice without delay.[42]   Like the majority parties, even
the Independent Socialists were totally unprepared for the news of the
impending military disaster.[43]

In the summer of 1919 the German government finally published a
White Book on the events leading to the armistice, in order to combat the
conservative and monarchist propaganda and to justify the action of the
revolutionary government in admitting its defeat by signing the armistice.[44]   These documents reveal the utter helplessness of the German High
Command in the face of the continuous allied advances, and they show
clearly that only the armistice saved the wreck of the imperial army from
a disaster which would have been unparalleled in history.   Only the
Athenians before Syracuse, or the French at Moscow, showed the indecision
and lack of appreciation of the real military situation which the Germans
evinced in the summer of 1918.

In a military state a successful revolution is only possible when the
army is permeated with the spirit of revolt.   Otherwise it remains a
permanent obstacle to a violent change of government irrespective of
the weakness of the established régime.   That the failure of the German
army leaders to gain the promised victory would bring about a military
revolution was clear to all.   The collapse of the army meant *par conse-
quent* the collapse of the bourgeois—liberal order of life and the emerg-
ence of the fourth estate with its idea of socialism from political, social
and economic repression, to power.[45]   The German soldiers, deprived of
their martial spirit of 1914 by the unsuccessful peace offensives, the military defeats and the desperate conditions at home, had lost the consciousness of fighting for a good cause.[46]

Forced by military necessity to sue for peace, the German military
leaders turned to President Wilson, hoping by invoking the fourteen
points to escape from destruction.[47]   That they accepted the President's conditions of peace, at which they and the German people had openly scoffed,
reveals the desperateness of their position.   Concerning this appeal to
President Wilson, General Groener wrote: "At any rate we did not
lighten the rôle which we had expected of him." [48]

---

[42] Haase, "Reichstagsreden," 184.

[43] Vetter, "Der Zusammenbruch der Westfront," 14.

[44] "Vorgeschichte des Waffenstillstandes." British official translation, "The History of Events Immediately Preceding the Armistice." Ludendorff published his defense against the accusations of the "White Book" in three pamphlets, August–September, 1919, which are included in "Urkunden der Obersten Heeresleitung."

[45] Moeckel, "Das Deutsche Bürgertum und die Revolution," 16.

[46] Nowak, "Der Weg zur Katastrophe," 288–289.

[47] Valentin, *Supra*, 375–383.

[48] Groener, "Die Liquidation des Weltkrieges," in *Preussische Jahrbücher*, February, 1920.

The Internal Collapse

As the powers of resistance and the morale of the German armies on the western front collapsed in the autumn of 1918 before the steady blows of the allied armies, so the internal front crumbled when the German nation gave up the unequal struggle after four years of false hopes, privations, and social, economic, and moral decay.[49] This collapse was all the more dramatic since the nation had entered upon the war with universal enthusiasm because of its belief that it had been attacked. From the Socialists who voted the war credits, to the Pan-Germans who joyously shouted, *"Vae Victis"*, the entire nation had united about the person of the last emperor to conquer a place in the world which would be worthy of Germany's imperial destiny.

Notwithstanding the superiority of Germany's war preparations over those of her enemies, innumerable mistakes were made at the outset. The one-sided adoption of the Schlieffen plan of crushing France while Russia was held off in the east proved a failure, not due to the fact that it was carried out by Epigoni, but to the lack of sufficient military strength and to the unparalleled resistance of the French.[50] Under the delusion that the war would be a short one, men and matériel were ruthlessly wasted during the first year in an attempt to reach a quick decision. Neither Austria, Bulgaria, nor Turkey possessed that military preparation which had been indicated by German General Staff reports.[51]

As the war progressed the powers of the General Staff increased, while the imperial ministry of Chancellor von Bethmann-Hollweg degenerated into a secondary government. After the failures at Verdun and the Somme, and the entrance of Rumania into the war, the German General Headquarters became the supreme military and political power in *Mittel Europa*. The nation lacked at this crisis a Bismarck, and the results were far reaching. Political life suffered under the military dictatorship. Countless sources of discontent were created by the enforcement of the innumerable war measures and regulations, while the varied policies of the German corps district commanders destroyed the advantages of this devolution of military authority.

More acute than the gradual political and military degeneration of the empire was the collapse of the economic life. Moltke, in emphasizing

---

[49] Steinhausen, "Die Schuld der Heimat," 56–79.

[50] Ludendorff and von Stein are largely responsible for the spreading out (*Verwässerung*) by the General Staff of the Schlieffen plan.

[51] Von Loebell, "Aus Deutschlands Ruinen," 30–31. The military and economic value of the German alliance with these states was, however, emphasized by Naumann in "Mitteleuropa." This great work was read extensively by the soldiers at the front. Cf. Oncken, "Das alte und das neue Mitteleuropa," for an excellent discussion of the probable relations of the empire with the great powers after the war.

the importance of agriculture, said: "The German empire will perish without a shot being fired if German agriculture collapses." [52]   Despite rigorous laws and the organization of a central food control, the food supply of Germany gradually declined, although it was supplemented by contributions from the occupied territory.   Contrary to official reports, the allied blockade and insufficient harvests reduced *Mittel Europa* to the verge of starvation.

As the war progressed, German agriculture felt the lack of agricultural laborers, horses, fertilizing material, and agricultural machinery. Official rules hindered rational work, while the maximum prices which were enforced throughout Germany only encouraged contraband trade and smuggling.   Critics were not lacking who declared that the conservative agrarian Pan-German system had perhaps failed worse in the field of war food control than in that of political and military leadership.[53]   As the allied blockade cut off the supply of raw materials from overseas, and as the reserve stocks were gradually depleted, the effect upon German industry became noticeable.   This was partly alleviated by the rapid development of arms and munition factories, which resulted in the growth of a great war industry.   The workmen secured higher wages, numerous strikes added to the seriousness of the national situation, and the constant economic agitation stirred up class hatred.[54]

From an economic standpoint, the most fatal step taken during the entire war was the adoption of the Hindenburg program.   This aimed to get the last ounce of economic strength out of the German people, and, although for a time it seemed to place the war industries abreast of the demands of the military authorities, it ultimately lead to economic destruction.   Wages were raised unnaturally by it, while the erection of factories upon non-economic sites lead to a shift of population and the creation of altered standards of life which produced a dangerous reaction upon the working classes.[55]

The political decline of the empire became apparent at the end of 1916. The peace offensive and the negotiations with President Wilson reveal a political incompetency scarcely equalled in the annals of Modern Europe. In January, 1917, only a portion of the government was convinced of the necessity of a peace of reconciliation.   Dr. Solf at that time could not agree to the indemnification of Belgium, which he finally accepted in August, 1918.   At the very moment when President Wilson was working

[52] Braun, "Kann Deutschland Durch Hunger Besiegt Werden?"

[53] Hoff, "Am Abgrund Vorueber, III."

[54] Bauer, "Konnten wir den Krieg vermeiden, gewinnen, abbrechen?" 40–43.

[55] *Taegliche Rundschau,* March 26, 1919.   Speech of Prussian Finance Minister Suedekum, 18–23.

for "a peace without victory", a settlement which would have maintained the integrity of the German empire, German statesmen through their foreign policy were destroying the moral credit of the nation abroad.[56] On January 29, 1917, the German Chancellor von Bethmann-Hollweg, with the approval of Ludendorff and Hindenburg, telegraphed the German terms of peace to Count Bernstorff, with instructions to deliver them, together with the note concerning unrestricted submarine warfare, to President Wilson. These peace terms provided for German annexations on the eastern and western fronts and for an enlargement of the German colonial empire. They were supported by the German political parties, including the Social Democrats. Scheidemann had informed Ludendorff that he was not opposed to the necessary annexations of territory nor to the proposed war indemnities.[57] Thus the adoption of unrestricted submarine warfare at the behest of the military dictators was the prelude to the general political collapse of Germany.

The empire was hurled to destruction primarily by the Pan-Germans, the politicians of the Fatherland party, and groups of annexationists who developed the war aims of the empire toward the goal of world conquest. Gothein asserts: "The blame for the moral collapse rests in the first instance upon those who sullied the pure thought of the war of national defense with demands for conquests." [58] From the first days of August, 1914, until the November revolution, Germany was deluged by the annexationists with pamphlets which either knowingly or unknowingly falsified the real situation. A great literature sprang up about the causes and the beginnings of the world war. To conceal the character of the fighting on the front became an art with German publicists, while the beginnings of unrestricted submarine warfare and the entrance of America were hopelessly distorted for the benefit of the German public.

As early as 1915 large economic groups in Germany were bent upon annexations. A memoir of the League of Landowners, Central Organization of German Industry, League of Industrials, German Peasant League, and National German Middle Class League, which was presented to the Imperial Chancellor, demanded annexations to secure the economic future of Germany. Intellectuals such as Meinecke, Schaefer, and Schumacher, later gave their assent to this plan.[59] These demands hastened

---

[56] Baumgarten, "Die Schuld am Deutschen Zusammenbruch," 23. That a secretary of state for foreign affairs in the midst of negotiations with a friendly power should have written such a document as the Zimmerman note is sufficient evidence of the real character of this imperial government.

[57] Ludendorff, "Urkunden der Obersten Heeresleitung," 342–344, 416.

[58] Gothein, "Warum Verloren wir den Krieg?" 92.

[59] *Freiheit*, May 16, 1919.

the collapse.[60]   Among the German publicists, Harden in 1915 demanded unrestricted submarine warfare and recommended Tirpitz for the post of chancellor of the empire.[61]   The foremost Pan-German demands were: unrestricted submarine warfare; the extension of the frontiers against Russia; the development of the idea of *Mittel Europa;* the collection of huge war indemnities; and the seizure of a greater colonial empire. Belgium was not to be allowed to regain her independence.   Economic control by Germany was declared important in order to prevent the exploitation of Belgium by her former allies.   Other writers maintained that Flanders and *Wallonien* should become separate protectorates of Germany, with the coast of Flanders under the immediate control of the empire.[62]   Meanwhile the failure of Germanization in Alsace-Lorraine was noted, and fiery demands were made during the war that the French influence should be completely uprooted.   The brutal tones of the Pan-Germans in this debate are characteristic of their general policy.[63]   These groups violently denounced the peace resolutions of the Reichstag.   They accused the *Internationale* of being a tool of their enemies.   In September, 1917, Kapp, von Tirpitz, von Wangenheim, and others founded the German Fatherland Party, destined to surpass all earlier war parties in demands for annexations and indemnities.[64]   The victory course of this party gained for it many adherents among the educated classes, but the great middle class and the proletariat were unmoved by the wild projects of the Fatherland group.

Antithetical to the Pan-Germans were the Independent Socialists. Their steady development since the middle period of the war was one of the most important factors in the fall of German imperialism.   Their policy, which was originally one of strict Marxism, became by 1918 decidedly revolutionary.   Developing from a group of Social Democrats who in 1914 opposed the voting of the war credits by the party, the Independent Socialists became an organization which regarded the war as ruinous for Germany.   Since the summer of 1917 their leaders had planned to overthrow the empire by a revolution.[65]   In this year the beginnings of revolutionary agitation are noticeable among strikers, particularly the metal workers.   In 1917 the seceding Social Democrats met at Gotha and founded the Independent Social Democratic Party of Germany.

---

[60] Lehmann-Russbueldt, "Warum Erfolgte der Zusammenbruch an der Westfront?"

[61] *Preussische Jahrbücher,* December, 1919.

[62] Zitelmann, "Das Schicksal Belgiens beim Friedensschluss." Wintzer, "Das neue Belgien."

[63] Berger, "Die Ursachen des Zusammenbruchs des Deutschtums in Elsass-Lothringen"; Hoppe, "Elsass-Lothringen," *Preussische Jahrbuecher,* January, 1919, 110.

[64] Deutsche Vaterlands-Partei, "Deutsche Ziele."

[65] Menke-Glückert, "Die November Revolution," 14.

It rapidly became the Radical Socialist Party and attacked the Majority Socialists as the servants of the expansionists. The leaders of the party were active in the great general strike of January, 1918. Their failure upon this field resulted in redoubled activity against the empire. The Independents declared: "Whoever protested against the German policy of force during the war was sent to prison, the penitentiary, or the trenches." [66]

The January strike was ruthlessly suppressed by the government with the effective aid of the majority parties, which then believed in a German victory. Thereupon the Independents concluded that only the armed rising of the workers would free the nation from the menace of imperialism and capitalism. Emil Barth, one of their leaders, organized a revolutionary committee, purchased arms, and secured the coöperation of Joffe, the soviet ambassador to Germany. Barth declared on the ninth of November: "Through my hands went for revolutionary propaganda and preparation several hundred thousand marks, which I received solely from comrades."

The Independent leader Vater of Madgeburg immortalized himself in Germany by boasting that the revolution had been systematically planned since January 25, 1918. Although the conservatives maintain that a widespread conspiracy existed against the empire, there is little evidence to support this view.[67] The Independent Socialists as a party failed to commence organized revolutionary activity until the outbreak was inevitable. According to Haase's statements, he first learned on November 9 that Barth had purchased weapons for the expected revolution of the proletariat. The national committee of his party had no connection with Joffe and was engaged only in the spreading of its own propaganda.[68] As late as the October 23 meeting of the Independent Socialists of Berlin the question of preparations for the coming revolution was discussed and several leaders protested against a policy which steered toward revolution.[69]

It is clear that the Pan-Germans by their wild demands for more sacrifices upon the altars of conquest were driving the nation, already weary of imperialism, to desperation. The Independent Socialists hoped after the failure of the January strikes to overthrow the empire by force. However, the definite collapse of the internal front was not due to the machinations of either party, but to other causes.

Public opinion gradually turned against the imperial government as the nation entered the fourth year of the war. The middle class, the

[66] *Freiheit,* March 24, 1919.

[67] *Taegliche Rundschau,* December 15, 1918.

[68] Zimmermann, "Der Zusammenbruch," 7–8.

[69] Däumig, "Das Raetesystem," 23–24.

small officials, and the industrial workers lead a precarious existence in the cities and towns. Owing to the breakdown of transportation, difficulties in supplying the population with coal became universal. There was lack of electric light and power in the cities and a scarcity of petroleum in the country. In 1918 the government established the meatless weeks, which heightened the effect of food control. To add to the general bitterness, contraband trade flourished, and, although the imperial currency depreciated, the wealthy class and the bureaucrats of the cities secured butter, eggs, and flour from the country. Hatred of the rich developed from month to month. The denunciation of war societies was general; they were accused of working only for themselves and their friends. The war orders were so numerous and conflicting that they were generally violated. Public morality and general moral standards declined. The most striking phase of the internal collapse was the degeneration of the efficient and honest Prussian and German official class. Bribery developed in a bureaucracy which before the war was impeccable.

While the great industrial corporations were declaring large dividends, the Social-Democratic press in ironical phrases was calling attention to the increasing misery of the masses. Many articles of household necessity were confiscated during the war. A petty bitterness was aroused in the middle class by the confiscation of door knobs, lightning rods, brass curtain-poles, and copper utensils. In agricultural regions the peasant houses were searched and articles of necessity taken away. As in all the warring countries, profiteers flourished; graft and greed for wealth were everywhere.[70]

Although the nation had borne these hardships with fortitude in the days of victory, it became exhausted when the military situation began to change. Realizing the danger, the imperial government endeavored by skillful propaganda to raise the declining national morale. The great speakers' offensive, commenced in the summer of 1918, is the final effort of militarism and imperialism to save itself. Undersecretary of State Solf on the twentieth of August, 1918, spoke on German war aims and the restoration of Belgium. On August 22 Prince Max of Baden delivered an able address to the chambers of Baden upon the celebration of the hundredth anniversay of the constitution of that grand duchy.

Meanwhile the allied advances in the west had revealed to the nation the extent of the military danger. The English successes against Cambrai caused Hindenburg to issue the pronouncement of September 4, warning against enemy propaganda and stating that he could force peace in the west in spite of the Americans. "Defend thyself, German army and German native land", was the new order of the day. On September 5 Ludendorff declared that he could handle the Americans, while the Crown

---

[70] Giesecke, "Im Kampf an der Inneren Front."

Prince stated that the word victory meant that Germany would maintain itself and not be overpowered.[71]

That the internal situation was indeed precarious was revealed by the speech of William II to the workmen of the Krupp factories at Essen. In an address full of pathos, the Kaiser called upon the workers to rally around him, but the assent of the Essen workmen was not the "yes" of the German proletariat. Vice Chancellor von Payer then declared on September 12 at Stuttgart that there would be no internal collapse and that the democratic reform of Prussia would be energetically carried out. The hour was past, however, when Germany would be satisfied with the abolition of the Prussian three-class electoral system. The Junkers and conservatives, who had blocked the Easter Program announced by the Kaiser in 1917, were now in the hour of peril scarcely willing to make even these long-promised concessions. The demand therefore grew that a new ministry should assume power and commence the belated work of democratizing Germany. The movement was developed rapidly by the Austrian Peace Offensive of September 14, which depressed Germany tremendously and opened up the question as to whether or not the German government had been informed of the real situation of its allies. The Chancellor's position became untenable under the attacks of the conservatives as well as the majority parties.

As soon as the imminent collapse of the western front became known to the party leaders, the downfall of the old monarchical system in Germany was certain. If the nation by fresh sacrifices were to continue the struggle, it must be given a share in the government. Eucken states, however, that the root of all evil was the lack of a strong national will and inner steadfastness.[72]

The destruction of the military dictatorship of General Headquarters, and the parliamentarization of the empire and the federal states became the program late in September of the Liberals and Catholics. These parties invited the Socialists to join them and to assume a share of the burden of government. The Socialists accepted, provided that Paragraph Nine of the Constitution, which forbade membership in Reichstag and Bundesrat at the same time, be abolished, and that they be given a portfolio. *Vorwaerts*, the official organ of the party, then published as their minimum demands: the recognition by the imperial government of the Reichstag resolution of July 19, 1917; the unequivocal declaration of a Belgian policy; the revision of the treaties of Brest-Litovsk and Bucharest; complete autonomy for Alsace-Lorraine; universal direct and secret suffrage; dissolution of the Prussian Parliament; representative government by the majority of the Reichstag; abolition of Paragraph Nine of

[71] Menke-Glückert, "Die November Revolution," 18.

[72] Eucken, "Was Bleibt Unser Halt?" 9–10.

the Constitution; freedom of assembly and the press; and the restriction of censorship to military affairs.[73]

This demand created a chancellor crisis, since the conservative Chancellor von Hertling had previously declined to grant autonomy to Alsace-Lorraine or to abrogate Paragraph Nine of the Constitution. He had also procrastinated in the question of Prussian reforms. The Cologne Socialist editor and deputy, Mierfeld, declared on September 23, that as Hertling was not the man to break with the old state, the Socialists would not enter the government under him. The following day the Chancellor discussed the general situation, but failed to make concessions. On September 26 he promised, however, that at the next session complaints would be adjusted. That adjustment never occurred. Foreign affairs now dealt the decisive blow. Suddenly the Macedonian front collapsed, and on September 25 the Bulgarian Minister-President Malinoff requested an armistice of the Allies. The blow to Austria, Turkey, and Germany was irreparable. On September 29 Bulgaria signed an armistice with Germany's enemies. The empire of the Hohenzollerns was doomed.[74]

Under the pressure of this tremendous weight, and conscious of the mortal danger of the empire, the majority parties of the Reichstag agreed hastily upon a common program. The committee of the majority parties met on the afternoon of September 28. It demanded of the government: the autonomy of Alsace-Lorraine, and the abrogation of Paragraph Nine of the Constitution. The Chancellor, who at first had decided to go to General Headquarters and carry through the new program, now announced that he would resign. On September 30 he was dismissed from office after recommending the coöperation of the parties in the government and proposing Prince Max von Baden as his successor.[75]

PRINCE MAXIMILIAN OF BADEN ATTEMPTS TO SAVE THE EMPIRE

With the fall of Chancellor von Hertling, the Kaiser and the military dictators made a last attempt to save the monarchy by liberalizing the empire. Two candidates had been proposed for the post of chancellor. Vice Chancellor von Payer was the choice of the majority parties, while Prince Max of Baden had been designated by the retiring chancellor. Both men were acceptable to the *bloc* which controlled the Reichstag. After a visit to General Headquarters, Prince Max was offered the chancellory by the Emperor.

Maximilian of Baden, born on July 10, 1867, was the nephew of the reigning Grand Duke Frederick II of Baden and heir presumptive to the throne of that grand duchy. A liberal in politics and a critic of the

---

[73] *Vorwaerts,* September 24, 1918.

[74] Nowak, "Der Sturz der Mittelmaechte," 331–332.

[75] Hertling, *op. cit.,* 181–187.

former government, Prince Max was considered nationally as an able and sincere statesman. His speech of August 22, 1918, at the celebration of the one hundredth anniversary of the Constitution of Baden, had found wide acceptance by Democrats and Socialists.[76] Possessed of prestige and ability, Prince Max arrived in Berlin determined, with the consent of the Kaiser, to establish a liberal monarchy and thus avert a revolution. "When I was called to Berlin", he stated, "our offensive had collapsed and the enemies were advancing victoriously. . . . The war was lost." [77]

The Prince went to the capital and commenced negotiations with the party leaders before his appointment was announced. Realizing that the empire was defeated, he wished to save the nation from unbearable conditions of peace by: internal democratic reorganization; a clear statement of war aims; the acceptance of the idea of a league of nations; and the opening of negotiations with the enemy states before the western front collapsed. Thus he would preserve Germany from her enemies. In internal affairs he wished to avert a revolution. He planned to carry out the political reforms demanded by the masses and to remove thereby the necessity for a violent overthrow of the government. The Reichstag was to be strengthened and the military dictatorship was to be abolished.[78]

Whatever might have been the fate of his original policy, which at least was the only one having even the remotest prospect of saving the empire, it was completely ruined by the dramatic intervention of the military dictator, General Ludendorff. While the Prince was negotiating with the party leaders, Ludendorff on the first of October demanded that a request for an armistice should be sent to President Wilson within twenty-four hours. Prince Max was filled with consternation and fought the ultimatum vigorously, while the party leaders, although prepared for inevitable defeat, were crushed by the suddenness of the military capitulation. Above all, Prince Max saw the depressing effect of a request for an armistice before the inauguration of his peace program. He made the counter proposal to General Headquarters that a detailed peace program should be announced by the new government. Ludendorff replied that the request for the armistice must be sent off within twenty-four hours— even if the old government had to make it.[79] The Prince was forced to yield, the new government was hastily formed, and the first note was dispatched to President Wilson. "The effect of the request justified my worst fears", said Prince Max. The request for the armistice was the signal for the external and internal collapse of the German empire.

[76] Egelhaaf, "Historisch-politische Jahresuebersicht für," 1918.

[77] Prince Maximilian, in *Preussische Jahrbücher,* December, 1918.

[78] *Ibid.*

[79] *Ibid.*

The intervention of Ludendorff, his demand for an armistice, and his repentance a week later, when he stated that he had been deceived in his judgment, illustrate how completely the military dictators at German Headquarters had lost their heads. The action of Ludendorff was unworthy of a great military leader. It reveals him as a political general and proves to what extent German militarism was capable of ruining the German people.[80]

On the afternoon of October 2 the armistice was discussed in a crown council. The Prince opposed it, for he saw its fatal effect more clearly than the military leaders. Owing to the masterful retreat of the German armies, their demoralization had been partially concealed from the Allies, and neither the Entente nor the Germans themselves were prepared for this confession of weakness.[81] On October 3 Prince Max was named Chancellor of the German empire and under the threat of a military dictatorship the note requesting an armistice was sent through the Swiss government to President Wilson.

Not even the military defeats on the western front demoralized the nation as much as did the publication of the first note to President Wilson.[82] A storm of protest arose against the German militarists, who were accused of deceiving the nation for years concerning the real military situation. Other groups declared that the German military leaders were incompetent. Germany's confession of defeat strengthened the war parties of her enemies. All talk of a peace of justice vanished from the Entente press, while in America the demand for unconditional surrender was almost universal.[83] On October 9 the President's reply was known to the German people. In questioning the character of the government of Prince Max, the President threw an internal question into the international exchange of notes, and from then on the abdication of the Kaiser was freely discussed in Germany.

Meanwhile the allied advances had not broken through the German armies, which continued to withdraw in fairly good order. Ludendorff attempted therefore a second time to influence the internal situation by declaring that he could hold out until winter on the western front. He sought to prevent further negotiations with President Wilson, but the Social Democrats countered his blow. Prince Max decided to continue the negotiations. He states that after the receipt of the first two notes he received reliable information from President Wilson that he would be satisfied with the restriction of the Kaiser's authority to the position of the English King.[84]

[80] Valentin, *Supra*, 384–385.
[81] Hindenburg, "Aus Meinem Leben," 389.
[82] Mühsam, "Wie wir belogen wurden," 9–25.
[83] *Auswaertiges Amt. Wochenberichte*, Nr. 42, 5018.
[84] Prince Maximilian, in *Preussische Jahrbuecher*, December, 1918.

The democratic reorganization of Germany proceeded rapidly apace with the armistice negotiations. On October 15 the Bundesrath agreed to alter Article II of the Constitution so that in the future Bundesrath and Reichstag were to give their consent to declarations of war and conclusions of peace. The same day the Kaiser placed the military forces under the control of the Chancellor. The reform movement resulted in demands in Bavaria, Baden, and Saxony for alterations of the state constitutions. On October 26 the amendments to the imperial constitution were adopted by the Reichstag and the last session under the empire came to an end.

The failure of the internal policy of Prince Max was due largely to the armistice negotiations with President Wilson. After Ludendorff had been defeated by Prince Max and the civil authority had been made supreme within the empire, the abdication of the Kaiser was prevented by powerful conservative influences, which prevailed upon William II to remain at the head of his armies. President Wilson's reply of October 8 to the German note seemed to demand the abdication, although the government sought to evade it by explaining the democratic character of the new government. On October 22 Prince Max stated in the Reichstag that if the Allies wished to continue the war Germany must fight to the last. But already the belief was gaining ground in Germany that all obstacles to an early peace must be removed and the conditions of President Wilson accepted.

The crisis occurred when the President's note of October 24 once more raised the question of the Kaiser's abdication. The conservatives favored a rejection of Wilson's terms and issued a manifesto calling for national resistance to the Allies. Hindenburg declared that he favored either an honorable peace or resistance to the last. On the other hand, the radical elements pressed for acceptance of the American conditions. The Poles, Danes, and Alsatians in the Reichstag talked quite openly of the dismemberment of the German empire in accordance with the fourteen points of Wilson. Ludendorff now intervened for the last time, demanding that no reply be sent to President Wilson. Friday, October 25, the Cabinet, supported by the Emperor, decided against Ludendorff. That day he signed the German army reports for the last time. On the twenty-sixth of October he was dismissed from the virtual command of the imperial forces.[85] His removal meant the defeat of the war party and the fall of military Prussia. Until his removal he was a dictator possessing almost imperial powers, and his dismissal, although his nominal chief, Field Marshal von Hindenburg, remained at the head of the General Staff, meant the end of the monarchy and the great German military system. On the twenty-seventh of October the German empire capitulated to the Allies in a note addressed to President Wilson.

[85] Ludendorff, "Meine Kriegserinnerungen," 616–617.

An imperial proclamation dated October 28, but not published until November 3, announced to the nation the formation of the liberal empire. The Kaiser proclaimed that "the imperial office is service to the people". Prince Max had ended the personal régime and given Germany its first parliamentary government, but his entire policy collapsed when his imperial master refused to abdicate. The rapid march of foreign events made this delay fatal. Austria broke out in revolution and on October 28 declared herself ready to negotiate with Italy. The next day Vienna dispatched parliamentarians to Italian Headquarters, but the Austrian front broke before an armistice could be signed. The collapse of the Hapsburg throne foreshadowed the end of the reign of William II.

The overthrow of the government of Prince Max was caused by the general rebellion of the nation against a system which, although it had been amended and altered, still seemed to perpetuate imperialism, militarism, and the bureaucracy. On November 4 Prince Max learned of the revolt of the German navy at Kiel. Soon tidings of revolts in southern Germany, the Rhineland and the Hanseatic towns indicated that the empire was doomed.

A proclamation was issued on November 4 enumerating as the achievements of the new government: the abolition of the Prussian electoral law; parliamentary government in the empire; sanction of war and peace by the Reichstag; control of military administration by the Chancellor; an amnesty for political prisoners; freedom of the press and assembly; development of Germany into a democratic state. The proclamation also stated that the replacements for the front were necessary because the German borders must be protected until the enemy agreed to an honorable peace. Meanwhile employment was to be provided for workers and support was to be given to the unemployed. The housing regulations would be improved. The proclamation concluded: "The secured future of Germany is our guiding star." An increase of the bread ration was then announced for December 1. These proclamations failed, nevertheless, to quiet the growing discontent. The majority of the German press now favored the immediate abdication of the Kaiser.

As a last effort Prince Max determined after the Kiel revolt to go to General Headquarters and secure the voluntary abdication of the Kaiser. Ebert promised to do his best to control the Socialists until the negotiation was completed. However, the afternoon of the same day Ebert and Scheidemann delivered an ultimatum to Prince Max, making their continuance in the government dependent upon the Kaiser's abdication. Prince Max later said: "This ultimatum forced me to resign. It meant the collapse of my policy, which was one of conviction, not of force."

Replying to the final note of capitulation dispatched from Berlin, President Wilson on November 5 informed Prince Max that Marshal

Foch had been authorized to conclude an armistice with the representatives of Germany. On the following day the German delegation, headed by Minister Erzberger, left Berlin for the front. It was not until the night of the eighth that the delegation reached the French lines and was conducted to the station of Rethondes, six miles east of Compiegne. There an armistice was finally signed by the Germans and the Allies which resulted in the ending of the world war. The armistice was signed by Germany because her army was defeated and incapable of further resistance. A military dictatorship of the Pan-Germans, a Bolshevist dictatorship of the Independents, or the government of Prince Max would equally as well as the coalition Socialist government have been forced to order the signing of the armistice. Although Erzberger was covered with abuse by conservatives and liberals, the blame for the débâcle rested upon the shoulders of the militarists, and not upon those of the diplomats and politicians.[86]

---

[86] Erzberger, in "Erlebnisse im Weltkrieg," 326–340, has written a detailed account of his negotiations. Von Liebig, "Der Betrug am Deutschen Volk," 45–52, is a violent attack on the peace negotiations. Valentin, *Supra,* 390–411, is a comprehensive study of the ministry of Prince Max.

II.

THE BEGINNINGS OF THE REVOLUTION

NAVAL MUTINY

The prelude to the German revolution was the revolt of the High Seas Fleet. That great naval power, which in the battle of Jutland threatened the supremacy of the British Grand Fleet, was the first force within the empire to turn against German imperialism and hasten its overthrow. The causes of this remarkable naval mutiny reach back to the early days of the war and are in part traceable to the defensive naval policy adopted by the German strategists, and to the demoralization of the fleet by constant drafts for submarine warfare. Although the morale of the navy was at its height in 1916, it declined rapidly after Jutland when the chief naval energies of Germany were directed toward the development of a submarine force.[87]

The lack of a naval tradition as in the American and British navies, the enervating character of the monotonous work of guarding the German coasts, and finally the failure of the provisioning system for the fleet, resulted in 1917 in a serious mutiny on the German battleships. While conditions on the light cruisers and destroyer flotillas, which came in contact with the enemy, were excellent, the battle fleet presented a terrible picture of systematic oppression. On the larger ships of the fleet the relations between officers and men reflected the caste spirit of German navalism, which had been modelled on Prussian militarism. That food conditions were improved in the summer before the outbreak does not detract from the value of the general statement that the mutiny was caused by improper provisioning, combined with oppression.[88] Several officers were killed in the 1917 riots, but the outbreak was suppressed promptly with an iron hand. Forty sailors were condemned by general courts martial, and of this number sixteen were shot. That greater severity was not exercised by the naval authorities was due to the personal intervention of the Kaiser, who, alarmed by the justice of the men's grievances, ordered Admiral Scheer to deal mercifully with the rebels. To satisfy the Emperor's demands, fourteen of the condemned men were pardoned. Historic precedents for this policy were found by the German authorities in the British treatment of their mutineers at Spithead and the Nore.

---

[87] *Cf.* von Tirpitz, "Erinnerungen," 337–339.

[88] Schaefer, "Der Krieg," 1914–1919, 3 : 130–138.

Among the rioters of 1917 were a number of Independent Social Democrats. Evidence was found that sailors returning from furloughs in the interior had spread their propaganda among the enlisted personnel. The admiralty promptly accused the Independent party leaders of aiding and abetting the revolt.[89] In the Reichstag, Admiral von Capelle, secretary of state for the navy, formally charged Dittmann, Vogtherr and Haase with fomenting the disturbances in the fleet. In an able speech on October 9, 1917, Haase cleared himself of this charge.[90]

The Pan-Germans covertly attacked the Kaiser for his interference with the punishment of the 1917 mutineers. Admiral Foss and Captain von Forstner state that it was the imperial amnesty which broke down the discipline on the ships.[91] Propaganda against the Pan-Germans was certainly disseminated throughout the fleet, especially after many strikers were sent in January, 1918, to the coast with naval replacements. As a large percentage of the navy was drawn from the Socialist districts of Germany, the efforts of agitators to revolutionize the sailors were considerably lightened. Russian methods were freely imitated and pamphlets were smuggled aboard ships in ever-increasing numbers. The correspondence of sailors with their families, although censored, kept the former in touch with the revolutionary movements of 1918.[92]

Although the morale of the German submarine forces was high in spite of losses and failures, that of the battle fleet declined rapidly after America entered the war. The failure of the submarine campaign and the collapse of the great offensive of the German army in the west completed this demoralization. As the end of the war approached it became apparent to the navy and the nation that England would demand the surrender of the German fleet as a condition of peace. By October, 1918, the Pan-Germans advocated the sending of the fleet out to fight a decisive battle with the Allies. While the armistice negotiations were taking place, they demanded that the fleet allow itself to be annihilated rather than to surrender. Agitators told the sailors that it would be a national dishonor to give up the fleet without a battle, and the commander of the *Markgraf* advocated blowing up the fleet rather than handing it over to the Allies.

The naval crisis was finally brought about by a decision of General Headquarters and Admiral Scheer that the fleet must be used to relieve the military situation in Flanders. On October 28 the admiralty issued orders to Admiral von Hipper to proceed with the fleet to the Belgian

---

[89] Scheer, "Deutschlands Hochseeflotte im Weltkriege," 412–415.

[90] Haase, "Reichstagsreden." 110; Verhandlungen des Reichstages, October 9, 1917.

[91] Von Forstner, "Marine-Meuterei," 26. Foss, "Enthüllungen über den Zusammenbruch," 27.

[92] Von Altrock, "Deutschlands Niederbruch," 42.

coast in order to protect the right flank of the retreating German army.[93]
Persius maintains that the instructions issued to von Hipper would have
lead to the desired decisive battle and to the useless sacrifice of thousands
of German lives.[94]

The plan of operations had indeed been worked out in advance, and
the fleet commander assembled his squadrons in the Aussenjade, while
the submarines, which were to cover the dash to the Flanders coast, were
sent to their stations.   Scarcely was the fleet concentrated in the Schillig
roadstead when the rumor ran through the ships that the admiral was
about to give battle to the Grand Fleet in order to prevent the surrender
of the ships at the armistice.   The mere painting of the afterstack of the
battle cruiser *Moltke* red, a German battle-sign, seems to have terrified
the heroes of Jutland.   Socialist agitators on the ships declared that an
attack on the English would hinder international Socialist aspirations and
that Admiral Scheer was trying to prevent the signing of peace.[95]   The
overwhelming majority of the sailors at once refused to fight, since the
war was to end in any event.   Secret signalling informed every crew of
the determination of the men not to sail.[96]   When the first order to proceed to sea was issued, the crews of the *Thüringen* and *Helgoland* refused
to weigh anchor.   The stokers in other ships mutinied, declaring: "If we
steam farther than Helgoland, the fires will be put out." [97]   Although several attempts were made by the admiral to take the fleet out, they all failed.

The sailors had won their first victory, but with the achievement of
their aims a semblance of order and discipline was restored throughout
the fleet.   Many naval officers had sympathized with the views of their
men.   Although the sailors did not seize control of the ships from their
officers, they formed sailors' councils, issued red brassards to the crews
and continued preparations for a general revolt at a more propitious
moment.   It was therefore not until the morning of November 6 that
the naval rebellion broke out in the city of Wilhelmshaven.

The mutiny of the fleet in the Schillig roadstead was merely the prelude to the revolution, because the mutineers lacked a political program
and were simply attempting to defend themselves against a supposed plan
to sacrifice the fleet.   However, the success of the first efforts of the
sailors quickly led to the formulation of political and revolutionary policies.   When the leaders of the mutiny were arrested, secret plans were
made for a general revolt on November 5.[98]

---

[93] Kuttner, "Von Kiel nach Berlin," 10–11.

[94] Persius, "Wie es Kam," 14. *Cf.* Scheer, "Deutschlands Hochseeflotte im Weltkrieg," 494. Tirpitz, *op. cit.,* 338.

[95] Kuttner, *op. cit.,* 12.

[96] Forstner, *op. cit.,* 8. Foss, *op. cit.,* 27.

[97] *Deutscher Geschichtskalender,* 3.

[98] Foss, *op. cit.,* 31.

After the failure of the Flanders operation, the fleet was dispersed. The first squadron was ordered to the Elbe River and the fourth squadron proceeded to the Jade. The third squadron, which was sent to Kiel, led there the revolt which destroyed the imperial system on the sea coast of Germany.[99] On Sunday, November 2, sailors from this squadron assembled in the Trades Union House at Kiel and voted to effect the release of their imprisoned comrades. Although the squadron commander ordered the alarm siganls blown, no one returned to the ships. That night a demonstration was held on the exercise square and a procession of sailors marched into the inner city, where it was fired upon by the watch. Immediately the sailors proceeded to arm themselves, and by the morning of November 4 they were in possession of the railway station, which they held against the infantry regiments of the garrison. The governor of Kiel was powerless to stop the movement, which soon spread to all the ships in the harbor. Socialist shipyard workers joined the rebels and a delegation of their leaders accompanied the sailors to the governor's office. There the mutineers presented an ultimatum containing fourteen points: the release of all political prisoners; complete freedom of speech; abolition of the naval censorship; appropriate treatment of the men by their officers; a general amnesty for all rioters; prohibition under any condition of the sailing of the fleet; avoidance of civil war; withdrawal from Kiel of all troops not belonging to the garrison; recognition of the authority of the sailors' council to protect private property; exemption of all sailors from military courtesies when off duty; unlimited personal freedom for all enlisted men off duty; dismissal without claim to compensation of all officers who do not accept the regulations of the sailors' councils; exemption of all members of the council from any duty whatsoever; countersigning of all future orders by the council; recognition of these demands of the council as general orders.[100]

Long before the delegation reached Admiral Souchon, he had informed Berlin of the revolt, and had been ordered to avoid further bloodshed. Meanwhile the imperial ministry had sent two representatives to Kiel to take charge of the situation. On this account the governor hesitated to accept the demands of the sailors, stating that a number of them were purely political and therefore beyond his jurisdiction. Finally he informed the delegation that two representatives of the government would arrive that evening and thus scured the postponement of the revolt.[101]

After a preliminary meeting a great procession of mutineers and Socialists proceeded to the railway station to greet Haussmann and Noske, the two government representatives. Immediately after their arrival, the

[99] Scheer, "Deutchlands Hochseeflotte im Weltkriege," 497.
[100] Kuttner, *op. cit.,* 14–17.
[101] Noske, "Von Kiel bis Kapp," 10–12.

latter made a rapid agreement with the sailors' council. The only point of difference was over the release of prisoners. That night the council issued a proclamation stating that Haussmann accepted their demands and promised their prompt execution by the government; that the military measures directed against the sailors would be broken up; that the fleet would be controlled in coöperation with the council; and that the council would examine the documents of those under arrest with the exception of men condemned because of dishonorable conduct.[102] Haase and Ledebour were promptly called to Kiel to take part in the examination of the arrested sailors. A great mass meeting was addressed on the evening of November 4 by Noske, who announced that the armistice would be signed shortly and that the sailors must maintain order. The close of his speech was answered by cries of: "Long live the republic." [103]

Thus the naval revolt triumphed at Kiel. Of the four infantry companies sent against the sailors on November 4, three joined the rebels and one was disarmed. The sailors boasted that day of the rout of the Wandsbecker Hussars. On November 5 the mutineers took possession of the ships and hoisted red flags. A few light craft refused to join the rebels and were promptly fired upon. The captain and a lieutenant of the battleship *Koenig*, which was in the dry dock, were killed while defending the imperial ensign. The submarines which remained loyal to the Emperor escaped from the harbor. Officers were disarmed and red cockades were assumed by the sailors. The brother of the Emperor, Prince Henry of Prussia, fled from the city. On the morning of November 5 the Prince's standard no longer waved above the tower of the royal castle.[104]

What had been originally a naval mutiny now became a great revolutionary movement. In the coast towns the proletariat made the cause of the mutineers their own. At Hamburg the workmen in the Vulcan factories decided to strike on the morning of November 5. Cooler heads secured a postponement until all Social Democratic leaders could decide upon the workers' demands. Nevertheless on that evening the Independent Socialists held a meeting before which a deputation of soldiers and sailors appeared. The Independent leader, Dittmann, recently released from prison by the government, was the principal speaker. He declared that the Kaiser would of course abdicate, that the coming republic would be a socialistic one, and that the present government with a prince at its head was a grim joke.[105] Duewill, a Hamburg Independent, demanded that the republic be proclaimed at once; that an official paper be printed

[102] Kuttner, *op. cit.*, 14–17.

[103] Noske, "Von Kiel bis Kapp," 11. Kuttner, *op. cit.*, 17–20.

[104] Menke, "Die November Revolution," 38–39. Von Forstner, *op. cit.*, 12. Noske, "Von Kiel bis Kapp," 20–21.

[105] Runkel, "Die Deutsche Revolution," 95–97.

for the revolutionists; and that a sympathetic strike for the Kiel workmen be declared at once.[106]

That night a procession of strikers disarmed officers in the city, removed insignia from soldiers, and prevented furloughed men from returning to the front. On November 6 war ships arrived in the harbor, whereupon the shipyard workers struck, and a great assemblage was held in the Holy Ghost Field. A soldiers' council waited upon General von Falk, but that official, who feared to use force against the rioters, fled from the city. Only a few days before the Kiel outbreak, he had said: "We live in an orderly state; internal disturbances cannot occur among us."[107] The city commandant finally accepted the demands of the soldiers' council in the Trades Union House. A revolutionary military control of the city was established, and the Hamburger *Echo* appeared as *The Red Flag,* the official organ of the workmen's and soldiers' council.[108]

In Bremen the revolution triumphed without bloodshed. For weeks the city had been agitated over the question of the extension of the suffrage. After the sailors revolted at Wilhelmshaven the Independent Socialists decided on November 6 to establish universal suffrage. That morning one hundred of the mutineers arrived under guard from Wilhelmshaven on their way to the prison camp at Rethen on the Aller. They were quickly freed by the workers, who were joined by the garrison of the city. A workmen's and soldiers' council was formed at once. Colonel Lehmann, the commander of the garrison, made an agreement with the rebels by the terms of which the military power was to be exercised by the Colonel, two officers, and four members of the soldiers' council.[109] The officers retained their swords and insignia. The bells of the cathedral were rung to celebrate the victory, and on November 7 the workers paraded through the city. Guards were posted to protect the town against a government invasion.[110]

On November 5 the revolution broke out in Luebeck, the third Hanseatic republic. Warships and destroyers landed detachments, occupied the railway stations, arrested the commandant of the city and his principal officers, and interned them in a hotel. The troops joined the sailors, and that night the newly formed soldiers' council proclaimed: "From this hour all power is in our hands. We herewith declare that by our cause our comrades at the front as well as at home are aided. The corrupt conditions and the military dictatorship of yesterday must be

---

[106] Menke, *op. cit.,* 11.
[107] Lambach, "Ursachen des Zusammenbruchs," 111.
[108] Kuttner, "Von Kiel nach Berlin," 19–20.
[109] *Ibid.,* 20.
[110] Menke, *op. cit.,* 12.

thoroughly cleaned up. The purpose of our rising is to secure an immediate armistice and peace." [111] The council also took steps to maintain order in the industries, to prevent plunderings, and to safeguard the control of the food supplies, which it left in the hands of the civil authorities.

Wilhelmshaven, which had been the scene of the original mutiny, finally joined the movement on November 6. Over sixty thousand sailors and shipyard workers held a demonstration that day and the station chief negotiated with a deputation from the soldiers' council which was formed by the rebels.

Not only did the revolt triumph in the principal German coast cities, but it also spread to the smaller towns and naval stations. On November 5 the men of the battleships *Posen, Ost Friesland,* and *Nassau,* then lying in Brunsbuettel, the west end of the Kiel canal, joined the movement and occupied the wireless station at Ostmoor. On November 6 the towns of Cuxhaven, Rendsburg, Warnemuende, Rostock, Bremerhaven, and Geestemuende fell into the hands of the sailors. At Rostock the workers struck, and at Schwerin the soldiers of the Eighty-sixth Ersatz Battalion joined the men of the Fokker works in overthrowing the old order.[112]

By the close of the first week of November the naval revolt, supported by the Radical Socialists of the Hanseatic republics, had triumphed along the German coasts. Originally without political aims the naval mutiny became a general revolt against the liberal empire of Prince Max of Baden. When the success of the coast uprisings became known in the interior there followed the revolt of town after town. In many cities of northern Germany the arrival of detachments of sailors marked the beginning of the rebellions. Although the Independent Socialists had in many instances planned uprisings for later dates, the sudden arrival of armed revolutionary soldiers and sailors furnished the leaders and the dramatic moment so essential to any revolt. It was the navy which destroyed the imperial rule in North Germany. When on November 9 Admiral Scheer urged the Kaiser to remain at the head of his fleets, the former admiral of the Atlantic replied in a disappointed voice: "I no longer have a navy." [113] "The German people," states Admiral von Tirpitz, "did not understand the sea. In the hour of its destiny it did not use its fleet." [114]

---

[111] Runkel, *op. cit.,* 94.

[112] Menke, *op. cit.,* 45. Kuttner, *op. cit.,* 19.

[113] Scheer, *op. cit.,* 499.

[114] Von Tirpitz, *op. cit.,* 387.

THE BAVARIAN REVOLUTION

The second and decisive blow which overthrew the German imperial system was the revolutionary outbreak in the kingdom of Bavaria. Here in the largest of the South German states the revolutionary movement had found fruitful soil, due to the prolongation of the war, to the gradual economic decline, and above all to the belief that the Bavarians were being involved in Prussia's guilt. Since the failure of the general strike of January, 1918, revolutionary plots had been formed in Bavaria. Hatred of Prussia had increased during the war, and popular agitation was directed against the Bavarian ruling classes, who were considered the accomplices of Prussia. The Bavarian monarch had failed to take Bavaria out of the war. The intellectuals of the state prepared the way for the revolution, while the two Socialist parties plotted to overthrow the monarchy. Even the Roman Catholic Church failed to check the revolutionary movement, although the population of Bavaria was overwhelmingly Catholic.

The leader of the Bavarian revolutionists was the venerable Kurt Eisner, an Independent Socialist writer. Of Jewish parentage, he was from 1898 to 1905 on the editorial staff of the *Vorwaerts,* but had been finally dismissed because he had favored revisionism as a party policy. On account of his participation in the January, 1918, strike, he had been sentenced to imprisonment and was released only after the general amnesty issued by Prince Max. Eisner was not only a publicist and stylist, but also a Socialist with statesmanlike ability. Convinced of Germany's guilt in starting the war, and of Prussian responsibility for its prolongation, he advocated the overthrow of the imperial system by force.[115]

On Sunday, November 3, Eisner issued a call for a meeting to demonstrate against the prolongation of the war.[116] Thousands assembled to denounce the reactionaries, and after the close of the meeting a large crowd went to the Stadelheim prison to free those who had been arrested during the January strike. Toward evening these men were actually released on telegraphic orders from Leipsic and brought back in triumph to the city. Bold spirits cheered that day for the republic.

On the night of November 5 two meetings were called by the Socialists to protest against the Pan-German demand for the continuance of the war. Unable to crowd the masses into the two halls, the leaders adjourned the meetings to the *Theresienwiesse,* where, under a clear sky, their orators uttered fiery protests against the robber knights who had ruined Germany. Both Socialist parties had now agreed upon joint action against the royal government, which was too weak either to make concessions to

[115] Menke, Glückert, "Die November Revolution, 1918," 46–50.
[116] Eisner, "Schuld und Sühne."

the revolutionists or to resist their demands by force. The *Muenchener Post* thereupon issued a call for a meeting on November 7 on the *Theresienwiese* of the entire population of Munich except those involved in the transportation of food supplies. The chief purpose of the gathering was to demand the abdication of the Kaiser. On Thursday afternoon over one hundred thousand people assembled in the meadow before the colossal statue of Bavaria. Twelve speakers demanded the abdication of the Kaiser, amid the plaudits of the masses. After the close of the meeting the civilians marched in a procession to the Column of Peace, while the soldiers present moved off in military formation to the barracks in order to release their comrades, who had been confined to quarters by the commandant of the city.[117]

The moment the revolutionary soldiers reached the Guldin School Barracks their comrades opened the doors and marched out. Thus the military revolt began and the garrison of Munich, after deposing its officers, joined the republicans. In the course of the afternoon the revolutionists seized the Maximilian II, Marsfeld and Tuerken barracks, while two hundred and fifty soldiers confined in the military prison as revolutionists were released. Soldiers in motor trucks with red flags patrolled the streets, and the capital passed without a struggle into the hands of the soldiers and workmen. The railroad stations, telephone and telegraph offices, army headquarters, government ministries, and the newspaper offices of the *Muenchener Neueste Nachrichten* were occupied by the rebels.

Under Eisner's direction, the workmen and soldiers elected delegates, who established revolutionary headquarters in the Mathaser brewery. That night this revolutionary government occupied the Parliament building and held the first session of the revolutionary councils in the Parliament chamber. Kurt Eisner presided over this assembly of workmen, soldiers, and peasants, which promptly proclaimed Bavaria a People's State. The Munich garrison formally adhered to the republican movement.[118]

On the morning of November 9 Munich awoke to find the walls of the city placarded with the proclamations of the Council of Workmen, Soldiers, and Peasants of the Free State of Bavaria. These announced that the new government would call a national assembly; work for a just peace; support a plan for a league of nations; and carry out fundamental social, economic, and political reforms. At the same time a proclamation was issued to the agricultural population of Bavaria, announcing the formation of the new government and calling for coöperation especially in the maintenance of better food conditions in the cities. Although the

[117] *Deutscher Geschichtskalender*, 65–76.

[118] Kuttner, *op. cit.*, 25.

new government was completely Socialistic, it declared that at a time when the productive powers of the nation were exhausted it was impossible to place the Bavarian industries in the hands of the commonwealth.

The fall of the Bavarian dynasty illustrates the weakness of the old government. The afternoon of the revolution King Louis III was walking in the English garden with his daughters when a private citizen advised him to go back to the palace. Scarcely had he returned when his ministers informed him that the republic had been proclaimed in the streets. The royal family hastily packed their hand luggage and left in an auto unattended. No effort was made to maintain the monarchy by force, and on November 13 the King formally abdicated the throne. The provisional government in announcing this fact in a proclamation stated that the former King and his family might remain in Bavaria as any other free citizens if they did not attack the new state.[119]

The establishment of the republic of Bavaria on November 8, 1918, signified the collapse of the Bismarckian empire and of those monarchial German states which had endured since the Middle Ages. As Eisner had previously denounced the government of Prince Max of Baden, his coup d'état at Munich indicated that either all Germany must be revolutionized or Bavaria would conclude a separate peace with the entente. Noteworthy is the success of Eisner, the idealist and foreigner, who, with the help of the Munich Radicals, seized control of Catholic Bavaria. His dramatic success electrified all Germany on the morning of November ninth. It heralded the triumph of German Radicalism and Socialism over the Conservative empire.

The Spread of Revolt

The mutiny of the German fleet resulted in the establishment of revolutionary governments in the Hanseatic republics and the coast towns of Oldenburg, Mecklenburg, and Prussia, while detachments of sailors advancing into the interior set up workmen's and soldiers' councils in the North German states. In the Rhineland the great city of Cologne passed into the hands of mutinous troops, and Hanover and Magdeburg by proclaiming council republics threatened the lines of communications of the imperial armies. However, the naval revolt and its repercussions were limited in their effect and alone would not have destroyed the liberal empire.

It was the overthrow of the Bavarian monarchy by the coup d'état of the Munich Socialists which gave the signal for the German revolution. On November 8 the principal cities of Saxony, Baden, Württemberg, Hesse-Darmstadt and the Thuringian states were in open rebellion. One by one the monarchical federal states were engulfed by the rising tide of

---

[119] *Deutscher Geschichtskalender*, 66–67. Runkel, *op. cit.*, 98–104.

revolution. Ministries were everywhere powerless to maintain the old order. The reaction from the military defeat of the empire had brought about the complete collapse of the Bismarckian state. Yet the administrative system of the empire and the several states continued to function long after the monarchical control had vanished. By the ninth of November the federal empire had ceased to exist. Revolutionary plots had either overthrown or weakened the monarchical states to such an extent that Germany only awaited the signal from the capital to abolish entirely the old order and to proclaim the Socialistic republic. Above all the movement lacked national leaders and cohesion, which accounted for the numerous delays in overthrowing Kaiserism.

In Berlin alone the liberal empire under the control of Prince Max of Baden still maintained a semblance of its former authority. The fall of his ministry was, however, only a question of time, since the maintenance of the empire had been made impossible by the refusal of the Kaiser to abdicate. In a single day, therefore, Berlin overthrew the empire of the Hohenzollerns, as Paris had once shaken off the yoke of Napoleon III after Sedan.

III.

THE NINTH OF NOVEMBER

ABDICATION OF THE KAISER

When William II was at the height of his power, the German historian, Karl Lamprecht, wrote: "The best source for a knowledge of the personality of the Kaiser will perhaps always be his speeches; other information from first as well as even second or third hand is, if it does not originate from intimates, to be received with pronounced distrust. However, it is not very easy to acquire an understanding of the speeches." [120] During the war the published utterances of the War Lord revealed more and more that he was incapable of great military or political leadership.[121] Nor did he show himself to be possessed of that ability and spirit of coöperation which had enabled his grandfather to utilize the genius of Bismarck and Moltke. In spite of many attempts it was even impossible for the Kaiser and the chiefs of his military, naval, and civil cabinets to maintain the fiction of the Hohenzollern genius. An excellent example of this imperial attitude was the reply which the Kaiser made on February 23, 1916, when Admiral Scheer asked him on what date unrestricted submarine warfare could be commenced. "To my question the Kaiser remarked that he dared not make the decision merely in accordance with the military propositions, whose justification he thoroughly recognized, since he had to bear the responsibility not only as supreme war lord, but also as head of the state. If he were to order the immediate commencement of unrestricted submarine warfare, it probably would meet with the complete approbation of the widest circles. He had, however, to take care that the advantages of unrestricted submarine warfare would not be outweighed by the results of the entrance of America into the war on the side of our enemies." [122] Unfortunately for himself and his dynasty, William II was unable to assume that leadership of his people which he so proudly proclaimed in this instance to the admiral of his fleets. After 1916 the Germans realized that Ludendorff and Hindenburg were the real dictators of *Mittel Europa*.

Surrounded since 1914 by a succession of military and political groups which were striving continuously to formulate war aims in conflict with a considerable portion of German public opinion, the Kaiser failed to follow,

---

[120] Lamprecht, "Der Kaiser Versuch Einer Charakteristik," 49–50.

[121] Rathenau, "Der Kaiser," 47.

[122] Scheer, "Deutschlands Hochseeflotte im Weltkrieg," 169.

as head of the state, a consistent policy, but varied from one extreme to the other, as expediency or necessity seemed to demand. Those very qualities which in the decade before the war had made him prominent as a European ruler, now aided in the destruction of that imperial system which he sought bravely to perpetuate. After the revolution, his former subjects accused him unjustly of lack of character, timidity, vanity, unreliability, and even personal cowardice. In their rage and vindictiveness the German radicals overdrew the picture, as formerly the Byzantine flatterers of the Kaiser had magnified his virtues and genius. At its best, the Hohenzollern monarchy under a military genius would have been unequal to the test of a prolonged modern world war. For that, the national and dynastic traditions were lacking in Germany. The greatest charge that can be brought against the Emperor was that he was unable to direct the affairs of state at the crisis of the nation's history.[123] During the great political debate in the National Assembly, July 28, 1919, on the causes of the loss of the war, Gothein said of the Kaiser: "He bears a substantial part of the blame for our misfortune." [124]

The publication in Germany of President Wilson's third note of October 23 made the abdication of the Kaiser a political necessity. From that day the monarch was doomed.[125] Socialist and enemy propaganda had so far undermined the position of William II that only a voluntary and worthy renunciation of the throne would have halted the revolutionary movement. In reality, what the enemy propaganda had been unable to accomplish in Germany was achieved by Ludendorff when he demanded on Sunday, September 29, that the government request an armistice with the Allies. From that moment President Wilson dominated the problem of ending the world war. Prince Max said, "Not the enemy propaganda nor the Independent Socialist agitation, but the war policy of the army caused the psychological catastrophe and the collapse of the internal front." [126]

The agitation of the Socialists for the abdication of the Kaiser was by the end of October accepted by the majority of the nation as the only means to escape from a perilous international position and to secure bearable terms of peace.[127] Influenced by public opinion, the Majority Socialists were forced to agitate the question in the ministry. The policy of Prince Max was in fact directed toward convincing the Emperor of the necessity of abdication, but the Prince believed that only a voluntary decision of the Kaiser would save the empire from destruction. Scheidemann, in a

---

[123] Foss, "Enthüllungen," 82.

[124] *Berliner Tageblatt,* July 29, 1919.

[125] Erzberger, "Erlebnisse im Weltkrieg," 323.

[126] Letter of Prince Max of Baden in *Berliner Tageblatt,* August 9, 1919.

[127] *Deutscher Geschichtskalender,* I Heft, 23–32. *Frankfurter Zeitung,* October 24, 1918.

memoir to the Chancellor, had, however, insisted upon the immediate abdication of William II. In an effort to convince the Emperor, Prince Max
sent Drews, the Minister of the Interior, to Spa, but the Kaiser declined to
renounce the thrones of Prussia and the empire.[128]

It was the refusal of the Kaiser to abdicate after the seriousness of the
situation had been respectfully laid before him by Drews which gave the
pretext for the Berlin revolution.[129] Max was unable to convince the
Kaiser, but the Socialists now felt themselves strong enough to force the
issue. In fact the agitation of the Independents and the disaffection within
their own ranks really forced the Majority Socialist leaders to take such
action in order to maintain their power over their followers. In a party
caucus the Social Democrats supported Ebert, who stated that the Kaiser
must abdicate in order that Germany might secure better terms of peace.
Then followed the ultimatum of the Socialists to Prince Max.[130]

Over the history of the last eight days of imperial rule at Spa there has
raged already in Germany a political controversy of the first magnitude.[131]
Field Marshal von Hindenburg, Generals von Plessen, von Marschall,
Count Schulenburg, and Admiral von Hintze have all drawn up supplemen-
tal reports to the official documents bearing upon the Kaiser's abdication.
Prince Max von Baden has also vigorously defended his position. The
essential facts are, however, undisputed.

As late as November 1 the Kaiser, when informed by Minister Drews
of the popular demand for his abdication, instructed that official to notify
the chancellor that he would remain at his post, convinced that his abdication would be the signal for the triumph of Bolshevism.[132] Both Hindenburg and Groener also rejected the idea of abdication at that time. The
Kaiser believed that only at Spa would he possess complete freedom of
political action and that there, supported by his loyal troops, he could maintain his crown.

Meanwhile the agitation for abdication increased in Germany, even
democratic and liberal papers supporting the movement. The navy revolted,
and the mutineers as well as the Independent Socialists in the Hanseatic
cities demanded a republic.[133] General Groener visited Berlin on November 5 and returned to Spa, convinced at last, as was the civil government
there, that the Kaiser must abdicate.

---

[128] Letter of Prince Max of Baden in *Berliner Tageblatt*, August 9, 1919. Runkel,
"Deutsche Revolution," 57–61.

[129] Egelhaaf, "Histor-polit. Jahresbericht für 1918."

[130] Runkel, "Die Deutsche Revolution," 64.

[131] Hindenburg's attack on Schulenburg in *Vossische Zeitung*, April 7, 1919.

[132] *Deutsche Tageszeitung*, July 27, 1919.

[133] Noske, "Von Kiel bis Kapp," 7–8.

On the morning of November 8 a large number of division, brigade, and regimental commanders from the front were assembled at Spa to report on conditions in the retreating army. Many declared that the veteran troops could be relied upon, but that the replacements and new drafts were untrustworthy. All agreed that the army would return to Germany under its old leaders, but not under the command of the Kaiser. Thereupon the Emperor ordered General Groener to prepare a plan of operation to maintain the empire by force. In the evening a war council discussed the proposed plan, Hindenburg and Groener agreeing that it was impossible to carry it out, Plessen favoring it. That night the soldiers at General Headquarters, who had heard of the revolts in Hamburg, Hanover, and Cologne, declared they would not defend the lives of the Kaiser and their officers against the German Republicans.

Prince Max had already informed the Kaiser on November 7 of the Socialist ultimatum. He followed up his report by telegraphing the Emperor, advising abdication and the calling of a constitutional assembly in order to destroy Independent and Spartacan propaganda. In reply the Kaiser telegraphed: "His Majesty has completely rejected the recommendation of Your Grand Ducal Highness in the throne question and considers it now, as formerly, his duty to remain at his post."

As the republic had in the interval triumphed in Bavaria, and as the fate of the empire hung, therefore, in the balance, Prince Max held, on the night of November 8, a twenty-minute telephone conversation with the Kaiser. He stated bluntly that abdication was necessary, that the military could not suppress the rising tide of revolution, and that he recommended as a final measure the naming of a regent and the calling of a national assembly before the Reichstag demanded it. In addition he informed the Kaiser of a second plan recommended by the interfractional committee of the Reichstag, which called for the abdication of the Kaiser, the renunciation of the throne by the Crown Prince, and the appointment of a regency for the Emperor's grandson.[134] "I believe," states Prince Max, "that if General Headquarters had told the Kaiser the truth about the army on the night of the eighth, he would have abdicated then." [135]

Advised by his Chancellor to abdicate while there was yet time, the defeated War Lord still clung tenaciously to his crown and symbols of former authority. At ten o'clock on the morning of November 9 he was, however, at last told the truth by his military advisers. Hindenburg requested his dismissal because of the plan of operations against the interior, and Groener declared that the field army could not be marched against the nation. Still the Kaiser clung to his plan of returning at the head of his

---

[134] Letter of Prince Max of Baden in *Berliner Tageblatt,* August 9, 1919.
[135] *Idem.*

Prussian troops. Toward the close of the military report the chancellery at Berlin telephoned to the Emperor, pressing for abdication.[136] Previous to this Admiral von Hintze had informed the chancellery that the army would wage a civil war for the Kaiser.

While the generals were discussing the abdication question in the park of the Kaiser's villa, the Crown Prince appeared and asked his father not to leave the army but to return to Germany with his army group. At one o'clock Colonel Heye arrived with a report of the conference of thirty-nine generals and regimental commanders held at Spa that morning. Twenty-three had declared it impossible for the Kaiser to reconquer Germany with the army. Fifteen were doubtful of the success of the operation. And only one officer believed it possible. All agreed that the army refused to fight longer either abroad or at home.[137]

Thus the War Lord learned the truth on the soil of that gallant country which he had ruthlessly invaded five years before. The scene was dramatic. Suddenly he announced that the Chancellor, the first adviser of the crown, as well as the army and navy, had deserted him. Even when he was told that the roads to the front and to the interior were closed by mutinous troops, he could only bring himself to agree to a conditional abdication as Kaiser. But before Berlin could be informed of this decision, Prince Max of Baden had on his own initiative announced the Kaiser's abdication in Berlin. "I am and remain King of Prussia and as such with my troops," the Emperor exclaimed, when told of the action of his Chancellor.[138] That too, however, soon proved impossible.

"Since William II dismissed Bismarck", wrote Baron von Wolzogen, "until November, 1911, when he was politely told by Bülow of the discontent of his people, he had often enough deserved deposition." [139] In the end the action of Prince Max on November 9 was equivalent to deposing the Kaiser. When the Chancellor of the empire ordered the Counsellor of Legation, von Schmidthals, to inform the German press of the Kaiser's abdication, William II was deprived of his throne.[140]

In the eyes of the Prussian Monarchists, Prince Max had really forced the Kaiser to abdicate and then advised him to go abroad to avoid civil war.[141] The Prince was denounced as a hypocrite, swindler, and traitor, who had betrayed the Hohenzollerns to the Socialists. He was even accused of having attempted to play the rôle of a Louis Philippe in order to make himself regent of the empire.

---

[136] *Deutsche Tageszeitung,* July 27, 1919.
[137] Menke, *op. cit.,* 58–60.
[138] *Deutsche Tageszeitung,* July 29, 1919.
[139] Von Wolzogen, "Harte Worte die Gesagt Werden Müssen."
[140] Von Liebig, "Der Betrug am Deutschen Volke," 51–52.
[141] Krieger, "Die Wahrheit."

On account of the revolutionary outbreaks in the rear of the armies, a peaceful return of the Kaiser to Germany was impossible.[142] Hindenburg wrote later from General Headquarters at Kolberg that the Kaiser only had three possible courses of action: to fight his way back to Germany with loyal regiments; to die at the head of his troops on the front; to go abroad. That he chose the latter policy was due to his desire to spare the nation the horrors of civil war. The Field Marshal also declared: "He had gone in order to spare the Fatherland additional sacrifices and in order to secure for it more favorable conditions of peace."[143]

On the night of November 9, without a word of farewell to his people, the Kaiser fled in his special train to the Dutch border. It was not until November 28, 1918, that he wrote a formal renunciation of the throne. His flight was followed by a torrent of abuse throughout Germany. Publicists proclaimed his guilt and called his desertion infamous.[144] Others sought after the German collapse to excuse his going abroad.[145] Von Plessen was accused of having prevailed upon his master to flee.[146] Unkingly, unmanly, the deathblow to dynasty and monarchy were general accusations brought against William II.[147] Many declared that it was at least cowardly to flee.[148] Finally the absurd cry was raised that the Emperor was insane.[149]

REVOLT OF BERLIN

The collapse of the liberal empire established by Prince Max of Baden was not due to a lack of statesmanship on the part of the prince, but to the sudden breaking up of the inner front under the pressure of military defeat. The final struggle with Ludendorff, the demands of President Wilson, the failure of the Kaiser to abdicate, and finally the general uprising of the German radicals, following the naval mutiny, all brought about

[142] Nowak, "Der Sturz der Mittelmaechte," 331–332.

[143] Letter of Hindenburg in *Berliner Tageblatt,* March 19, 1919. Hindenburg, "Aus Meinem Leben," 401–402.

[144] Binder, "Die Schuld des Kaisers," 34.

[145] Krieger, "Die Wahrheit über die Angebliche Abdankung." Hagenau, Peter, "Ein Wort für Wilhelm II." Grossmann, Fritz, "Was Sind Wir Unserm Kaiser Schuldig?" (The first pamphlet is one of a number of popular defenses written by soldiers. The latter are typical pamphlets filled with fulsome praise which, though naïve, is sincere.)

[146] Binder, "Die Schuld des Kaisers."

[147] *Die Wahrheit,* I Heft, 16. Wulff, "Die Persönliche Schuld Wilhelms II."

[148] Von Hoensbroech, "Wilhelms II Abdankung und Flucht." Rump, "Paul Reichsgraf von Hoensbroech als Gefolgsmann der Hohenzollern."

[149] Friedlander, Prof. Dr., "Wilhelm II, Eine Politische-psychologische Studie," Halle, 1919. Kleinschrod, Dr. Franz, "Die Geisteskrankheit Kaiser Wilhelms II?" Worishofen, 1919. Tesdorpf, Dr. Paul, "Die Krankheit Wilhelm II," Munchen, 1919.

the overthrow of the last imperial ministry. Only the support of the Majority Socialists enabled this government to exist as long as it did.[150]

The fundamental policies of the ministry of Prince Max are outlined in a proclamation issued November 4, announcing as the important things accomplished by the government: equal suffrage assured for Prussia; a new government formed from representatives of the majority parties of the Reichstag; the confidence of the Reichstag required by the Chancellor and his co-workers to carry on their administration; fundamental powers transferred from the person of the Emperor to the representatives of the people; the approval of the Reichstag required for making war and peace; the establishment of the subordination of the military to the civil powers; the proclamation of a general amnesty and the granting of freedom of press and right of assembly. Until peace was signed the proclamation stated that the people must maintain order and assist the army leaders and the government to protect the borders of the empire and to restore the economic life of the nation in order to assure the existence of the returning soldiers and sailors. The conclusion was worded as follows: "Still much remains to be done. The transformation of Germany into a people's state, which shall not stand behind any state of the world in political freedom and social betterment, will be firmly carried out. . . . The assured future of Germany is our guiding star." [151]

This proclamation was signed by the Chancellor, the Vice Chancellor, the Vice President of the Prussian Ministry, the Minister of War, the Secretary of State for the Navy, and Secretaries Solf, Count von Roedern, von Krause, Ruedlin, von Waldow, Baron von Stein, Scheidemann, Groeber, Erzberger, Haussmann, Bauer, and Trimborn.[152]

To accomplish this transformation of Germany, Prince Max was now ready for even more radical measures. The idea of a national assembly, which would give to Germany a new constitution modeled after the English monarchy, appealed to him. He negotiated with the majority parties and attempted by this policy to maintain the solidarity of his ministry. The question of the abdication of the Kaiser now predominated the political situation at Berlin. On November 6 Prince Max issued another proclamation to the German people, stating that the entente had accepted the fourteen points, excepting freedom of the seas, and that Marshal Foch would make known to the German plenipotentiaries the terms of the armistice.[153]

---

[150] Ahnert, "Die Entwickelung der Deutschen Revolution und das Kriegsende," and Buchner, "Revolutionsdokumente, I," contain collections of periodical and pamphlet literature as well as documents.

[151] Runkel, "Die Deutsche Revolution."

[152] *Deutscher Geschichtskalender,* I Heft.

[153] Kuttner, *op. cit.,* 25. Menke-Gluckert, *op. cit.,* 47. Egelhaaf, *op. cit.* Runkel, *op. cit.,* 107.

Noteworthy is the fact that until the final collapse, Berlin contained the strongest forces of the imperial government. The Hohenzollern dynasty had raised Berlin from a provincial town to the rank of a world city, the third of Europe. The capital had shared generously in the prosperity of the empire after the Franco-Prussian War and had become one of the greatest manufacturing centers on the continent. Art and science had given to this modern city a peculiar lustre.

Its population of almost three millions had accepted the empire as the source of its wealth, order, and fame. To the nobles and bureaucrats, Berlin was the capital of an empire destined with invincible armies and fleets to dominate the policies not of an entire continent but of the world. To the middle class of the city, Prussian commerce, industry, and finance proved the superiority of an irresponsible paternalism over the democracies of the west. Finally the working classes, disciplined by the forces of trade unionism and social democracy, took a secret pride in that imperial government which had elevated the city to such a commanding position among the industrial centers of the old world.

It required four years of war and blockade, combined with the military, diplomatic, and political blunders of the ruling classes, to shake the loyalty of the Berlin bourgeoisie and proletariat to the empire.

Since the summer of 1916 revolutionary plots had been formed in Berlin. When the naval mutiny of 1917 occurred there were not wanting Socialist conspirators in Berlin to take advantage of a possible spread of the revolt. In January, 1918, General von Kessel suppressed the general strike in Berlin with efficiency and brutality. But from that time on, a definite plan was worked out by Independent Socialists to overthrow the empire. The Berlin revolutionary committee, which included Barth and Däumig, established connection with comrades on the front and the industrial workers in the capital. Although surprised by the request for an armistice, these revolutionists planned to seize the opportunity created by the military defeat and loss of courage at home, to establish the Socialistic republic. At a meeting held November 2 in which Haase, Liebknecht, Dittmann, Barth, Däumig, and Ledebour took part, the question of striking the first blow was discussed. The majority were in favor of commencing the revolution November 4, but Haase and Dittmann, uncertain of victory, had the uprising postponed. Among these revolutionary conspirators was a certain Lieutenant Walz of the Berlin garrison. He was arrested on November 6 and charged with treason. In order to save his life, he revealed the plot to the military authorities. Thus the government learned of the extent of the Independent Socialist agitation for the republic.

As early as 1916 a section of the German General Staff had found time during the Verdun and Somme battles for the preparation of "a battle and mobilization plan in case of a revolution." General von Linsingen, an able general from the eastern front, was in 1918 Acting Commander-in-Chief in Berlin and prepared to carry out this General Staff plan to the last. His military measures were worked out in detail and included even the formation of reliable companies of citizens.[154] From November 6 on there was a general tension in Berlin. Except for incomplete official bulletins, the censor suppressed all news of the naval revolt along the coasts. Rumors, however, only exaggerated the extent of the mutiny. November 7 was the anniversary of the coup d'état of the Russian Bolshevists, which the Independents prepared to celebrate. Five assemblies were scheduled for that night in Berlin, but Linsingen forbade their meeting. At the Koenigsbau the police drove the Socialist masses from the hall.

Linsingen then informed Berlin in a proclamation: "In certain circles the plan exists to form, in violation of legal regulations, workmen and soldiers' councils after the Russian model. Such organizations violate the existing orders of the state and threaten public security. I forbid by authority of Paragraph 9b of the Law concerning the state of siege, every formation of such unions and participation therein. The Commander-in-Chief in the Marks, von Linsingen, Major General." [155] A second order summoned all officers on leave in Berlin to report at headquarters with full field equipment. That night Linsingen seized at the Lehrter Station the first small columns of sailors and soldiers arriving from Hamburg, and confined them in the Moabit prison. The gas, electric, and waterworks were occupied by troops, and the telephone and telegraph offices were closed, thus cutting off all communication with revolutionary Germany. The day was, however, past in Prussia when the militarists could overawe the masses with paragraphs of the law or bayonets of the monarchical guard. Linsingen could not rely upon his own troops, and the civil government had been rendered powerless by the ultimatum of the Socialists.

After his resignation Prince Max had continued in office by direction of the Emperor, seeking to maintain the popular movement in democratic and legal channels. The majority parties were in a panic, and on the eighth of November hurriedly voted to extend the democratic electoral law to all federal states in the next session of the Reichstag. By an almost unanimous vote the government decided to propose abdication to the Emperor. Meanwhile the entire Prussian cabinet resigned.[156]

The government was no longer mistress of the situation either in Berlin or the empire. Its plenipotentiaries were already on their way to meet Marshal Foch, and Hindenburg was certain to accept the allied conditions irrespective of their severity. That the publication of these terms would

---

[154] Kuttner, *op. cit.*, 3–5.

[155] Kuttner, *op. cit.*, 26.

[156] *Deutscher Geschichtskalender*," I Heft, 35.

end the reign of William II was clear to all. Prince Max wished above all to preserve the unity of the *reich,* to save the monarchical principle and to control the revolution in peaceful channels. He was not, however, a Louis Philippe, and was unable to attempt a coup d'état which might have placed Germany in his control as regent.

The stopping of railway transportation led, on November 8, to a demonstration of furloughed soldiers who were thus detained in Berlin. They marched from their barracks to the commandery in order to secure commutation of rations, but were joined by civilians, who thought that they were demonstrating out of sympathy for the Kiel revolt. Before the *Vorwaerts* building the procession cheered for the republic.[157]

On the night of November 8 Berlin appeared to be on the eve of a serious revolt. Armed revolutionists had succeeded in entering the city, while the Independent Socialists had distributed weapons to their followers. A large majority of the workingmen were fully prepared for the uprising. On the other hand, General von Linsingen had occupied all strategic points with troops, fully equipped and wearing steel helmets. Armored cars and trucks patroled the center of the city. The party office of the Independent Socialists was closed by the police, who arrested Barth and Däumig. Trusted Jaeger Battalions of veteran infantry were then brought in haste to the capital.[158]

These last efforts, however, were frustrated by an order from Prince Max to the commander to refrain from attacking the masses. Thereupon General von Linsingen resigned. Aware of the disaffection among his own troops, he realized that even Prussian militarism could not save the monarchy in Berlin. Not even the Independent Socialists had, however, believed that Prussian militarism in the hour of revolution could be so weak and so defenseless. The spirit of General von Prittwitz no longer inspired the Berlin garrison.

It is of primary importance that, after the Kaiser bade Prince Max to remain in office until he had made a final decision concerning his resignation, the Majority Socialists still supported the ministry. During a conference with Prince Max they even extended their ultimatum until the signing of the armistice. Here is an indication of their weak and vacillating policy, which seemed to be governed by political expediency and by a due regard for the plans of the Independent Socialists. Handbills distributed by the Majority Socialists on the evening of November 8 announced that a part of their demands were accepted; that equal suffrage would be established in Prussia and all other federal states by imperial law; that immediate parliamentarising of the Prussian government was assured with an

---

[157] Runkel, "Die Deutsche Revolution," 122.

[158] Menke-Glückert, *op. cit.,* 49. Kuttner, *op. cit.,* 27.

increase of Socialist influence in the imperial government, that the *levee en masse* had been given up and that the settlement of the question of the Kaiser's abdication had been extended to the signing of the armistice.[159]

The original demand of the Majority Socialists for the abdication of the Kaiser had been made in the hope that by this step they could reach the goal of democracy without a civil war. After the sudden increase of disorder in the empire, the Socialists extended their ultimatum until the signing of the armistice, but the action of the leaders came too late. The German workmen demanded energetic action; the Majority Socialists therefore withdrew from the government and attempted to unite with the Independent Socialists.

Early Saturday, November 9, the general strike broke out spontaneously in the Berlin factories. From the General Electric Works, the German Arms and Munition Factory, and the Schwartzkopf and the Loewe Works, the strike spread to almost all the Berlin industrial plants. Agents of the Independent Socialists were active everywhere. At 10 a. m. a workmen's council of the Social Democrat party officially confirmed the strike, and an extra edition of the *Vorwaerts* announced it to the masses. As the factories were emptied of the workmen the Independent Socialists prepared for street fighting.

That no attempt was made to maintain the empire was due first to the orders of Prince Max to the military and secondly to a general revolt of the garrison of Berlin. The center of the city was held by strong military forces, while a northern reserve was posted in the Garde Fusilier Barracks and the Fourth Guard Regiment Barracks and a southern reserve of three battalions held the Augusta Barracks.

Early in the morning the Fourth Naumburger Jaeger Battalion mutinied, deposed its officers, and elected a soldiers' council. It then sent delegates to the *Vorwaerts* building to declare that the battalion would not fire on the people, but would aid the Socialist leaders. The Alexander Regiment, to whom the Kaiser had once said that in case he gave the order they were to fire upon their own fathers and mothers, joined the revolt, and was harangued by the Socialist Deputy, Wels. The famous *Lehrregiment* and the First Guard Reserve Regiment mutinied and armed the people at their barracks. In the southern portion of the city the Sixty-fourth Reserve Regiment deposed its officers. In all, fourteen units of the Prussian army mutinied on November 9 and refused to fire a shot for King and Fatherland. At the barracks of the Guard Fusilier Regiment in the Chaussee street, the loyal officers fired upon a procession of soldiers; otherwise no fighting occurred in the morning. The entire garrison of Berlin simply refused to maintain the empire by force.

---

[159] *Deutscher Geschichtskalender*, I Heft, 35.

Although the Independent Socialists had proclaimed a revolution, they made no attack upon any government office, nor did they attempt to set up a provisional government. At noon the Majority Socialist newspaper *Vorwaerts* issued an extra sheet stating: "The Workmen's and Soldiers' Council of Berlin has voted for the general strike. All factories stand idle. The necessary provisioning of the population will be maintained. . . . A great part of the garrison in closed formations with machine guns and artillery have placed themselves at the disposal of the Workmen's and Soldiers' Council. The movement will be directed in common by the Social Democratic Party of Germany and the Independent Social Democratic Party of Germany. . . . Workmen and soldiers provide for the maintenance of peace and order. Long live the Socialistic Republic."

Meanwhile what remained of the imperial government of Germany was centered at the chancellery in the Wilhelmstrasse. At 9 :15 a. m. the Chancellor was informed that the German Field Armies would no longer recognize the Kaiser as commander-in-chief. At 10 a. m. reports reached the chancellery of the mutiny of the Alexander Regiment, Fourth Naumburger Jaeger Regiment, and Jueterbogker Artillery. As the Jaegers were considered the most reliable troops of the Berlin Garrison, their revolt was regarded as sealing the fate of the Kaiser. In despair, Wahnschaff exclaimed to the Prince that only the abdication of the Emperor could save the monarchy. Prince Max spent the morning in frantic efforts to secure the Kaiser's abdication, but it was not until 11 o'clock that he was informed the decision had been made and that the formula was being discussed.

At that hour the strike of the workmen and the mutiny of the troops had become general throughout the capital. At any moment the masses might have proclaimed the deposition of the Kaiser and established a provisional government. Prince Max, therefore, determined to act upon his own authority in a last desperate effort to give the crisis a constitutional solution. He accordingly issued the following decree: "The Kaiser and King has decided to renounce the throne. The Imperial Chancellor will remain in office until the questions connected with the abdication of the Kaiser, the renunciation by the Crown Prince of the throne of the German Empire and of Prussia, and the setting up of a regency, have been settled. On behalf of the regency he intends to appoint Deputy Ebert as Imperial Chancellor, and he proposes that a bill should be brought in for the establishment of a law providing for immediate promulgation of universal suffrage and for the election of a Constituent German National Assembly which will finally settle the future form of government of the German Nation and of those peoples which may be desirous of coming into the empire."

The news of the Kaiser's abdication spread like wildfire through Berlin and assured the strikers and soldiers of a Socialist victory. Red flags were hoisted over the *Vorwaerts* building and other Socialist headquarters. Agitators harangued the mobs which surged through the Unter den Linden from the Palace to the Reichstag building. Cockades and insignia vanished from the uniforms of officers and soldiers.

While the proletariat demonstrated against the empire, the Majority Socialist leaders, Ebert and Scheidemann, commenced negotiations with the Independents. Ledebour, Dittmann, and Vogtherr, Independent leaders, had spent the night in the Reichstag building. Their party had planned to seize power on the following day, but the Majority Socialists, although weakened by the events preceding the abdication, were still in control of the situation. The Independents refused to accept the conditions of the Majority Socialists and postponed a meeting of the two parties with the newly-formed workmen's and soldiers' council of Berlin.

From a window of the Reichstag Scheidemann read the Kaiser's abdication, and announced: "The monarchial system has collapsed. A great part of the garrison has joined us. The Hohenzollerns have abdicated. Long live the great German republic. Ebert is forming a new government to which both Social Democratic parties will adhere. Deputy Gohre, who has been assigned as adjutant to the military commander-in-chief, will attest all military orders. Nothing dare destroy the great victory which we have achieved. Let us maintain peace, order and security."[160]

At three o'clock Ebert, Scheidemann and the members of the workmen's council, Prolat and Heller, went to the chancellery and informed Prince Max that only the formation of a Socialist government could save Germany. In accordance with the provisions of his decree Prince Max thereupon requested Ebert to assume the office of imperial chancellor.

Only in a nation trained by an autocratic military government to habits of obedience could such a course have been possible. Prince Max represented here the attempt to legalize the revolution in imitation of the bourgeoisie of France in 1830. Up to the last he clung to the monarchial principle. Ebert and Scheidemann sought on the other hand to establish a democratic republic by peaceful means and with an avoidance, if possible, of extra legal methods. The Independents alone wished to break with the past, to overthrow by force the capitalistic and bourgeois state, and to erect a Socialistic republic. As for the Pan-Germans and bourgeoisie they played a miserable part on this day of proletarian victory. Those who had preached world conquest as the goal of Germany were unwilling to defend even the capital of their king against a Socialist rebellion.

Ebert actually made an attempt to assume the office of Imperial Chancellor. Immediately after assuming office he issued a manifesto to his countrymen worded as follows: "Fellow citizens! The former Imperial

---

[160] *Deutscher Geschichtskalender,* I Heft, 36.

Chancellor, Prince Max of Baden, has with the consent of all the secretaries of state, turned over to me the safeguarding of all the affairs of the
Imperial Chancellor. I am about to form a new government in agreement
with the parties, and will shortly inform the public concerning the result.
The new government will be a people's government. Its effort must be to
give peace as quickly as possible to the German people and to strengthen
the freedom which it has won." To all the officials and employees of the
empire Ebert announced: "The new government has taken over the conduct of affairs in order to preserve the German people from civil war and
starvation and in order to carry out its just demands for self determination." He called upon all administrative officials irrespective of their
political beliefs to remain at their posts in order to save the Fatherland
from misery and anarchy.[161]

Even before the announcement of the Kaiser's abdication the Majority
Socialists had commenced negotiations with the Independents for the
formation of a united Socialist government. The Independents, however,
demanded: the establishment of a Socialistic republic with executive and
legislative power in the hands of trustees of the proletariat and soldiers;
the exclusion from the government of the bourgeoisie, with the exception
of technical department ministers; an agreement merely for a provisional
coöperation of three days in order to sign the armistice; and finally complete equality of leadership in the united cabinet. By the evening of
November 9 the Social Democrats replied to the six points of the Independents, stating: that the constituent assembly must decide the question
of a Socialist republic; that the establishment of a dictatorship by a
portion of a social class was contrary to their democratic principles; that
their party must reject the demand to exclude the bourgeoisie from the
government; that the Independents must remain in the government until
the meeting of the National Assembly; and finally, that they accepted the
demands of the Independents concerning the department ministers and
the principle of equality in the cabinet.[162] Thus the first revolutionary
day passed in negotiations between the Socialist factions. The Majority
Socialists had one great advantage: they were in possession of the Reichstag Building and Chancellery. Both parties now appealed to the workmen and soldiers for support in forming a provisional government. The
fate of Germany was placed in the hands of the proletariat of the capital.[163]

On the night of November 9 the workmen's and soldiers' council of
greater Berlin met in the chamber of the Reichstag. Barth, the chairman
of the assembly, paid tribute to the victorious revolution of the Berlin
proletariat and of the garrison. The meeting then decided to elect on

[161] *Deutscher Geschichtskalender*, I Heft, 36–37. *Bekanntmachungen*, 1050.
[162] *Deutscher Geschichtskalender*, I Heft, 38.
[163] Germanicus, "Zum 9 November," is a typical reactionary account of the revolt.

the following day workmen's councils in the factories. One delegate to the council was to be elected by every one thousand workmen, the smaller factories uniting to elect one delegate. Soldier delegates were to be elected, one to each battalion or independent unit, by the garrison in their respective barracks and military hospitals. It was finally voted that the elected members should meet in the *Zirkus Busch* at five o'clock in the afternoon to choose the provisional government. That night the Workmen's and Soldiers' Council issued a proclamation calling for the maintenance of order and the protection of the provisioning system of Berlin. It was signed by the deputy of the chancellor and the minister of the interior, by representatives of the people's committee, by representatives of the soldiers' council, and by the Berlin commission of labor unions.

The call for the maintenance of order was not unwarranted, since street fighting broke out toward evening. Late in the afternoon Karl Liebknecht and his Spartacan followers occupied the Palace, hoisted the red flag, and ordered the bells of the illuminated cathedral to be rung in celebration of the proletarian victory. The soldiers' council occupied the police presidency and army headquarters.[164] At night street fighting occurred between groups of loyal officers and revolutionary soldiers. Machine guns were used in the *Friedrichstrasse* and before the Library and the University on the *Unter den Linden*.

The only organized resistance to the revolution was made by a group of officers, cadets, and palace officials who gathered in the royal mews and there barricaded themselves. During the entire course of this revolutionary day only fifteen people were killed. To these martyrs was accorded on November 20 a public funeral and they were buried in Friedrichshain beside the heroes of 1848.[165]

FORMATION OF THE REVOLUTIONARY GOVERNMENT

Berlin awoke on the morning of November 10 to a realization of the fact that, although the monarchy had been overthrown in a single day, unless a coalition Socialist government was formed at once civil war would break out between the Socialist factions. The *Vorwaerts* earnestly pleaded for a union of all Socialists to complete the victory of the revolution, to prevent the self-destruction of the proletariat and to avert a condition of chaos. The Independents also saw the necessity of a compromise. Opposed to a coalition government were, however, the Spartacans, the extreme left of German Socialism, who in their party organization demanded: the disarming of the police and royalist military and the arming of the people; occupation of all civil offices and commands by commissioners of the workmen's and soldiers' council; seizure of all arms,

---

[164] Runkel, *op. cit.*, 116.
[165] Kuttner, *op. cit.*, 28–29.

ammunition, and war industries by the councils; control of transportation by the councils; abolition of military justice and establishment of voluntary discipline; taking over of the government by the Berlin workmen's and soldiers' council until the formation of a national council of workmen and soldiers; elections of workmen's and soldiers' councils with full legal and executive powers by the entire grown working people in city and country and without regard to sex; abolition of the dynasties and states and formation of a unified Socialist republic; immediate resumption of relations with brother parties abroad; immediate recall of the Russian embassy to Berlin.

The Independents were determined, however, to unite with the Majority Socialists, and on November 10 a deputation arrived at the chancellery with the ultimatum of their party. This declared that the Independent Social Democratic Party was ready to enter the cabinet under the following conditions: the cabinet to be composed entirely of Socialists who will be commissioners of the people; the departmental ministers to be technical helpers assisted by two adjutants chosen from the Social Democratic parties; the period of Independent coöperation not to be limited; the supreme political power to be in the hands of the workmen's and soldiers' councils, which are to be summoned from all Germany to a general assembly; the question of electing a National Assembly to be discussed after the consolidation of revolutionary conditions; Haase, Dittmann, and Barth to be delegated by the party to the cabinet.[166]

The Majority Socialists had already formed a government under the leadership of Ebert and Scheidemann. Their followers were in possession of the Reichstag and the government offices, while the commander-in-chief in the Marks had been appointed by them. Hindenburg at General Headquarters recognized their authority. Notwithstanding the opposition of Independents and Spartacans, the Social Democrats formed the majority in the Berlin Workmen's and Soldiers' Council. The party therefore might have ruled alone and, by convoking at once a National Assembly, it might have perpetuated itself in power. But its policy had been since November first one of compromise. A proclamation issued by Ebert on November 11 stated: "The Kaiser has abdicated and his eldest son has renounced the throne. The Social Democratic party has taken over the government and has offered entrance into the cabinet on the basis of complete equality to the Independent Social Democratic Party."

The Majority Socialists accepted, November 10, the conditions of the Independents and a revolutionary cabinet composed of the Social Democrats, Ebert, Scheidemann, and Landsberg, and the Independents, Haase, Dittmann, and Barth, was immediately formed. This government was at once recognized by the army, the bureaucracy, the principal federal states,

---

[166] *Deutscher Geschichtskalender,* I Heft, 42.

and the overwhelming majority of the German people. Although the Socialists thus seized the power of the state, they did so with the consciousness that they were the only class which had opposed that policy of conquest which had ruined Germany. Within a day the monarchical German people acknowledged this government.[167]

"The cause of freedom", said Ebert at the close of the events of November 9, "has experienced today in Germany one of its greatest days of victory. The German people have conquered and the old established rule of the Hohenzollerns, Wittelsbachs, and Guelphs has been overthrown. Germany has completed its revolution. After the abdication of the Kaiser, Prince Max, who had already handed in his resignation, formally bestowed the chancellorship upon me. Actually the people have by their will made me chancellor. . . . Monarchism and imperialism are gone from Germany. The constitutional national assembly will establish a government which shall represent as near as is humanly possible the will of the people. Germany's future state is the republic and the free German nation will regard itself as fortunate to become an equally respected member of the international league of free nations." [168]

The fundamental characteristic of the German revolution was the efficient control of the movement by the forces of the barracks and the labor unions. Unsupported by the intellectuals and lacking therefore great leaders, the revolution developed rapidly and overthrew the empire without apparent effort. The explanation of this success is of course the fact that the imperial system had ceased to be recognized by the people and functioned merely as an apparatus. Every genuine revolution possesses an ideal, uses force to achieve its ends, and organizes society in conformity with its principles. In Germany the ideal of political and economic democracy, grasped by the great masses of the nation, overthrew the power of the imperial government.

Just as every revolution of necessity overthrows the decadent political structure by force, so every revolution develops extremists after initial success and creates thereby the possibility of anarchy. There has never been a genuine revolution in which the victory of the revolutionists over the old order meant the final possession of power. No sooner is the political and social structure weakened by the fall of the established régime, than the struggle of classes, parties, and class groups for power begins. In the inevitable internal struggle, only a decision of arms brings the capitulation of the extremists. The history of the German revolution from November, 1918, until the adoption of the constitution is that of a constant struggle of radical parties for power.

---

[167] Delbrück, in *Preussiche Jahrbücher*, January, 1919.

[168] Runkel, *op. cit.*, 121.

In the external struggle for world conquest the Pan-Germans had ruined the empire and ultimately suffered defeat. Now in the internal conflict the Socialists completed the military defeat by adding to it internal dissolution.[169]

THE FALL OF THE PRINCES

The practical deposition of William II on November 9 in Berlin brought to an ignominious end that German empire which Bismarck had founded with blood, iron, and secret diplomacy. In the second week of November all the other German thrones collapsed. Although the Bavarian dynasty and the Hanseatic oligarchies had capitulated to a revolutionary democracy before the ninth of November, the majority of the German federal princes had been able to hold their thrones until the Kaiser abdicated. As they were equally involved in the ruin of the Hohenzollern empire, the lesser monarchical governments collapsed without any resistance to revolutionary Socialism.

The fall of the Bavarian monarchy was followed by that of the kingdom of Württemberg. Here the democratic royal house was quickly involved in the general monarchical disaster. In forming a provisional government on November 9, the Württemberg Socialists established at Stuttgart close relations with the rest of revolutionary Germany. The King of Württemberg abdicated in a dignified document and refused to hoist the red flag over his palace because it was his private property.[170] So weak were the Socialists in Württemberg that they called upon the bourgeois parties to form a coalition government with them.[171]

The grand duchy of Baden, under the rule of the able house of Zähringen, had long been the most democratic state in Germany. Here, however, in the most liberal of the monarchical states, the revolutionary movement began with the revolt of the soldiers, the formation of revolutionary committees, and the resignation of the civil and military authorities. A provisional government was formed on November 10 and on the fourteenth the Grand Duke abdicated. No resistance was offered by the monarch whose nephew had deposed the Hohenzollern Emperor. Of all the German princes, Friedrich von Baden played the worthiest part in the revolution.

On November 10 King Friedrich August III of Saxony ingloriously renounced his title, stating that he would allow no defense of the throne and that the people could get along by themselves in the future.

The Grand Duke of Saxe-Weimar offered violent resistance to those who would depose him until he was promised personal security. The

[169] Lederer, "Einige Gedanken zur Soziologie der Revolution," 11–20.
[170] Runkel, "Die Deutsche Revolution," 134.
[171] Menke-Glückert, *op. cit.,* 66.

Duke of Brunswick was forced to abdicate to avoid deposition and possible assassination. In Oldenburg the Socialists held a great demonstration on November 7, which was followed shortly afterward by the abdication on November 11 of the Grand Duke, Friederick August. The Grand Duke of Hesse abdicated on November 10, as did also the Prince Heinrich XXVII of Reuss Younger Line.

The Prince of Lippe-Detmold abdicated on the eleventh, Adolf of Schaumburg-Lippe on the fifteenth, and Duke Karl Eduard, formerly the Duke of Albany, on the thirteenth. In the next few days the rulers of Anhalt, and Altenburg abdicated. On November 14 the Grand Duke, Friedrich Franz IV of Mecklenburg-Schwerin, who was also regent of Strelitz, issued a decree renouncing the throne for himself and his house. Thus ended the ancient Obotrite monarchy.

The last German ruler to abdicate was the Prince of Schwarzburg-Rudolstadt, head of a picturesque district in the forest of Thuringia. He had escaped for only a few days the fate of his royal brothers.[172]

The war destroyed the German monarchies which were not strong enough to survive the tasks imposed upon them.[173] They blocked the reorganization of Germany, were opposed to democracy, and, therefore, fell. The monarchical ideal was damaged, perhaps permanently, by these inglorious abdications. The red flag floated over the palaces, while royal mottoes vanished from the courts, the newspapers, and the commercial world. The republican spirit of 1848, which had been crushed by the reaction, was indeed avenged in 1918. Just as Versailles stands as a monument of royal extravagance so the innumerable royal palaces of Germany will remain symbolical of an era of political tutelage.

---

[172] *Deutscher Geschichtskalender*, "Die Deutsche Revolution," I Heft, 93–151, contains the important acts of abdication issued by the German rulers.

[173] Naumann, "Die Demokratie," 5–7.

IV.

SOCIALISM AND SOCIALIZATION

The Social Democratic Party During the War

To understand the history of the November revolution it is necessary to comprehend the tripartite character of German socialism, for the history of the revolutionary movement from the signing of the armistice until the adoption of the constitution is almost entirely that of the struggle of the three socialist factions for control of the state. It was the great tragedy of the German proletariat that at the moment of triumph over the autocratic and capitalistic empire, the socialists were divided into hostile groups, and had been so divided since the beginning of the war. One hundred years after the birth of Karl Marx the German proletariat seized control of the national government, but were unable to establish socialism. Majority Socialists, Independent Socialists, and Spartacans, all considered themselves the true representatives of Marx and Engels, and waged a fratricidal war with one another. That the Marxian teaching was thus capable of different interpretations emphasizes its inner contradictions and its failure to remain entirely in accord with the reality of historical development. Now Marxism is not only an economic theory but it is also a *Weltanschauung*. As an economic theory the teaching of Marx is evolutionary, but as a political and historical interpretation of human progress it is distinctly revolutionary.[174]

The Communist Manifesto of 1847 prophesied the fall of the existing economic system, the supplanting of the capitalistic organization of society by the dictatorship of the proletariat, and the achievement ultimately by humanity of the goal of stateless communistic society.[175] The demand for secularization, for the expropriation of the expropriators, comes first from Marx. Marx erred in stating that the increase of the misery of the masses would be the result of the development of capitalism. Other economic factors have distinctly altered this conception. Karl Renner, the Austrian Socialist and statesman, wrote in his work, "Marxismus Krieg und Internationale": "The capitalistic society, as Marx experienced and described it, does not exist any more." Bernstein sought by Revisionism to hold together what was possible of Marxism and to build then a foundation for new evolutionary tactics.[176]

---

[174] Gisbert, "Von Marx bis Lenin" in *Preussische Jahrbücher*, September, 1919, 391–400.

[175] Weber, "Der Sozialismus," 17.

[176] *Preussische Jahrbücher*, September, 1919, 400.

Immediately before the war the industrial workmen improved the general conditions of life and work in Germany. Better food, clothing, dwellings, heating, lighting, and even luxuries were secured for the proletariat than at any time since the industrial revolution. In opposition to the law of misery, German writers now spoke of the law of social development or the law of social solidarity of interest. Kumpmann asserted, "As long as the national economy develops the standard of life of the employer class, so long will that of the workmen improve." [177]

The growing Socialist Party of Imperial Germany, conscious of the national economic development, waited therefore quietly to take the inheritance in accordance with this evolutionary theory; but during the war the inheritance was dissipated by the economic collapse of the Fatherland.[178]

The German revolution was not due primarily to economic causes. There was no miserable proletariat which rose against capitalism, nor was there any considerable agitation against capitalists and employers. The revolution was distinctly not the fulfilment of the economic development prophesied by Marx. When millions returned from the fronts and it was imperative that they should be able to find an economic field of activity, there was no systematic attempt made to seize the industries of the nation. It is especially significant that the hatred of the revolutionary masses was directed not against the capitalists and factory owners but against the army officers and bureaucrats.

It would be erroneous, however, to conclude that the socialistic movement was not the predominating one of the revolution nor socialism the great ideal of the advancing German proletariat.[179] Orthodox socialism struggled for power in Germany against liberalism, anarchism, and state socialism. The parole of socialism was and is "through equality to true freedom, *l'égalité des faits*". The decline of Marxism as a diagnosis of history and as a prophetic view of social and economic development has not destroyed the value of socialism.[180] To the masses socialism still appears to be the means of dividing equally the Marxian surplus value among the entire proletariat, as a result of which all cares will disappear; the hours of work will be reduced; the years of labor will be shortened; and misery will vanish.[181] Although critics have pointed out the limited character of this annual surplus value in even the great industrial states, that fact has not diminished the belief of the proletariat in socialism.

[177] Kumpmann, "Die Neuere Entwickelung," 46.
[178] Naumann, "Die Demokratie," 14.
[179] Goetz, "Deutsche Demokratie," 43.
[180] Kumpmann, "Die Bedeutung der Revolution," 5.
[181] Rathenau, "Kritik der Dreifachen Revolution," 33.

Ebert said, "Work is the religion of socialism." Scheidemann declared, "Developed from scientific principles, socialism is the highest organization of mental and manual labor." [182]

This organization has, however, a negative and a positive side, evidenced by the necessity on one hand of dispossessing the bourgeoisie and on the other of organizing the seized possessions for higher productivity. Socialism aims positively not at dividing but at holding together, substituting for individualistic production the systematic planned production of the entirety. The earnings from capital form the mass which is divided; but if production declines the profits from capital become of little value to the proletariat. Kuttner states: "Socialism is only capable of existing when it makes us richer as a whole—not if it makes us poorer. . . . To work toward that conception in which misery and suffering are past and forgotten ideas, in which the people are not only in possession of political rights but also in complete possession of the cultural achievements which have come down to us in ever increasing manner from our ancestors; to work toward that condition in which order, well-being, good manners and contentment, spiritual striving and robust activity form the normality of human life, that is the most beautiful and the finest task of the German Republic." [183]

The doctrines of socialism had been fearlessly advocated in imperial Germany by the Social Democratic Party. Notwithstanding the assaults of the government, the conservatives, and even the democratic parties, it had grown rapidly as a revolutionary group from the end of the Bismarckian era until the outbreak of the world war. It had built up a party organization and a party machinery unequaled by any other political group in the Fatherland. Although in the first decade of the century it had produced no great men comparable with Lassalle, Marx, Engels, and Bebel, it had nevertheless trained able organizers and efficient leaders. The party had survived the shock of revisionism, and, aided by a truly Prussian discipline which did not disdain bureaucratic methods, it had achieved a great victory in the Reichstag elections preceding the war. Refusing to play practical politics, denouncing parliamentarism, and expecting confidently the revolution, this party met its first great disaster in the outbreak of the world war. Powerless to prevent the inevitable world conflict, the party found its millions of voters involved in the maelstrom of war and nationalism. The German rising of 1914 with its nationalistic and patriotic fervor threatened to destroy the doctrine of socialism as the ideal of the Teutonic proletariat.

In the historic session of the Reichstag in the palace of William II, the socialist party leaders accepted the imperial amnesty. On August

---

[182] Vorwaerts, December 25, 1918.
[183] Kuttner, "Von Kiel bis Berlin," 15.

4, 1914, they voted the war credits and thus entered the field of national politics. This policy of August fourth was supported by the overwhelming majority of the German labor unions and party organizations.[184] In acting thus the party broke with all its traditions and apparently even for the time with the old dogmatism which taught that all history was in the final analysis a class struggle. That materialistic interpretation of history ceased to be as a result of coöperation with chancellors and military authorities, a living dogma of the party.

From another viewpoint this parliamentary policy of the socialists was a direct result of the suspension of the class struggle in Germany by the war. The achievements of the imperial social legislation inaugurated by Delbrück and Bethmann-Hollweg, the development of revisionism, the influence of South Germany, and finally the supremacy of the labor unions over the party had all tended by 1914 to bring about closer coöperation between Social Democrats and the bourgeois parties of the left.[185]

The nationalistic policy of the unions was expressed by their leader, Legien. When the Socialists adopted on August 4 the policy of national defense, they were enthusiastically supported by the overwhelming majority of the proletariat.[186] It was not until the allied blockade had forced upon the nation ration systems, contraband trade, and wage agitations, that the parliamentary policy of the leaders was questioned by the masses. Defeatism developed then throughout Germany, and the proletariat, unlike their leaders, were blind to the social and economic results of military defeat. Yet the original attitude of the proletariat toward the war had been nationalistic, and indeed the foundation stone of German unity in 1914.[187]

During the war the goal of the Social Democrats was the control of the Reichstag. Evolutionary democracy was to be established by participation in parliamentary life. Scheidemann declared in 1916 that the party had become strong enough to look forward to possessing political power.[188] Succinctly stated, German socialism rejected the dogmas of the past in order to secure an immediate parliamentary success. Since 1917 the Socialists formed one of the three majority parties of the Reichstag.[189]

---

[184] Jansson, "Arbeiterinteressen und Kriegsergebnis.

[185] Legien, "Warum muessen die Gewerkschaftsfunktionaere sich mehr am inneren Parteileben beteiligen?"

[186] "Sozialdemokratie und nationale Verteidigung," the official defense of the socialists' war policy. Kautsky, "Die Internationalität und der Krieg," 34.

[187] Heyde, "Abriss der Sozialpolitik," 52–55. Lensch, "Die Deutsche Sozialdemokratie und der Weltkrieg."

[188] Scheidemann, "Es Lebe der Frieden."

[189] Delbrück, in *Preussische Jahrbücher,* January, 1919, 142–143.

The success of this parliamentary policy was not achieved, however, without the sacrifice of that *union sacrée* of all German socialists, which had existed since the heroic age of Marx and Lassalle. Party unity, which had survived the shock of revisionism, was destroyed by the world war and the success of Bolshevism. Before the Social Democrats voted the war credits on August 4, 1914, a majority of the party voted to oppose any attempt on the part of the imperial government to give the war a character of one of conquest. In that fateful party caucus, Hugo Haase, then leader of the party, with thirteen other comrades voted against any support of the capitalistic empire. On the other hand patriotic socialist leaders, as the brilliant Ludwig Frank, were determined in any event to support the government. Under these circumstances, party unity was in a precarious condition. The right wing of the party was frankly nationalistic, the center was determined to maintain the war of self-defense as proclaimed by William II, while the left wing of the socialists was distrustful of the imperialists and opposed to any sacrifice of socialist principles even at the expense of a considerable loss of followers. The party discipline of the Social Democrats was, however, so strong and the influence of the German rising so powerful that the radical minority accepted the views of the majority and voted for the war credits. Indeed it was Haase himself who as spokesman of the party uttered those famous words: "In the hour of danger we will not desert our own Fatherland." [190] The united socialist support of the war was, however, of short duration. With the development of Pan-Germanism, the crisis was quickly reached.

The victories of the Central Powers in 1915, which profoundly affected the German proletariat, were received by the Pan-Germans with jubilation and led to an enlargement of the annexationists' demands. A prominent socialist, Wolfgang Heine, exclaimed in February, 1915, that the defeat of the enemy was the only war aim of the German Social Democrats.[191] Eduard David wrote about the same period a pamphlet entitled: "Are We Conducting a War of Conquest?" [192]

By publishing certain French plans for dividing Germany, which were being disseminated in the Entente states, the large industrial interests, financial groups and patriotic societies sought to strengthen their propaganda campaign for the annexation of Belgian, French, and Russian territory. In the historic Reichstag session of December 9, 1915, Chancellor von Bethmann-Hollweg finally showed that the imperial government accepted a part of the Pan-German plan of conquest. Speaking of eventual

[190] *Verhandlungen des Reichstags.* Dreizehnte Legislaturperiode. Zweite Session, Aug. 4, 1914, 9.
[191] Hildebrand und Heine, "Zwei Reden."
[192] David, "Führen wir Einen Eroberungskrieg?"

terms of peace, he declared that Germany must have a guaranty in the Belgian question. After describing recent German victories, the Chancellor exclaimed: "The open way to the Near East marks a milestone in the history of this war. . . . Neither in the east nor in the west dare our enemies of today possess gates of invasion through which they can tomorrow threaten us again and sharper than before." As spokesman of the bourgeois parties, Deputy Spahn, a Centrist, demanded that the necessary annexations be made. Speaking as the representative of four million voters, a socialist replied: "We request the renunciation of all plans of conquest." On December 21, 1915, the government asked the Reichstag for additional war credits.[193]

THE INDEPENDENT SOCIALISTS

The newly announced but long suspected imperial policy led to an immediate split in the socialist ranks. By a narrow vote of 66 for to 44 against the voting of the credits, the party caucus agreed to support the government. From then on Hugo Haase became the leader of those socialists who denounced the truce with the capitalistic empire and the abandonment of the dogmatisms proclaimed at Erfurt in 1891. In an able speech in the Reichstag on March 24, 1916, Haase reiterated the minority position. At this time David accused him of prolonging the war by his policy of opposition.[194]

In April, 1917, these secessionists met in a party convention and formed the Independent Social Democratic Party of Germany. They reaffirmed the fundamental principles of Marxian socialism, denounced all compromises and opportunism, and secretly adopted a revolutionary policy.

From then on the Independents worked to overthrow the empire. By seizing a portion of the socialist organization and by rapidly building up new party machinery, they became in an incredibly short time politically efficient and thoroughly organized. The success of Bolshevism, despite the support of the treaties of Brest Litovsk and Bucharest by the Majority Socialists, encouraged the Independents in their revolutionary policy. Through them the plan of establishing revolutionary workmen's and soldiers' councils was spread throughout Germany and even to the fronts. Believing in the possibility by means of the dictatorship of the proletariat of a quick transformation of the capitalistic state into the state of the future, they prepared plans for the immediate socialization of the means of production and distribution in Germany.

---

[193] *Verhandlungen des Reichstags,* 22 Sitzung, 9 December, 1915, 436–438.

[194] *Verhandlungen des Reichstags,* 37 Sitzung, 24 March, 1916.

THE SPARTACANS

Scarcely were the Independent Social Democrats organized as a minority party, than there appeared upon their left a revolutionary and communistic group of extremists calling themselves the Spartacan Alliance. Karl Liebknecht, son of William Liebknecht, was the founder of this section of socialists which ultimately became the Communist Party of Germany. The development of this new school of thought with its exotic interpretation of Marx is the direct result of the world war and the rise of Bolshevism. It is the most significant fact in the recent history of German socialism.

The first German to recognize the empire's responsibility for the outbreak of the war, and to denounce the moral guilt of the German and Austrian leaders, was Karl Liebknecht. Within the first year of the war he refused to support the nationalistic policy of his party. On May 1, 1916, he delivered on the Potsdam Square in Berlin a revolutionary speech against the empire.[195] For his opposition to the traditional solidarity and discipline of the Socialists he was expelled from the party. For summoning the masses to overthrow the criminal government of Germany he was promptly arrested and imprisoned. Nevertheless his protests against the nationalistic war policy of the Social Democrats were supported by Rosa Luxemburg, the ablest personality of the women's socialist movement. As a result of the work of these leaders, a group of communists without representation in the Reichstag began advocating the adoption of the Russian revolutionary methods of 1905, the immediate socialization of industry, and the beginning of a world revolution of the proletariat.

On the fifty-seventh birthday of William II the first of a series of open political letters, signed Spartacus, appeared in Germany. They were addressed to the leaders of the Social Democracy and advocated the reorganization of all socialistic groups upon an international basis. Spartacus declared that the establishment of a permanent socialistic society was only possible in case the entire European continent was revolutionized. National revolutions were to be regarded as a means to achieve this end. A letter entitled "Retrospect and Prospect", published August 12, 1916, revealed Liebknecht as the author of most of the Spartacan letters. These communications circulated throughout Germany and were even sent to the fronts. After September 20, 1916, the letters were no longer hectagraphed, but printed.[196] Notwithstanding police and censors, the Spartacan literature denouncing the war and advocating the cause of

---

[195] "Ein Jahr Sozialdemokratischer Reichstagsarbeit im Kriege," 8–12, contains the official Social Democratic report of the Liebknecht affair.

[196] *Tägliche Rundschau,* March 4, 1919.

communism, continued to be read in the interior of Germany. Wide publicity was also given to certain Spartacan letters by the Chemnitz *Volksstimme*. This socialist paper published the bitter attacks which accused Haase and the Independents of timidity and lack of vision. "Our goal is communism", Spartacus declared, "Freedom's golden land of anarchy." [197]

Although the deeds of the Roman gladiator who had lead his companions and slaves in the great uprising were unknown to the German proletariat, the classic name of this new communistic group nevertheless aided the spread of its propaganda. With characteristic German thoroughness, publicists noted that as early as 1849 the poet and revolutionist, Gottfried Kinkel, had chosen the name *Spartacus* as the title of a weekly paper. Others recalled that in 1877 Johann Most, publisher of the *Freiheit,* before his flight to the United States, declared to the Berlin workmen that Spartacus was the only great man in Roman history.[198]

The origins of Spartacism are traceable to the communistic movement within the German social democracy. The formulation of its program is, however, the result of the success of Bolshevism. Lenine's interpretation of Marx was readily accepted by the Spartacans, and the soviet system adopted as the fundamental part of their program. Karl Liebknecht and Rosa Luxemburg sought to raise the masses at once against the bourgeois state. Blindly convinced of the truth and practicality of their ideas, they prepared a fanatical rising of the German proletariat. The Bolsheviki evinced a keen interest in the Spartacans as true exponents of their own ideals, and they financed the Spartacan efforts to overthrow the German empire.

"All power to the workmen's and soldiers' councils" became the slogan of the Spartacans. Rosa Luxemburg prepared a consistent and clear political program modelled largely on Bolshevism. She drew the line sharply between the communistic Spartacans and the Social Democrats and Independents. The Majority Socialists were denounced as practical politicians, opposed to immediate socialization and advocating bourgeois doctrines of democracy and the rule of the majority, while the Independent Socialists were scorned as opportunists who had abandoned the true gospel according to Marx. Spartacus declared, "The workman has no Fatherland to defend." [199]

Although small in numbers, the Spartacan Alliance was, long before the November revolt, the revolutionary party of Germany. Its ideology was that of the Bolsheviki and its goal was the world revolution. "All reason is on the side of communism", wrote a Spartacan sympathizer,

---

[197] Wolffheim, "Knechtschaft oder Weltrevolution."
[198] Lentulus, "Wer war Spartakus?", 4
[199] Von Altrock, "Deutschlands Niederbruch," 46.

"for the decision of the communist to emerge from the world of this war gives to him such a moral superiority that nothing on earth can stand beside him." [200] When the November revolution delivered Germany into the hands of the socialists, the Spartacans were one of three factions capable of establishing a provisional government.

THEORIES OF SOCIALIZATION

As the German socialists differed in their interpretations of Marxism, so too they were at variance concerning the character of that transition economy or period of socialization which was to precede the establishment of "stateless communistic society". In the same manner that the doctrine of the dictatorship of the proletariat appealed to the political ideals of the Republican Revolutionists, the doctrine of socialization fired the imagination of those who believed themselves to be enmeshed in economic slavery.

During the world conflict the failure of German capitalism had become apparent to the proletariat and a return after the war to the old economic conditions was considered impossible.[201] The problem of socialization was one, therefore, with which the German socialists were concerned before the armistice. According to Karl Kautsky, the proletariat in this transition period must consider the welfare of all classes, must maintain international relations with the proletariat of all lands, and must prevent an international economic war. He concluded: "The day of victory depends upon great historic factors which affect large masses of humanity." [202]

Socialization is defined by the socialists as the ultimate taking over by the people's state of all the means of production in the hands of private capital.[203] This had been promised by all socialists as the first fruits of the revolution which was to usher in economic freedom. Socialization was to elevate at once the economic and the idealistic situation of the working class to a place of equality in the process of production; and to increase the national wealth by raising the powers of production and distribution.[204] A large portion of the German workmen were obsessed with the naïve thought that socialization meant the possession of all factories by the employees and the seizure of the much prized "surplus value" by simply raising wages.[205] The belief that the logical way to distribute the surplus value was by wage increases resulted in

[200] Erhart, "Dieser Friede wird kein Brest-Litovsk," 15.

[201] Froelich, "Der Weg zum Sozialismus."

[202] Kautsky, "Sozialdemokratische Bemerkungen," 157.

[203] Karl Buecher in *Preussische Jahrbücher*, May, 1919.

[204] Heinemann, "Ziele und Gefahren der Sozialisierung." Stroebel, "Die Sozialisierung."

[205] Heuss, "Deutschlands Zukunft."

hundreds of revolutionary strikes, riots, and local revolts. Although all three socialist sections agreed in their definition of socialization, they differed on the question of the method of carrying it out.

Of all the internal problems which confronted the Majority Socialists in the revolution, none gave it more difficulty than that of socialization. To establish a strong revolutionary democratic government for the entire *Reich*, to preserve order, to maintain the national economic life, to conclude a just peace with Germany's enemies—these were the aims of the Social Democrats. These factors therefore vitally affected the policy of socialization which had been the goal of the party since its foundation.[206]

Addressing the Berlin socialists, Hermann Mueller said: "It is a misfortune that our party received the portfolios of office at a time which is as unfavorable as possible for socialization. The entire economic life has collapsed. Almost all assumptions for socialization are lacking. . . . We do not dare experiment; we must proceed cautiously." [207]

That which the undoubted majority of the proletariat demanded as their revolutionary right was now impossible unless Germany's economic life was to be reduced to the level of Russia's. Credit, food supplies, raw materials, transportation, markets, all were essential to socialization, and all were wholly or partially lacking. Party leaders therefore cautioned the masses that progress toward socialization would be slow. Even Independent publicists informed the proletariat that socialization was a matter of decades, and not of days. Promises were made to the people; commissions were appointed to study ways and means; laws were prepared to carry out the beginnings of factory councils and special socialization; but the old economic order remained virtually intact.

Yet the socialists realized that certain industries could be immediately socialized without damage to themselves or to the state. But the ability of the party to carry through such a measure was lacking. Opposed to socialization was the overwhelming majority of the bourgeoisie, and to establish socialism meant, therefore, to adopt dictatorial methods toward a majority of the nation. The socialist statesmen were, however, in this instance, consistent, for they recognized that principle of majority rule which they formerly championed against the imperial autocracy.

Socialist writers also pointed out certain limitations to the general process of socialization.[208] The principle of rentability demanded that no industry should be socialized which would require extensive subsidies from the state. Other industries possessing peculiarities of shop technique, such as the constant introduction of new methods, were not suited

---

[206] *Deutscher Geschichtskalender,* II Heft: "Die Deutsche Revolution," 50 Lieferung, 11–12.

[207] *Vorwaerts,* 7 April, 1919.

[208] Staudinger, "Profitwirtschaft oder Versorgungswirtschaft."

to immediate socialization. As a general rule all industries which had shown a tendency to concentrate, such as the electrical, iron and chemical industries, were considered to be in an economic condition suitable to state control. Another immediate group comprised the transportation system, and the lumber industry. "The chief thing in socialization", said Eduard Bernstein, "is the placing of production and our economic life under the control of the commonwealth."[209]

The Independent Socialists, the only Reichstag party which had actively prepared for the revolution, regarded the socialization of the means of production and distribution as its final goal. When on the ninth of November they sought to safeguard the revolution by presenting their minimum demands to the Social Democrats, it was partly due to the fear that those practical politicians would liquidate rather than finish the revolution. The Independents regarded the National Assembly as an institution which would enable the bourgeoisie to regain control of Germany. Their demand that the supreme political power should rest with the Workmen's and Soldiers' Council was not an attempt to imitate Soviet Russia, but to safeguard socialism against the inevitable reaction.

Determined to complete the revolution by the progressive socialization of the means of production, the Independents wished this work to be carried out solely by the proletariat. Once socialization was well under way the other revolutionary questions could be easily solved. Their slogan was: "The working classes alone can establish socialism." The two great tasks were: the abolition of private ownership of industry and the establishment of the socialistic order in production and distribution.[210]

Unlike the Spartacans, the Independents did not believe in immediate socialization as a political rather than as an economic measure. Their program called for a gradual, progressive, and consistent carrying out of the Marxian theory.[211] The council system was emphasized as necessary to socialization because it alone was able to supplant the administrative apparatus of the capitalistic state. The Independents realized that certain industries could be quickly socialized, while others could not be taken over by the state without an economic disaster. They recognized also the danger of state socialism to the movement and strenuously opposed the taking over of single factories by the workingmen. The Independents found it difficult to convince the radical workers that socialism was not the taking over of the industries by groups of workers in factories, but by the entire proletariat. Above all they emphasized the necessity of controlling the banks and the system of credit; the necessary raw materials; and the sources of food supply in order to make socialization possible.

[209] *Das Neue Reich,* Nr. 2, 8.
[210] Frölich, "Weg zum Sozialismus," 2.
[211] *Prussische Jahrbücher,* March, 1919, 343.

Their program was therefore similar to that of the Majority Socialists except that they did not believe in a policy of socialization which required coöperation with the bourgeois parties of the National Assembly.[212]

During the period of the war and revolution, a fourth and non-socialistic theory of socialization was propounded by Walther Rathenau, head of the General Electric Company. Author of numerous pamphlets, his doctrines commanded national attention and evolved a storm of criticism and denunciation. Rathenau, however, defended his theories with unusual ability.

Analyzing Germany's situation, he wrote: "Before us is the lion, Lenine; at our left, the dragon of world competition; in our midst, the chimera, Spartacus." [213] Rathenau attacked the socialist doctrine of the "equalization of goods". The theories that if all surplus values were divided equally the general well being would be assured, and that if capitalism were abolished poverty would disappear, are erroneous. While socialism demands equality and well being, "organized economy" demands the increase and cheapening of production. By means of social legislation, Rathenau would establish a national control of industry. His reformatory aims are: national economic unification; the ennobling of work; the shortening of the hours of labor; the equality of standards of life; the abolition of proletarian conditions; the responsibility of the individual to the commonwealth and of the commonwealth to the individual; the change of rule into leadership and of submission into self-determination. "Economic anarchy" would then be supplanted by organization; education would become the highest duty of the state; class differences would be abolished, and political responsibility would be assured by the establishment of socialization and the creation of the council form of government.[214]

THE OPPOSITION TO SOCIALIZATION

Although a vociferous and insistent minority of Germans demanded immediate socialization, the voices of the critics of this panacea were even louder. Criticism of socialization came from socialists, labor unionists, economists, intellectuals, the middle class, and finally the capitalists. The socialist leaders were convinced that socialization was a slow process and criticised the impatience of their followers with the government's policy.[215] They were supported by the majority of the labor unions, which declared that the first year of the revolution was not the time for socialization and that the process in any event would be a slow one. The

---

[212] "Frölich," op. cit., 20–22.
[213] Rathenau, "Nach der Flut," 7.
[214] Rathenau, "Kritik der Dreifachen Revolution."
[215] Hoffmann, "Sozialismus oder Kapitalismus," 14.

unions also protested against the interference of the workmen's councils
in economic disputes, and arrogated to themselves the control of the
socialization movement in Germany. Their goal was the securing of
favorable tariffs in all industries, and as they were bound to carry out
the wage and labor contracts made with employers, they exercised a
conservative influence upon the proletariat. Bernstein, one of the greatest
socialist theorists, had stated that a long reform work was necessary
before the general socialization of production could take place. In this
he was supported by the unions.[216] Kautsky declared: "The difference
between the establishment of the republic and socialism becomes here
apparent; the former under favorable conditions can be carved out in a
few hours, while the erection of socialism demands decades of work." [217]

To the intellectuals and economists socialization was either "a leap in
the dark" or *"Herumexperimentieren am siechen Wirtschaftskoerper"*.
Publicists wrote that where competition ends, there progress ceases.
Eucken assailed the scheme of socialization as oppression in the guise of
social freedom.[218] Democrats asserted that the nation's industries could
not recover and provide work for the returned soldiers, if the blind cry
of socialization continued.[219] Naumann boldly announced that although
the socialists had complete political power, socialization would prove to
be impossible.[220] Even socialists realized the difficulty of socialization, due
to the federal character of Germany. It was this fact for example which
vitally affected the socialization of Saxony.[221] Jesuit writers attacked
socialization as well as other revolutionary doctrines, and presented a
Catholic plan for the reconstruction of German economic life.[222]

Other publicists pointed out that even if the coal mines, iron and steel
works, chemical plants, insurance companies, and electrical corporations
were nationalized the problem of socialization would be still unsolved.
By estimating the national wealth at three hundred billion marks and the
amount invested in stock companies at twenty-one billions, these critics
showed that only seven per cent of the entire wealth of the German people
was invested in the shares of corporations. As it was obviously impossible
for all the German factories and corporations to become communal or
state property without economic disaster, socialization would have to
proceed deliberately, if at all. As Kautsky, Bernstein, and Cunow all

[216] *Preussische Jahrbücher,* March, 1919, 343–345.

[217] *Die Freiheit,* December 6, 1918.

[218] Eucken, "Deutsche Freiheit," 33.

[219] Cohn, "Die Zukunft," 9.

[220] Naumann, "Die Demokratie," 14.

[221] Neurat, "Die Socialisierung Sachsens."

[222] Pesch, "Socialisierung." Pesch, "Neubau der Gesellschaft."

noted the necessity of compensation for the owners of nationalized industries, this factor presented a further complication to the problem of socialization. Minister Simon announced on behalf of the government that there would be no confiscation of property by the republic, but that the owners of nationalized property were to be fully compensated.[223]

Finally, critics declared that, with the elimination of the acquisition of private property, the technical and organizing processes in industry would cease, and production would decline. Nationalization would create a group of contented workmen as a result of the first steps toward socializations; but it would inevitably lead to diminished production. Kautsky believed, however, that custom, discipline, and attraction would keep the proletariat at work after the social revolution. The general conclusion of the non-socialist critics was that only a small portion of the means of production could be socialized, while the rest must be left under private ownership and control.

The November Revolution failed to carry out the socialist ideal of the nationalization of industries. German socialism was frankly unequal to the task and was forced to attempt the solution of the larger problems of the reconstruction of the state and the recognition of its international obligations as a result of the war. For years the German socialists had cried: "Proletarians of all lands unite"; but they themselves remained hopelessly divided. This disunion caused the failure of the German attempt to establish a socialist state. Socialization was, however, the great ideal of the November Revolution, and a rational socialization remains the one hope of the German proletariat.

---

[223] May in *Preussische Jahrbücher,* March, 1919.

V.

THE STRUGGLE OF PARTIES FOR POWER

The Six Commissioners

The Majority Socialists and Independent Socialists had seized power in Germany with the consent of the nation, because they were the only parties which had opposed the ruinous policy of the Pan-Germans. In imitation of this revolutionary federal government, since Germany remained a federal republic, the two Socialist parties established coalition governments in the several states. Everywhere the Socialists had political power in their own hands. The old imperial system with its twenty monarchies and autocratic methods had vanished within a week, and the historic German monarchical spirit had temporarily disappeared. The revolutionists gained at once for Germany: popular sovereignty; a general amnesty for political prisoners; the eight-hour day; equal suffrage; the right of assembly; freedom of the press; suppression of militarism; supremacy of the trades unions; and abrogation of the war legislation affecting laborers. The triumph of these ideas proves that the German revolution of November was a genuine one.[224]

Yet the government of the Six Commissioners was hopelessly disunited; did not possess a program and was confronted with the gravest of revolutionary problems. The Majority Socialists wished to reëstablish internal order, to create democratic governments in the several states, to convoke a national assembly, and to conclude a preliminary peace with the Entente. The Independent Socialists desired to develop the political power of the proletariat, to establish the council system, to commence progressive socialization, and to prepare the nation for socialism. Under the immediate pressure of the general collapse, the Independents held back, however. The well grounded fear that the masses of returning soldiers might mutiny, really forced the Independents to accept the plans of the Social Democrats.[225] Shall socialization of the means of production and distribution be carried out at once, or shall only those industries be socialized which have shown a tendency toward centralization? Shall a national assembly be convened to express the will of the German people, or shall the revolution be developed along Russian lines? These questions divided the provisional Socialist government as well as the masses of the German people. Many Socialists, who before the war had preached

---

[224] For a typical revolutionary pamphlet see Harz, "Die Revolution als Lehrerin und Erloeserin."

[225] Daümig, "Raetesystem," 16.

the doctrine of the unified state, chafed at the delay in calling the national assembly together. Others attacked the provisional government for reorganizing the ministries of Prussia and other states and thus perpetuating German federalism. The Independents denounced the Commissioners because they opposed the development of the revolution and were hostile to the Executive Committee of the Berlin Councils.[226]

However, from November 10 to December 29 the Six Commissioners completed a great amount of constructive work. Their common activity began when they agreed to the terms of the armistice. On November 12 Ebert, Haase, Scheidemann, Landsberg, Dittmann, and Barth issued the following proclamation to the nation:

The government, which has issued from the revolution and whose political control is purely socialistic, places before itself the task of realizing the socialist program. It proclaims immediately with full force of law the following decrees:

1. The state of siege is abolished.
2. The rights of union and assembly are under no restrictions. Officials and state employees are also unrestricted in the enjoyment of these rights.
3. The censorship does not exist. The theatre censorship is abolished.
4. Expression of opinion in speech and in writing is freed from control.
5. Religious freedom is guaranteed. No one shall be forced to perform any religious act.
6. An amnesty is granted for all political crimes. All proceedings on account of such misdeeds are quashed.
7. The law concerning the Fatherland Relief Service is abolished with exception of the regulations for the settlement of disputes.
8. The domestic servant regulations as well as the special laws against agricultural laborers are annulled.
9. The enactments concerning the protection of labor, abrogated at the beginning of the war, are herewith declared again in force and effect.

Further social and political ordinances will shortly be published. Not later than January 1, 1919, the eight-hour working day will come into force. The government will do everything within its power to provide sufficient opportunity for work. An ordinance has been drawn up concerning the protection of those without means of support. It divides the burdens between the *Reich,* state, and municipality.

In the sphere of sickness insurance, the obligations of working men's insurance will be increased beyond the prevailing limit of two thousand five hundred marks.

The housing problem will be attacked by the requisition of unusued dwellings.

The government is working on the problem of national food administration.

The government will maintain established production; will protect property against interference by private parties; and will preserve the personal freedom and security of the individual.

[226] Cohen-Reuss, "Der Aufbau Deutschlands," 3–7.

All elections to public offices are henceforth to be carried out according to the equal, secret, direct, and universal franchise upon the basis of the proportional voting system for all male and female persons of not less than twenty years of age.

This electoral law is valid also for the constitutional assembly, concerning which further regulations will be issued.[227]

This proclamation represents the first democratic victory in the coalition government, since it pledged the Socialists to call a constituent assembly. The fear of a mutiny of the army or the apprehension that the general strike of the defeated army and navy would spread over the Fatherland and produce universal anarchy held the Independent Socialists in line with the Social Democrats. German democracy was saved in November, 1918, because its communist opponents failed after their first defeats to unite upon a practical program of political action.

The Return of the National Forces After the Armistice

During the general rejoicing of the proletariat over the revolution, the government announced, on the eleventh of November, the terms of the armistice. The evacuation of the left bank of the Rhine and the neutral zone, the loss of rolling stock and matériel, the surrender of the fleet, and the continuance of the blockade, appeared especially severe to the nation. All parties regarded the returning armies as a possible danger to the orderly progress of the revolution. Grave fears were felt that all discipline would disappear and that the mutinous troops would sweep over Germany, destroying local governments, disorganizing transportation and the system of food control.

Although revolutionized, the German military organization under Hindenburg and Groener remained practically intact on the western front. Division, corps, army, and army group staffs continued to function, while brigade, regimental, and battalion commanders maintained a semblance of discipline in their units. Even in defeat, the veteran German infantry diivsions proved loyal to their leaders; and, counselled by soldiers' committees, obeyed orders. Above all Hindenburg remained at his post in Spa, and the General Staff commenced at once the work of moving the armies and their supplies into the interior of Germany.[228] Contrary to the accusations of its enemies, the revolutionary government made an effort to maintain discipline in the face of the enemy as well as at home. On November 12 the government authorized General Headquarters to maintain strict discipline in order that the army might be

---

[227] Deutscher Reichs-und Staatsanzeiger Nr. 269; Von Volkmann und Böttger, "Die Rechtsverordnungen des Rates der Volksbeauftragten vom 12 November, 1918."

[228] For an excellent account of the work of the general staff in connection with the return of the armies see von Kuhl "Der Deutsche Generalstab," 199–206.

brought home safely. The proclamation required: the relation between officers and men to be one of mutual trust; military discipline and order to be maintained under all circumstances; soldiers' councils to have a voice in the regulation of the commissary, furloughs, and disciplinary punishment, and to aid in preventing disorder and mutiny; similar rations to be issued to officers, officials, and men; equal increases of pay and equal extra field pay to be given officers and men; arms to be used against Germans only in case of self-defense or to prevent plunderings.[229]

When the armistice was signed the German armies were fighting a series of battles to cover their retreat to the Antwerp-Meuse line. The battles on the Lys, Aisne, Meuse, Scheldt, and in the Argonne, indicated the approaching collapse of the German forces. On November 12 the evacuation of the occupied territory and the march into the interior of Germany commenced. The I, II, III, IV, V, VI, VII, XVII, XVIII, and XIX Armies and Army Detachments A, B, and C retreated through Lorraine, the Rhine Palatinate, and the Rhine Province to the interior of Germany.[230]

On the other fronts the retreat of the armies was not carried out in such a systematic manner. At the conclusion of the Palestine battle on October 30, 1918, the German forces there were in full retreat. After September 15 German troops were retreating in Macedonia and Serbia. On September 29 there occurred the action between German forces and Bulgarian rebels near Sofia. By November 2 the last German forces crossed the Save and Danube rivers and entrenched on the soil of the Dual Monarchy. The German troops in Asia Minor as well as the forces in Syria fell back on Constantinople. Other detachments from the Caucasus marched through the Ukraine toward the German frontiers.

The Army Group of Mackensen in the Balkans consisted of the XI Army, the forces in occupation of Rumania, and troops from Turkey and the Caucasus. These forces commenced on November 12 to retreat to Germany through Hungary and Austria.

The evacuation of the Ukraine by the Army Group of Kieff, composed of the XX Corps Staff and four depleted divisions, was commenced November 16, 1918, and was not completed until March 16, 1919. Meanwhile the X German Army, with the consent of the allied and associated powers, continued to occupy Lithuania, Latvia, and portions of White Russia.[231]

[229] Reichs-und Staatsanzeiger, Nr. 269, November 12, 1918.

[230] "Die Rückführung des Westheeres," 3–10.

[231] "Die Schlachten und Gefechte des Grossen Krieges," 1914–1918. "Quellenwerk . . . vom Grossen Generalstab." General von der Goltz, "Meine Sendung in Finnland und im Baltikum," is an able account of German military activities in the Baltic states after the armistice.

The last great achievement of the Prussian military organization was that it brought the armies of the western front back home quickly and without mishap. German efficiency and the praiseworthy discipline of the veterans kept these retreating divisions from degenerating into mobs. The old Prussian spirit lasted long enough to march the troops back from the west. Although Socialist pamphlets stated that the soldiers' commissioners, without silver on their shoulders, really saved the wreck of the army, these assertions were true only in isolated cases.[232] It was the Prussian officer, loyal to his Fatherland in revolution, who was responsible for this success, the last great act of the Army of Frederick, Scharnhorst, and Moltke.

Grave disorders occurred, nevertheless. The Soldiers' Councils in the Rhineland had the greatest difficulty in maintaining order. Cordons of troops were placed at all the Rhine crossings to pick up stragglers and deserters. Along the lines of communication mutinous troops lost supplies amounting to billions of marks. Here the collapse was worse than after Jena. Officers left their commands and soldiers plundered depots and trains. In Belgium the soldiers often sold or abandoned weapons and supplies to the population. Yet when the officers fled from Belgium the councils saved supplies valued in millions. So serious did the situation become that the government issued a proclamation stating that the commissary of the comrades on the western front was in danger and that the plundering and confiscation of stores in depots or in transit must be stopped.[233]

On November 28 Hindenburg issued a general order, stating that all soldiers were to remain with their units until properly demobilized, and that the classes of recruits of 1896 to 1899 would be released as quickly as possible. Efforts were also made to stem the tide of hatred against the officer class. This hatred of the officers had resulted in the removal by the enlisted men of many regimental and company commanders. In many instances the officers were deprived of their side arms, epaulets were torn off, and infamous treatment was accorded to those who, by their arrogance and inability, had ruined the morale of the army. These conditions were more general among the reserves and line of communication troops than at the front. Here and there conflicts broke out between staffs and soldiers' councils. Generals von Boehn and von Mudra refused to recognize the commands of the councils. At other demobilization points the councils disarmed the veterans and deprived them of their imperial cockades. In Berlin the officers shortly after the revolution

---

[232] Vetter, "Der Zusammenbruch der Westfront," 14.

[233] Bekanntmachungen über den Ernteverkehr nebst den anderweitigen Gesetzen und Verordnungen wirtschaftlicher Natur aus den Jahren 1915–18, 24. Nachtrag, 1051.

formed a new political organization, the German Officers' Alliance, for their own professional protection. This was followed by the formation of the National Union of German Officers by a few political malcontents.[234]

While many soldiers' councils wasted or destroyed great quantities of food or raw materials, the majority of them formed useful auxiliaries to the army staffs. Mistakes were made everywhere and the maintenance of order was always difficult. Thirty-nine per cent of the German regular officers had been killed in battle, yet this class was violently attacked by revolutionists. However, the policy of the army leaders was supported on the whole by the veteran soldiers, and when three hundred representatives from the soldiers' councils of two hundred and twenty divisions met on December first at Ems, they represented an almost conservative force in a period of anarchy.[235]

In the east the condition of the German troops, which were as a general rule inferior to the western units, varied according to locality. The army of occupation in Poland, especially the Lorraine Landsturm, hastily evacuated the country, abandoning valuable supplies. Prussian regiments actually allowed themselves to be disarmed by Polish legionaries, while Polish troops in Posen and portions of West Prussia and Silesia regarded those territories as already a part of Poland. As the thin line of German troops retired in the Baltic States, notably at Minsk, Lithuania, and Courland, they were followed by the red army of the Soviets. The Latvian regiments fled before the Bolshevists. The army of Mackensen was interned by the Allies in Hungary.[236]

The naval demobilization did not present such difficulties, although the revolutionary spirit had destroyed the morale of the splendid fleet which fought at Jutland. The Berlin government issued an order on November 12, 1918, that officers were to wear the insignia of their rank, and that the councils were to aid them in maintaining discipline. All damage to ships and matériel must cease, and everyone was ordered to carry out the terms of the armistice. "We will have peace only if we loyally carry out the prescribed terms of the armistice", the government declared.[237] Difficulties were experienced in surrendering the fleet. Sailors demanded a premium of 500 marks to make the voyage to the British internment ports. English naval forces entered Kiel, Wilhelmshaven, and Danzig, to observe the carrying out of the armistice, while the Allies maintained a blockade in the Baltic as well as in the North Sea.

---

[234] D. O. B. *Schriften*, Heft I.

[235] *Deutscher Geschichtskalender*, 190.

[236] *Preussische Jahrbücher*, January, 1919.

[237] *Reichs und Staatsanzeiger*, Nr. 269.

The general result of the demobilization of the imperial army and navy was the acceptance of the revolutionary conditions by the overwhelming majority of the enlisted men. It was a naval force which had in fact first mutinied against the empire. As a general rule these demobilized forces formed the nucleus of a military support which was far more conservative than even the Social Democrats had expected. The influence of the German veterans upon the course of the revolution was destined to be decisive; for it was the German army which helped in a large measure to save the nation from the chaos of Bolshevism.

THE WORKMEN'S AND SOLDIERS' COUNCILS

The most characteristic political and economic development in the first phase of the revolution was the formation throughout Germany of workmen's and soldiers' councils. Everywhere these revolutionary forces seized local power and arbitrarily altered the established political and economic life. As revolutionary administrative bodies, they brought about the radical democratization of the German state governments.

The council system owes its origin to the Russian Revolution of 1905, which developed during the struggle with the Czar new and highly efficient revolutionary organizations called the Workmen's Deputies Councils. These were created in the large Russian industries and formed the backbone of the revolutionary movement. They failed in their revolutionary efforts because of the loyalty of the Russian army to Czarism. However, the creation of soldiers' councils during the revolution of 1917 formed the basis upon which, combined with the workmen's deputies councils, the Bolsheviki erected the soviet system. Although German Socialists had previously sought to develop the English shop steward system into a revolutionary organization, they adopted in 1917 the Russian methods. Viewed from the standpoint of efficiency, these methods, which gave the masses active participation in government, were better suited for the establishment of the dictatorship of the proletariat and ultimately of Marxian socialism than were German parliamentary tactics. Proletarian impatience with union and party secretarial methods also accounted for the spontaneous adoption of the council system in November, 1918.[238]

The goal of the councils movement was the completion of the socialistic revolution and the formation of communistic society. The system itself was two-sided: political and economic. Politically it united legislative and administrative power in the councils, discarded periodical elections, restricted the franchise to the proletariat, and placed the political power of the state virtually in the hands of the workmen of large industries. Starting with the commune the industrial workmen formed, according to occupation,

[238] Cohen-Reuss, "Der Aufbau Deutschlands und der Raetegedanke," 8–16. Feiler, "Der Ruf nach den Raeten," 29–31.

councils of one thousand workers, which elected leaders. The delegates of all the communal councils then formed a council for that commune which assumed all the functions of government. City officials, magistrates, and police were displaced by the council and its committees. Communes were organized into districts and districts into provinces. The provinces then were subordinated to the national congress of all councils. This congress was to choose an executive council which was to be elected twice a year and was to be subject to recall. It was to exercise the supreme power of the state.[239]

The proletariat demanded active participation in government and not merely the right to vote. What the Socialist party organizations and labor unions had done to create a proletarian bureaucracy was in a measure obverted by the recall provision of the council system. There again the immediate idea was Russian, although the prototype existed in the Paris Commune of 1871. Actually the council system eradicated this evil more effectually than syndicalism or the shop steward plan. The best answer to the charge that the Germans slavishly imitated what Russia had produced is the history of the council movement in Germany from November, 1918, until March, 1919.

The economic side of the council system aimed to bring about socialism by the aid of the proletariat and to create an economic organization in which the proletariat would have complete control of the national economic life. Besides the political councils, shop councils were to be organized according to industries. They were, like the political councils, to be formed into districts and provinces. The provinces elected delegates to the Central Economic Council, which exercised the supreme power of the state in questions of economic policy. Conceived as a bold measure to carry through the economic revolution, the chief function of the Central Economic Council was to be the maintenance of the processes of production under socialism.[240]

However, from an economic standpoint this organization appeared both dangerous and superfluous. Claiming to protect the interests of the workingmen, the strong and well organized labor unions were already in the field. Their opposition to the economic councils vitally affected the development of the idea, and ultimately the government took a middle ground in preventing any competition between the shop councils and the unions.[241]

The theory of the council system was by November, 1918, generally known throughout Germany. Its doctrines had been spread by Russian propagandists, Socialist organizers, and even by bourgeois publicists. The

---

[239] Daümig, "Raetesystem."

[240] Fröhlich, "Der Weg zum Sozialismus."

[241] *Preussische Jahrbücher,* May, 1919.

actual workings of the system were, however, quite at variance with the general theory.[242]

Although the workmen's and soldiers' councils of the Hanseatic States and South Germany, as well as the soldiers' councils on the fronts, had been the bearers of the revolutionary standards, it was not until the revolt of Berlin that the national triumph of the council idea was assured. The meeting of the first workmen's and soldiers' council on Red Sunday, November 10, in the Circus Busch, marked the beginnings of this new revolutionary system for Germany. Over three hundred delegates were present. From the start the meeting was divided into factions of Socialists, Independents, Spartacans, and Bourgeoisie. A strong soldier sentiment favored a compromise, and Ebert's announcement that the two Socialist parties had agreed to work together was loudly cheered. But on the election of the executive committee the Independents and Spartacans sought to nominate a list which contained only their own members. At once a violent opposition developed, which resulted in the election of a committee composed of six Socialists and six Independents. Thereupon the assembly assumed supreme power in Germany until the meeting of an all-German council, and confirmed the election of the government of Six Commissioners already installed in the Wilhelmstrasse. A proclamation was then issued to the proletariat of Germany, announcing the formation of the Socialistic republic.[243]

It was only after this meeting that the coalition government was assured of power. That night a conference was held between the Six Commissioners and the Executive Committee of the Councils and a serious attempt was made to define the powers of the two governing bodies. It was agreed that the Council should remain in permanent session in the former Prussian House of Lords and that it was to be the real governing power. The provisional government was to be responsible to this Berlin Council. While theoretically this conference established the dictatorship of the proletariat, actually it created a governing organization which was conservative socialist in character. Thus this conference strengthened the position of the Majority Socialists. On November 12 the Council issued a proclamation stating that all communal, land, national, military, and administrative authorities were to continue their regular activities. This was the second great conservative step of the Council and effectually checked the demoralization of the German administrative system. The Berlin Independents on November 14 issued placards in Berlin, signed by Dittmann and Haase, declaring that the Councils were the supreme political power in Germany, and that the Social Democrats were already failing to develop the revolution. This attack was

[242] Geyer, "Sozialismus und Raetesystem."

[243] Poster of Workmen's and Soldiers' Council, November 12: "Aufruf an das werktaetige Volk."

followed by others accusing the Socialists of supporting the military authority of the bloodhound, Hindenburg, and the plan of calling a national
assembly. "If the Berlin government lifts up its horn on high", declared
the Independents, "then the class-conscious proletariat will raise their
weapons in order to sweep away the traitors to the revolution." Yet the
Independents wavered in their opposition and actually agreed, after prolonged debate, to the calling of the National Assembly for February 19,
1919.

The second important meeting of the Berlin Councils was held November
19. The chairman of the committee, Richard Mueller, said in his opening
speech: "We will not have a democratic but a socialistic republic. The
way to the constituent assembly goes over my dead body." A resolution
providing for a meeting of a national congress of workmen's and soldiers'
councils was then passed. The Independents regarded the fall of the provisional government as certain, since the Berlin Council called the bourgeois
demand for a National Assembly an attempt to rob the workers of the fruits
of their victory. However, on the same day that the councils met, the city
government placarded Berlin with the announcements of voting lists for the
National Assembly.[244]

Other speakers asserted that the coming congress must elect an authorita-
tive control council and that it must give Germany a constitution adapted to
a proletarian democracy. The reality of the situation was on the other hand
explained by Scheidemann, who stated that the National Assembly was not
being called to legalize the revolution, but to lay the permanent foundations
of the future national state. Only thus could a government be erected
capable of negotiating with Germany's enemies. The Entente would not
recognize a dictatorship nor would it lift the "hunger blockade" for such a
government. If Russian aid were invoked by the revolutionists, German
unity would collapse and the Entente would occupy Berlin before the
Soviets could assist the German proletariat.

Meanwhile the rule of the workmen's and soldiers' councils throughout
the empire was rapidly reducing Germany to a condition of anarchy. Millions of marks were squandered by these revolutionary organizations. In
hundreds of cities and towns they stopped food transportation, confiscated
supplies, deposed officials, removed directors and teachers from the public
schools. The general orders of the Berlin government were disregarded in
many instances by the local councils which considered themselves as sovereign within their own sphere of activity.

The division of power between the government and the Central Council
of Berlin caused widespread opposition throughout Germany. The assump-

---

[244] Poster of Berlin City Council, November 19: "Aufstellung der Waehlerlisten
für die Nationalversammlung."

tion of control over the empire by the Berlin Council aroused general indignation in southern Germany. Bavaria, Württemberg, and Baden denounced the radical terror of Berlin and openly stated that the necessity might arise for the South to take its fate in its own hands. Throughout the Rhineland the cry of "Away from Berlin" was raised. Even socialistic Saxony opposed the arrogance of the Berlin councils in assuming revolutionary control of Germany. The Minister-President of Hesse, Ulrich, denounced the Berlin authorities because of their failure to maintain order.

In an effort to remedy these intolerable conditions, the provisional government called on November 22 a conference with the Executive Council. The result of this meeting was an agreement that the executive power was to be vested for the future in the government, while the councils were to act as "an organ of control". Until the meeting of an all-German congress of workmen's and soldiers' councils, the Executive Council of Berlin was to exercise supreme power in Germany. It could appoint and dismiss the cabinets of the *Reich* and Prussia. It could also give its opinion on the appointment of the "technical ministers". On November 23 an official notice of this conference was published, and the Executive Council issued a call for a congress of delegates to meet in Berlin on December sixteenth.

In the proclamation, the Executive Council disclaimed any attempt to assume dictatorial powers, urged the maintenance of national unity, pointed out the dangers to peace and the food situation, and authorized the existing councils to send delegates, since the time was too short to establish an electoral system for the proletariat.

On the same day the Berlin Executive Council issued a proclamation to all the German councils warning them against interferences with the food administration, the control of raw materials, or the administrative work of officials who were loyal to the new régime. Confiscations of public funds, interference with ship, railway, and postal transportation, and arbitrary arrests without the consent of local officials, were prohibited. Finally all councils were directed to alleviate the housing situation, to conserve the food supplies, to maintain the health regulations, and to aid the transportation of soldiers from the fronts.

This November conference was a victory for the Majority Socialists in the government as well as evidence of the ability of Ebert, Scheidemann, and Landsberg. Scheidemann showed marked sagacity in his analysis of the political and economic situation and in his determination to adhere to the democratic program of his party. The victory of the government was made easier by the strength of the Majority Socialist group in the Executive Council. Not the arguments of the majority leaders, however, but the fear of the disunion of Germany, forced the Councils to reach an agreement with the Six Commissioners.[245]

---

[245] Menke-Glückert, *op. cit.*, 101.

Before the meeting of the Congress of Workmen's and Soldiers' Councils, the provisional government of Germany called a conference for November 25 of the representatives of the revolutionary federal states. The purpose of this conference was to establish better relations between the states and the provisional government and to discuss the questions of peace and national reorganization. Since the revolution of November 9 the national unity had been in constant danger. Under the influence of Lauffenberg, the Hanseatic Republic of Hamburg had attempted to negotiate with Soviet Russia. Eisner had sent Professor Foerster as Minister of Bavaria to Switzerland and opened negotiations directly with Clemenceau. Heads of governments in other federal states had publicly denounced the radical misrule in Berlin.

At the conference which was held in the Congress Hall of the Imperial Chancellery, Kurt Eisner as the representative of Bavaria attacked two ministers of the central government, Solf and Erzberger, whom he declared to be compromised by their activities during the war. He announced that the Entente would not negotiate with the leaders of the old system, and that a presidency of five or seven uncompromised men should direct the negotiations for peace.[246]

Other representatives advocated the immediate convocation of the National Assembly. All recognized the necessity of concluding peace, reorganizing commerce and industry, and adopting a republican constitution for Germany. The conference resolved finally that the unity of Germany must be maintained; that the National Assembly was to be convened as soon as possible; that in the interval the workmen's and soldiers' councils were to be the representatives of the will of the people; and that the provisional government should attempt to bring about a preliminary peace with the enemies of Germany.[247]

The summoning of a congress of workmen's and soldiers' councils to meet in Berlin was the first great step taken since the fall of the empire to reëstablish German unity. Although a proletarian movement, it was hailed by the bourgeoisie as the first serious attempt to reëstablish order throughout the nation. This sentiment was voiced by Ebert on December first in a speech to the Berlin Socialists in which he said that the great German revolution would not found a dictatorship or an enslavement of Germany, but would firmly establish German freedom. On December 9 the Berlin Council drew up an order of business providing for a discussion of the questions of the National Assembly, the socialization of the economic life, the conclusion of peace, the erection of a socialistic republic, and the election of an executive council for all Germany.[248]

---

[246] Scheidemann, "Der Zusammenbruch," 218, 221, 223.
[247] *Deutscher Geschichtskalender,* I Heft, 58–63.
[248] Runkel, "Die Deutsche Revolution," 167.

During this period Liebknecht at the head of the Spartacans attempted by continuous street demonstrations to pave the way for the proclamation of the dictatorship of the proletariat. On the night of November 21 a mob of Spartacans attacked the Police Headquarters, but were repulsed with severe losses. That day Liebknecht had announced to his followers that when the world revolution was completed, the proletariat of France, England, and the United States would feed Germany.

On December 6 several conservatives in the Foreign Office, including Count Matuschka, Rheinbaben, and von Stumm, chief of the intelligence department, planned an anti-revolutionary coup d'état. At the head of several hundred soldiers and students these precursors of the counter revolution marched to the Chancellery, proclaimed Ebert President of Germany, and occupied the Prussian House of Lords, where they arrested the Executive Committee of the Councils. Although order was soon restored by the provisional government, the report spread among the workers that a reactionary conspiracy had deposed the people's Commissioners. That night two Spartacan processions attempted to reach the Wilhelmstrasse, but were repulsed by troops of the guard with a loss of forty killed. At this time Spartacan attacks took place at Hamburg, Halle, Duesseldorf, Schwerin, and Dortmund. On December 6 the Spartacans of Munich seized the principal newspaper offices and forced the Social Democrat Auer to resign from the ministry.[249]

Berlin was the scene on Sunday, December 8, of demonstrations by the Majority Socialists, Independents, and Spartacans. That night Liebknecht proceeded with thousands of his followers to the *Wilhelm Platz,* which was entirely filled with Berlin communists. From an automobile Liebknecht harangued the mob, while the people's Commissioners stood silent in the darkened rooms of the Imperial Chancellery. Pointing to the large hall, where the Congress of Berlin had met in 1878, Liebknecht shouted: "There they sit, the traitors, the *Scheidemaenner,* the social patriots. We have shown that we have power to take the whole nest of them, but I demand for tonight only the cry: 'Long live the social revolution, long live the world revolution.'"

At this dramatic moment the Independent, Emil Barth, appeared on an illuminated balcony of the Chancellery. He had been one of the revolutionary conspirators who had planned to overthrow the empire, but the masses greeted him with shouts of derision and scorn. Barth boldly denounced Liebknecht for his opposition to the Socialist government, and the mob dispersed after a violent debate between the two revolutionary leaders. This demonstration was not without its effect upon the Independent leaders, who saw that their coöperation with the Majority Socialists

---

[249] Scheidemann, "Der Zusammenbruch," 230–231.

was estranging their radical followers from the party. The left wing of the Independents now openly advocated an alliance with the Spartacans.[250]

THE FIRST CONGRESS OF THE COUNCILS

The meeting on December 16 of the first congress of German workmen's and soldiers' councils in Berlin was the most important event since the outbreak of the November Revolution. The future of Germany was in the hands of this assembly of the victorious proletariat, and for the first time since November 9 the nation had an opportunity to express its opinion upon the great revolutionary questions. Liebknecht correctly said that the members of the congress had to decide whether they would develop further the revolt begun in November to a socialistic revolution of the German proletariat. The high character and abilities of the men attending the congress was an indication of the success of the educational work of the Socialist party during the last decade before the fall of the empire. A majority of the members were earnest and politically intelligent. They were also aware of the problems facing the nation, and they were determined to arrive at a prompt solution of these difficulties.

In the crowded hall of the Prussian House of Deputies, Richard Müller formally opened the congress with an address of welcome. He pointed out the necessity of consolidating the gains of the revolution and said that the first problem was to decide whether or not the proletariat should maintain the dictatorship until the end of the revolution. Stating that the workmen's and soldiers' councils were the only achievement of the revolution, he added that their relations with the government must be altered and that the troops must take an oath to defend them. For the government, Ebert said that there was only one source of law in Germany: the will of the people. The national goal was the erection of a state of law. The victorious proletariat would overcome first the political class differences and then the economic inequalities until finally complete equality would be established. Democracy would form the rock upon which the working class would build the house of Germany's future.

Thus the great question of the revolution was brought before the congress in the first morning session at the very moment which the Spartacans had chosen to assure the triumph of the communist cause. Great crowds of striking workmen assembled that morning in the Avenue of Victory near the statue of Otto the Lazy and marched to the House of Deputies. Before its portals, Liebknecht, in a speech to the strikers, denounced the idea of a national assembly, demanded the disarming of the army leaders and counter revolutionists and the arming of the revolutionary working classes. To the armed strikers he shouted: "Whoever

---

[250] Scheidemann, "Der Zusammenbruch," 220–221. Runkel, "Die Deutsche Revolution," 168–170.

votes for the National Assembly, votes for the rape of the working class."
Thereupon a deputation of these Spartacans entered the hall and demanded in the name of two hundred thousand workmen: a socialistic
dictatorship with all power in the hands of the councils; the abolition of
the present government and the old administrative system, and the formation of a "red army". Their petition was noted, but the congress refused
to allow Karl Liebknecht and Rosa Luxemburg to attend the meeting
with full voting privileges. Then the Spartacans brought a procession of
youths to the congress. These young communists demanded: the six-
hour day for workers under sixteen years of age; abolition of military
service, and the enactment of a law establishing the age of majority at
eighteen. Tumultuous scenes occurred during these interruptions and
order was maintained with difficulty.

Within the congress, the Majority Socialists defended the government
against the assaults of the Independents and Spartacans. Landsberg accused Müller of aiming at the dictatorship, and said that just before the
congress met the Executive Committee had debated the question of re-
moving Ebert from the government. "If the Berlin Executive Council
wished to defend itself against the suspicion of a dictatorship," he said,
"it should have called this congress the first day after the revolution."
The delegates from southern and western Germany supported the accusations of Landsberg.

On the second day of the congress George Ledebour accused Ebert of
insincerity in declining the presidency and charged him with the fateful
crime of December sixth. Boasting that the Independents had planned
and organized the revolution of which the other parties now enjoyed the
fruits, he shouted: "Ebert is a mark of infamy for the government."
During the afternoon session, thirty soldiers entered the meeting bearing
pasteboard shields, representing the units of the Berlin garrison. They
demanded: the formation of a supreme military council chosen by all the
soldiers' councils of Germany; the abolition of all insignia of rank; the
disarming of all officers and returning troops, and the maintenance of
the discipline and revolutionary character of the army by soldiers' councils. Speaking from various parts of the hall, these soldiers required the
congress to debate these propositions at once. A violent discussion broke
out between the Independents and the Majority Socialists over the question. Haase himself sought to have this ultimatum laid on the table until
the following day. The session finally ended amid scenes of tumult and
strife.

The third day of the congress was the decisive one and marked the
turning point in the history of the German revolution. Amid a storm of
protests, Cohen-Reuss moved that the elections for the National Assembly should take place on January 19, 1919. Supporting his motion, Cohen-

Reuss made a masterful speech, describing the hopeless condition of Germany which was drifting toward a fearful catastrophe. In the course of his address he said: "Only a strong central authority, which is supported by the sturdy foundation of the general will of the people, can save our nation. No central power can secure authority for itself either at home or abroad if it is not supported by the overwhelming majority of the German people. The only organization which can carry out the will of the people is the German National Assembly for which every German can cast a vote. Workmen's and soldiers' councils can never be the expression of the universal will of the people. Bolshevism in Russia has discredited socialism for decades. The Entente will occupy this city if Germany does not develop order. Björn Björnson has just informed me that the French minister in Christiana has said within the last few days: 'Things are favorable for us in Berlin; if conditions continue thus, we will be there in four weeks.'"

The great majority of the congress accepted this view of the necessity of calling a National Assembly. Although the Independent and Spartacan leaders violently attacked the motion, they could not even control their followers. Dittmann, one of the Independent leaders, exclaimed: "The masses wish the National Assembly; no doubt can exist concerning that; the leaders must therefore become the instruments of the masses." Finally the question was put to a vote and carried by 400 to 75.[251]

It was then moved by Luedemann that: "The national conference of the workmen's and soldiers' councils of Germany, which represents the entire political power in Germany, transfers, until further regulation by the National Assembly, the legislative and executive power to the Council of the People's Commissioners. The congress authorizes further a central council of the workmen's and soldiers' councils, which will exercise the right of watching over the German and Prussian cabinets. This council has the right of appointing and dismissing the Commissioners of the *Reich* and Prussia until the definitive regulation of the relations between the central government and the several states. In order to control the conduct of business in the offices of the national ministries, assistants to the secretaries of state will be designated by the Council of the People's Commissioners. Two assistants who will be chosen from the two social democratic parties will be placed in each of the ministries. Before the appointment by the Commissioners of all technical ministers and assistants, the Central Council is to be consulted."

The Independents denounced the powers given by this resolution to the Central Council as inadequate and demanded explanations. Landsberg declared that the bill would establish parliamentary control of the government by the Central Council. The Independents then moved to make

---

[251] Runkel, "Die Deutsche Revolution," 185–190.

the council system the foundation of the constitution. This was defeated by a vote of 344 to 48. As a final test of strength the Independents moved to allow the Central Council to reject or accept all laws before they were promulgated. This was also defeated, and the motion of Luedemann was then adopted.

Embittered by their defeat, the Independents now demonstratively left the hall, declaring that they would not take part in the election of the Council. This was the first great mistake which the Independents made, since the list of candidates of the Majority Socialists was then adopted and the control of the revolutionary government passed into their hands.

The other work of the congress was unimportant. Numerous radical measures, advocating the abolition of state elections, the formation of a unified republic, and the union of the Socialist parties, were rejected. To the attacks of the Independents, Scheidemann replied that the answer of his party would be given on January 19, 1919.

The congress of the revolutionary proletariat had demonstrated the strength of the Majority Socialist Party and the desire of the nation to carry out its democratic policies. It was the German proletariat itself which, in voting to call a national assembly, established the principle of democracy above that of class rule. The congress demonstrated also the astounding weakness of the Independents. It brought to light their lack of parliamentary leaders and made their position in the provisional government precarious. It is to the credit of the German councils that at a time when anarchy, starvation, and invasion were threatening the nation, they took the first steps to establish order and democracy.[252] In the words of Ebert: "The dictatorship of the Junkers had plunged the German people into the deepest misery and every other dictatorship would be for the people equally unbearable." [253] Although the Central Council of the German Socialistic Republic announced that it had taken over the affairs of Prussia and the empire, the nation was assured that democracy would be established.[254]

THE JANUARY SPARTACAN UPRISING

The decision of the proletarian congress of workmen's and soldiers' councils to convene the National Assembly and thus to establish democracy in place of the dictatorship of the working classes, was the signal for the attack of the Independents and Spartacans and the prelude to civil war. Although still in the government, the Independents planned to overthrow the rule of the Majority Socialists, while the Spartacans aimed

[252] Däumig, "Raetesystem," 18.
[253] Deutscher Geschichtskalender, "Die Deutsche Revolution," II Heft, 200–259.
[254] Official Poster of Central Council, December 21, 1918.

at the immediate establishment of communism with all power in the hands of workmen's and soldiers' councils.[255]

Before the meeting of the congress, Rosa Luxemburg announced that the revolution must be secured from lowering enemies; that the power of the national and local councils must be developed; that a red guard should be organized; that dynastic property and the large estates should be confiscated; and that the entire administrative system of the old police state should be destroyed. To the armed Spartacans she exclaimed: "The abolition of the rule of capitalism, the realization of the socialistic order of society, this and nothing less is the historic theme of the present revolution. Only in the Internationale, in the world revolution of the proletariat, is the German revolution anchored."

In the same manner as the Parisian mob had dominated the Convention, the Spartacans of Berlin had planned to control the congress of councils. Their failure aroused them to political frenzy. To the Spartacans, the convocation of the National Assembly meant the creation of a bourgeois counterweight to the revolution, the perpetuation of the old imperial bureaucracy, and the beginnings of a counter revolution. Spartacus demanded: the six-hour day in order to have time to educate the workers; the cancellation of all war bonds excepting those held by small subscribers and saving banks; the nationalization of all banks, large industries, and great agricultural estates; and the exclusion from the socialistic state of all bourgeois elements.

Denouncing the bourgeois democratic aims of the Majority Socialists, Rosa Luxemburg exclaimed: "The national assembly is an obsolete inheritance from former bourgeois revolutions, a shell without contents, a relic of the period of narrow-minded townsmen's illusions about the united people, about liberty, equality and fraternity." Karl Liebknecht asserted that the political power of the masses was declining daily, that bourgeois elements had entered the councils, and therefore that the working classes must hold fast to what had been conquered, drive out the ruling classes and seize power. In accord with the Berlin leaders were the Spartacans of the other German industrial centers. In Hamburg, Bremen, Brunswick, Magdeburg, Leipsic, Dresden, and Munich, the communists denounced the calling of the National Assembly as a betrayal of the revolution and the restoration of the old imperial bureaucracy. To gain control of the remnant of the German army, the Spartacans commenced publishing the *Rote Soldaten*, the official organ of the Red Soldiers' Alliance. Here they advocated the directing of the military movement into proletarian channels, which would result in the completion

---

[255] Bernstein, "Die deutsche Revolution," 100–161, is a detailed account of the collapse of the coalition socialist government and the course of the Berlin communist rebellion of January, 1919.

by force of arms of the socialistic revolution. This military propaganda was remarkably effective, winning over thousands of war veterans and republican soldiers to the Spartacan cause.

On December 23 the sailors, who had occupied the Royal Palace and mews of Berlin, attempted a revolt when they were ordered by the government to evacuate their quarters. Wels, the Commandant of Berlin, was seized by them, and bands of mutineers occupied the Chancellery and the central telephone and telegraph offices. Ebert and Landsberg were actually confined in the Chancellor's palace by a group of sailors which had occupied the Wilhelmstrasse. Ebert was able, however, to communicate with the Minister of War, Scheuch, by means of a secret telephone connecting the two offices. Scheidemann, who was absent from the Chancellery when it was surrounded by the sailors, also made every effort to rescue his colleagues. Toward evening the veteran troops of General Lequis, who remained loyal to the government, advanced from their barracks to the Chancellery. Thereupon the sailors abandoned their effort to overthrow the government.[256]

Ebert now made an effort to secure the release of Wels, who was confined in the cellar of the Royal Stables. This failed, and Radke, leader of the sailors, informed the government that he could no longer be answerable for the life of Wels. Therefore the government ordered General Scheuch to rescue Commandant Wels.

After fruitless negotiations, the Guard Cavalry Division commenced on Christmas morning an attack on the palace and stables. In the struggle for the possession of the palace, sixty-eight combatants were killed. The action was, however, indecisive; the government, afraid to take energetic measures, compromised with the sailors, who ultimately evacuated the palace.

The Independent members of the provisional government seized upon this opportunity to resign and to denounce the Majority Socialists for ordering reactionary troops commanded by veteran officers to fire upon the people. The Central Committee of the workmen's and soldiers' councils, however, supported Ebert, Scheidemann, and Landsberg; and on December 27 it confirmed the appointment of Noske and Wissel to the vacancies created by the resignations of the Independents.[257]

Thus a Majority Socialist government was established in Germany with the consent of the representatives of the councils of workmen and soldiers. This governing body was supported by the entire bourgeoisie. Therefore it appeared certain that the forces of order and democracy would triumph, unless a communist coup d'état overthrew the Berlin

---

[256] Scheidemann, "Der Zusammenbruch," 233–234.

[257] Egelhaaf, *op. cit.*, 26.

government. The vacillating policy of the Independents strengthened the Spartacans, who continued their preparations for the overthrow of the Social Democrats. With the Independents in opposition, the Spartacans believed that it would be an easy task to raise the Berlin masses against the government and to establish a genuine proletarian rule. The central secretariat of the Spartacans sent an ultimatum to the Independents, demanding the calling of a party convention before the end of December and the immediate adoption of a revolutionary policy. Although the left wing of the Independents was in favor of accepting this ultimatum, the party finally rejected it. It announced as its reasons for this action: the difficulties of convening its representatives, and the necessity of carrying on an active campaign for seats in the National Assembly.

Däumig, a radical Independent, later expressed his views of the dictatorship as follows: "Our goal is the realization of democracy, namely, the creation of economic and political equality as well as the equality of rights. Let us examine the world democracies: In the great American democracy, the dictatorship of the trust magnates rules the land, and the American workmen can tell of Pinkertons and other oppressors. A dictatorship of imperialists, who under the names of liberals or conservatives are interested in colonial policy, rules England and the British Empire. A dictatorship of financiers in conjunction with professional parliamentarians rules France. Why should we be afraid of the dictatorship of the proletariat?" [258]

Undaunted by this refusal to cooperate with them, representatives of the German Spartacan Party met on December 30 in convention in Berlin. Karl Radek, the able Russian leader and propagandist, appeared secretly at the convention and pronounced in favor of civil war if necessary to establish the dictatorship of the proletariat. Liebknecht, Rosa Luxemburg, Franz Mehring, and Levy also spoke in favor of immediately completing the work of revolution.[259] The delegates then proceeded to draw up a party program and to formulate twenty-four military, political, social, and economic reforms which would pave the way for communism. "The sanguinary hallucination of the world empire of Prussian militarism", stated the preamble of the party platform, "vanished on the battlefields of France, and the band of criminals who had started the world war, plunged Germany into a sea of blood, and deceived her for four years, were decisively defeated. Society was thus placed before the alternative either of continuing the capitalistic system with new wars, chaos, and anarchy, or of establishing complete socialism as the only salvation of humanity."

---

[258] Däumig, "Raetesystem," 24.

[259] Runkel, *op. cit.*, 191.

Eight immediate measures were declared necessary by the platform to safeguard the revolution: the disarming of the police, officers, bourgeois soldiers, and all members of the ruling class; the seizure by the workmen's and soldiers' councils of all arms and ammunition as well as munition plans; the arming of the entire male proletarian population as a workers' militia; the formation of a standing red guard for protection against the counter revolution; the abolition of military and iron discipline and the adoption of the principle of the election and recall of officers by their enlisted men; the removal of all officers and cadets from the soldiers' councils; the displacement of all bureaucrats of the former régime by trusted men of the councils; the formation of revolutionary tribunals to condemn: those guilty of starting and prolonging the war, the two Hohenzollerns, Ludendorff, Hindenburg, Tirpitz, and their fellow criminals as well as the counter revolutionists; the immediate confiscation of all food in order to safeguard the ration system.

In the political and social spheres, the program contained eight minimum reforms: the suppression of all federal states in order to create a unified Socialist republic; the removal of all former administrative officials and appointment of workmen's and soldiers' councils in their stead; the election of workmen's councils according to industries by the entire agricultural and industrial proletariat of both sexes, as well as the election of soldiers' councils by the enlisted men with the exclusion of all officers and capitulants; the election by all councils of delegates to a central council, which shall choose an executive committee to act as the supreme organ of executive and legislative power; the control of the activity of the executive committee by the central council, and the right of recall of all delegates who fail to act according to instructions; the abolition of all class distinctions, orders, titles, and the creation of complete judicial and social equality for both sexes; incisive social legislation, shortening of the hours of labor because of the enervation due to the war, and establishment of the six-hour working day; prompt and thorough alteration of the food, health, and educational systems in the interests of the proletarian revolution.

The immediate economic demands were: the confiscation of all dynastic property and incomes in the interests of the commonwealth; the annulment of all state and other public debts as well as war loans except subscriptions up to an amount to be established by the councils; the expropriation of all agricultural estates except peasant small holdings and the formation of socialistic agricultural coöperative societies; the expropriation by the socialistic republic of all banks, mines, metal works, and large industrial and commercial corporations; the confiscation of all private property above a certain amount to be fixed by the councils; the control of the entire means of transportation by the councils, the election of shop councils in all factories in order, by agreement with the work-men's councils, to control the internal affairs of the factories, to regulate the conditions of labor, to control production, and eventually to take over the direction of the factories; the establishment of a central strike commission which shall insure to the growing national strike move-ment a uniform socialistic control.

Finally the platform advocated active preparations for the revolu-tionary rising of the world proletariat, and asserted of Spartacus: "He is the social conscience of the revolution. Crucify him, yell the secret enemies of the revolt and the proletariat, the capitalists, the small citizens, the officers, the anti-semitic press lackeys of the bourgeoisie, the *Scheide-maenner,* who, like Judas Iscariot, sold the workmen to the bourgeoisie. . . . Spartacus refuses to work with the *Scheidemaenner* or the bour-geoisie. Spartacus will seize power only if it is the undisputed wish of the great majority of the proletarian masses in all Germany, who must first accept the aims and battle methods of the Spartacans. The victory of the Spartacan Alliance stands not at the beginning but at the end of the revolution; it is identical with the victory of the millions of the socialistic proletariat. Thumbs in their eyes and knees on their breasts." [260]

More important than the formulating of this revolutionary platform was the decision concerning the immediate policy of the party toward the national elections. Although at the last moment Liebknecht and Rosa Luxemburg doubted the success of civil war, the communist party voted 63 to 23 to prevent the election of a National Assembly. They were con-vinced that, if the assembly once met, their program would be defeated and the revolution would be over. Many of the communists sincerely believed that a civil war which established the dictatorship of the prole-tariat would save Germany from her enemies by ushering in the world revolution. Radek boasted to the convention that the Russian proletariat would join with their class-conscious German brethren to fight the menace of Anglo Saxon capitalism on the Rhine. Liebknecht himself stated that the party goal was international communism and could be reached only by destroying the capitalistic classes in the Entente states, which alone barred the way toward the world revolution. He believed that it would be necessary to destroy all existing conditions in order to establish com-munistic society, and saw in the coming revolution the only salvation for Germany. Clemenceau had stated that he would burn Paris if it would save France; and the Spartacans now announced that they would lay Germany in ruins, convinced that from the ashes of the empire a new and greater nation would arise.[261]

---

[260] *Revolutions-Bibliothek,* Nr. 3, "Das Programm der Kommunistischen Partei Deutschlands (Spartakusbund)," 47–111.

[261] Lensch, "Am Ausgang der Deutschen Sozialdemokratie," 33.

The military leader of the Spartacan revolt was Robert Eichhorn, Police President of Berlin. Supported by Russian propaganda, gold, and weapons, he prepared at the Police Presidency to arm the masses of the capital and to overthrow the government. Rifles and machine guns were supplied to workmen from the Schwarzkopff and Daimler works as well as other factories, and instructions were issued to the communist guards to disarm those hostile to Spartacus.

The Prussian government became aware of Eichhorn's activities and ordered him removed from office. On Sunday morning, January 5, Eugen Ernst, the newly appointed successor of Eichhorn, and Lieutenant Fischer attempted to take possession of police headquarters, but the Spartacans refused to surrender the building. This attempt to remove Eichhorn from office was the signal for the first uprising of the German communists.[262]

On the fifth of January, 1919, the Spartacan rebellion broke out in the capital of Germany. That day the Spartacan and Independent newspapers, *Rote Fahne*, and *Die Freiheit*, called for demonstrations in the Siegesallee against the Majority Socialist government. Great crowds were addressed by Eichhorn, Liebknecht, and Ledebour, who described the Majority Socialists as bloodhounds, and denounced them for convening the National Assembly of the reactionaries. Meanwhile a committee of leaders organized the revolt and prepared to occupy the principal government offices, public buildings, the Brandenburg Gate, and the barracks of the city.

The first step was the seizure that night of the principal newspaper offices of the capital with the object of preventing the appearance of the social democratic and bourgeois press. The Wolff Telegraph Bureau, and the *Vorwaerts*, *Mosse*, and *Ullstein* offices were promptly occupied. At the *Vorwaerts* building eighty men of the security police surrendered without a struggle. Everywhere the Spartacans were successful, and their leaders believed that within twelve hours the government of the Majority Socialists would cease to exist. Liebknecht and Eichhorn prepared to assume the rôles of Lenine and Trotzki.

The morning edition of the *Vorwaerts*, the official paper of the Majority Socialists, appeared on the sixth of January under Spartacan control and printed a proclamation demanding: the disarming of all counter revolutionists; the arming of the proletariat; the formation of a red army; the union of all revolutionary troops with the workers for joint action; the seizure of power by the councils; and finally the overthrow of the traitors: Ebert and Scheidemann. In conclusion this Spartacan manifesto announced: "You have now reconquered the *Vorwaerts*. Hold it

[262] Noske, "Von Kiel bis Kapp," 66–67.

and fight for it with tooth and nail. Do not let it be snatched from you. Make it the paper which it should be: a pioneer on the road to freedom. Finally show your bravery in further battles and victories." [263]

With the seizure by the Spartacans of the Brandenburg Gate, the government printing offices, the provision office, several barracks, and railway stations, the terror began in Berlin. Liebknecht, Ledebour, and Scholze formed a provisional communist government and sent a detachment of Spartacans to occupy the Ministry of War.[264] Three hundred communists under the command of a sailor actually invaded the War Office and demanded its surrender. Armored cars were driven by the Spartacans into the Wilhelmstrasse and fighting broke out between them and the loyal troops who defended the government in the Chancellery. Radek, the representative of the Bolsheviki in Berlin, drove ostentatiously up and down *Unter den Linden* watching the progress of the rebellion. At night the Spartacans captured the Railway Building, where a small detachment of government troops surrendered.

During the day's battle, many government troops gave up their arms without fighting, and the marine division declared its neutrality. Had the Spartacans possessed able military leaders and abandoned their speech-making for fighting, they could have easily overthrown the Socialist government in the Wilhelmstrasse and established the soviet system in Berlin.

At last the vacillating Socialist government acted when thousands of Social Democrats assembled before the Chancellery and asked for arms. To this living wall of defense Scheidemann said: "We will call together the entire population of military age, and it is self-understood that we will not place umbrellas in their hands."[265] Noske, the revolutionary governor of Kiel, was appointed on the night of January 6 Commander-in-Chief in the Marks and Governor of Berlin. At that moment Eichhorn's Security Police were in open rebellion and the Republican Guards were reported by the Commandant to be unreliable. Colonel Reinhardt, the new Minister of War, announced to the People's Commissioners that the only loyal forces near Berlin were the troops of Lieutenant General von Hoffmann. Noske therefore accepted the advice of the General Staff officers and withdrew to the little village of Dahlem on the road to Potsdam, where he established his headquarters. Here a determined effort was to be made to organize a force of government troops capable of defeating the Spartacans.

There is no doubt that only an able and energetic Social Democrat could have organized the scattered forces of the imperial army at this

---

[263] Runkel, "Die Deutsche Revolution," 202.

[264] Ledebour's Testimony in *Die Freiheit*, May 22, 1919.

[265] Menke-Glückert, *op. cit.,* 131.

crisis of the revolution. Under Noske's orders the troops of General von Hoffmann, the units near Berlin and Potsdam, the Jaeger of General Maercker in the camp at Zossen, and finally the Kiel Marine Brigade were concentrated for action against Berlin. To protect his left flank, Noske occupied the government munition plants at Spandau, which had been seized by radical workmen.

Only the lack of military leadership had prevented the Spartacans from seizing control of Berlin on January 6. On that day over one hundred thousand armed communists and Independents had occupied the entire *Unter den Linden*. Unorganized fighting broke out in various parts of the city between the Spartacans and detachments of soldiers.[266] In an effort to stop the bloodshed, the Independents, Dittmann, Kautsky, and Breitsheid, offered to mediate between the Majority Socialists and the Spartacans; but the latter refused to accept the government's terms for the surrender of the occupied buildings. The fighting therefore continued. All transportation ceased. Liebknecht, addressing his followers, said that the fall of the government was only a question of hours. Yet he narrowly escaped death at the hands of an enraged mob in the Leipzigerstrasse. Meanwhile Noske completed his preparations to occupy the capital with the skeleton regiments of the old imperial army, which were stationed at Dahlem and neighboring camps. On January 8 he announced in a proclamation to Berlin: "Spartacus fights now to secure complete power over the state. The government, which will bring about within ten days the free decision of the people concerning their own fate, is to be overthrown by force. The people shall not be allowed to speak. Their voices shall be suppressed. You have seen the results. Where Spartacus rules all personal security and freedom are abolished. . . . The government is therefore taking the necessary measures to suppress the reign of terror and to prevent its recurrence once for all." [267]

The government counter-attack on the Spartacans began January ninth with an attempt to retake the Mosse Publishing House, which had been converted into a communist stronghold. Colonel Reinhardt and Major von Stephani attacked the *Vorwaerts* building with their small forces. Minenwerfer, flame-throwers, and 10.5 cm. howitzers were used against the stronghold, while the defenders replied with machine guns. Unable to withstand this attack, three hundred Spartacans finally surrendered. The other newspaper buildings were then recaptured.

On Saturday, January 11, Noske and Colonel Deetjen entered the *Wilhelmstrasse* at the head of 3,000 veteran infantry. The week of terror was over. To Colonel Reinhardt belongs the credit of holding the Spartacans at bay until Noske and General von Luettwitz mustered sufficient

[266] Noske, "Von Kiel bis Kapp," 68–74.
[267] Runkel, "Die Deutsche Revolution," 202–211.

THE STRUGGLE OF PARTIES FOR POWER

forces to occupy the capital. The unorganized Spartacans had been unable to withstand the assaults of the remnant of the Prussian army. Eichhorn moved his headquarters to the Boetzow Brewery in north Berlin, while the government troops surrounded on Sunday, January 12, the principal Spartacan stronghold, the Police Presidency. This huge building was badly defended and no attempt was made to hold the Alexander Square or the Subway Station. After a preliminary bombardment with howitzers, the Presidency was stormed by the government troops. The last Spartacan command was then defeated at the Silesian Railway Station and by Wednesday, January 15, the entire city was in the hands of the government.

The first great rising of the Berlin communists had failed and the first attempt to establish the dictatorship of the proletariat had collapsed. Lacking proper military organization and unable to secure the support of a majority of the revolutionary troops stationed in Berlin, the Spartacans were defeated by small but disciplined government forces equipped with artillery and commanded by able officers of the old army. Nevertheless it took the weak Socialist government sixteen days to put down the rising. Reinhardt, however, was constantly hampered by the soldiers' councils, while many Berlin troops declared themselves neutral.[268] Berlin, the former capital of militarism, presented the strange spectacle during these days of a remnant of the Prussian guard fighting under the banner of the Socialist republic. The conclusion is, therefore, that, if Liebknecht had carefully prepared a military coup d'état, Bolshevism would have been established in January, 1919, in Berlin.

After their final defeat the Spartacan leaders disappeared. Eichhorn and Radek fled from the capital. A report was circulated that Liebknecht and Luxemburg had gone to Holland. Liebknecht, however, wrote to the *Rote Fahne:* "We have not fled, we are not defeated, even if they throw us in irons. We will remain here and victory will be ours. Spartacus is still the fire and spirit, the heart and soul, and the indomitable will of the proletarian revolution. Spartacus represents also the longing for happiness, and the readiness for battle of the class-conscious proletariat. For Spartacus is the personification of socialism and world revolution. The Golgatha way of the German revolution is not yet ended, but the day of salvation nears." [269]

Realizing that these leaders were still in Berlin, the government made every effort to capture them. On the night of January fifteenth Karl Liebknecht and Rosa Luxemburg were taken prisoners in the Wilmersdorf suburb and brought to the headquarters of the Guard Cavalry

---

[268] Delbrueck in *Preussische Jahrbücher,* February, 1919.

[269] *Cf.* Radek, "Rosa Luxemburg, Karl Liebknecht, Leo Jogiches."

Division in the Eden Hotel. Rosa Luxemburg was brutally murdered by government troops and her body thrown into the Landwehr Canal. Karl Liebknecht was, while being taken to Moabit prison, shot by his guards, ostensibly because he tried to escape. Thus political murder ended the revolt which a remnant of the old imperial army had suppressed. Liebknecht and Luxemburg perished not at the hands of the Majority Socialists, but of those Prussian militarists whom they had fought all their political lives. Their murder stamped out the fiery protests of communism against democracy, and their followers, deprived temporarily of leaders, were promptly scattered. When informed of the murder of Liebknecht and Rosa Luxemburg, Scheidemann said: "I sincerely regret the death of the two, and for good reasons. They have day after day called the people to arms and ordered a violent overthrow of the government. They have now become themselves the victims of their own bloody terroristic tactics."[270] The bourgeoisie and the Social Democrats openly rejoiced over the death of the two communist leaders who had threatened the peace of the defeated and exhausted Fatherland and had not shrunk from plunging the capital of Germany into civil war. The failure of the German communist rising was the signal for the triumph of German democracy in the national elections which were held on January nineteenth.

---

[270] Scheidemann, "Der Zusammenbruch," 238.

VI.

THE CONVOCATION OF THE NATIONAL ASSEMBLY

THE POLITICAL PARTIES

The victory of the Social Democrats over the Spartacans and Independents in the first congress of the workmen's and soldiers' councils resulted in the decision to hold the elections for the National Assembly on January 19, 1919. At once the activities of the political parties were revived throughout Germany. The November revolution, which had swept away empire, army, thrones, and dynasties, had little affected the German political parties. Party organization and party machinery remained practically unaltered since the last period of the war. The announcement of a definite date for holding the national elections served therefore to increase the activities of the bourgeois parties, as well as to call to arms the party organizations of Majority Socialists and Independents. Even the Communists were affected by the electoral controversies in the great industrial centers, and in certain instances took part in the campaign.[271]

With great rapidity the old monarchical parties reorganized themselves, abandoned their old platforms, adopted new party names, and advocated democratic measures for preserving the state from anarchy. The old conservative party of Prussia and Germany became the German National People's Party. The Conservatives, the Pan-Germans (the Fatherland group), and the majority of the Junker class joined this party. The old slogan of the defense of throne and altar had, however, become obsolete. The throne had been swept away; the king was in exile; and the altar had taken care of itself even in a socialistic republic.

As the champion of liberalism in the new state, the right wing of the old National Liberal Party formed the German People's Party. It attacked radicalism, ultramontanism and internationalism, and advocated a political union with Austria as well as cultural relations with the Germans beyond the seas.

The Centre Party had been freed from the menace of disintegration by the anti-clerical policies of the revolutionary Prussian government. During the revolution a witty Liberal proposed that the Centre should erect a monument in honor of the Independent Minister of Public Worship, Adolf Hoffmann, for preserving the unity of the Catholic Party.

---

[271] Bergsträsser, "Geschichte der politischen Parteien," 109–125. "Handbuch Deutscher Zeitungen 1917 Bearbeitet im Kriegspresseamt" contains complete information concerning the party newspapers.

The party now assumed the name of Christian People's Party, and, under the influence of the Cologne leaders, sought to gain non-Catholic support. While leaving to one side the question of monarchy or republic, the party denounced the attacks on private property and the nationalizing of the means of production, and advocated housing reform, the improvement of working conditions for laborers and peasants, religious freedom, and religious instruction in the schools.

As the new party of democracy, the left wing of the old National Liberal and the Progressive People's parties united to form the German Democratic Party. Various minor groups entered the political arena, not without distinct local success. Of all the parties, the Social Democrats and Independents alone retained their old party names and platforms. The Spartacans were the only party which refused to take part in the election campaign.

The German Nationalists, who united in one party the former Conservatives, Free Conservatives, and Christian Socialists, adopted a program which was almost revolutionary in character. It championed a strong state, with authority based upon the free will of the people, which should improve the national weal and social welfare. Specifically the party advocated: parliamentary government; freedom of speech, person, and conscience; equal suffrage; security of private property; liquidation of the war societies; a solution of the housing problem; the repopulation of arid districts; the protection of officials, teachers, soldiers, employees, and the war-wounded; the simplification of the national administration and taxation; and the coöperation of women in public life. Upon the issue of socialization the party declared for the adequate protection of employees and workers and for the rational socialization of the means of production.[272]

This remarkable platform was a direct attempt to hold the party together during the storm of revolution. Because of its championship of the Church, the evangelical orthodox groups supported the party. As the campaign progressed, the German Nationalist leaders openly avowed their monarchical sentiments and championed the rights of private property and inheritance. They accused the Democrats of being under the control of Jewish capitalists, and attributed the revolution to the treason of the Social Democrats toward the liberal empire.[273] Throughout Germany the Nationalists conducted a sharp and aggressive campaign.[274] Although many of their leaders had supported the Pan-German and Fatherland movements, they boldly accused the Socialists of being the cause of the

[272] Runkel, "Die Deutsche Revolution," 224. Menke-Glückert, op. cit., 125.

[273] Laube, "Das Wahre Gesicht der Parteien."

[274] A typical conservative pamphlet is Captain Karl von Mueller's "Das Betoerte Deutsche Volk."

ruin of Germany. It would be a fatal mistake to believe that the millions of German monarchists and conservatives had been converted to democracy by the November revolution.

The second great movement in German politics was toward liberalism. The new German People's Party appeared here as the heir of the liberalism of Benningsen and of that national liberalism of the Nineteenth Century empire. It announced that the way toward internal peace and a greater Germany led over the ground of republican government. Nevertheless the party denounced the revolution and declared its achievements to be: national economic, financial and moral collapse. It accused the Socialists of proclaiming a new commandment: "Thou shalt not work for thy employer, thou shalt thyself have a share in the profits of labor." [275] Stresemann asserted: "Whoever is of the opinion that the ninth of November created a new Germany does not belong in our midst; his political conceptions are far removed from those which inspire us." [276]

Leidig declared that the chief characteristic of the party is and remains liberalism, a liberalism which is not afraid to take a definite stand upon the issues of the day.[277] Freedom, justice, and national unity were indeed the great ideals of the German People's Party. It did not demand that all its members should become republicans at heart, but it did call for coöperation and united efforts to reëstablish the national life. The party specifically denounced: all class rule, strikes, "levelling democracy", socialization, communism, Spartacism, Bolshevism, and anarchy.[278]

The Centre, the great Roman Catholic Party of Germany, was seriously affected by the revolution. Its strongholds in southern Germany passed temporarily under the control of the Radical Socialists, while the advance of the allied armies into Germany placed the Catholic Rhine lands under foreign control. This latter fact was destined to have an important bearing not only upon the life of the party but also upon the course of the revolution itself. Erzberger's connection with the revolutionary government also profoundly influenced the policies of this party.

As early as November fifteenth the leaders of the Centre issued a manifesto denouncing class rule and demanding the convocation of a National Assembly. Until then the party declared it would recognize only the Reichstag as the sovereign power in Germany. When the executives of the revolutionary government issued on November 30, 1918, the electoral regulations for the coming election of a constitutional conven-

---

[275] "Bericht Über den Ersten Parteitag der Deutschen Volks Partei."

[276] Stresemann, "Die Politik der Deutschen Volks Partei."

[277] Leidig, "Liberalismus und Demokratie," 13.

[278] Steinmeyer, "Neudeutschland auf der Grundlage von Freiheit, Recht und Einigkiet," 16.

tion, the Centre Party, already menaced by the disintegrating influences of the revolution, determined to publish a statement of party principles to its followers.

On December 30 the national committee of the Centre drew up a party platform which recognized the new democracy, and attacked class rule, materialism, mammonism, and anarchy. Concerning the political reorganization of Germany the platform advocated: the immediate framing of a constitution by the National Assembly in a safer place than Berlin; the maintenance of the unity and federal character of the *Reich*; universal suffrage with proportional representation; popular governments in the states and nation; opening of all offices to all classes; and the adoption of a bill of rights.

In foreign affairs the platform read as follows: the immediate conclusion of a preliminary peace; the establishment of international law; the creation of a league of nations with obligatory arbitration, disarmament, and abolition of secret treaties; the protection of national and religious minorities in all nations; economic freedom of development and freedom of the seas; international regulation of labor legislation and insurance law; popular education for the understanding of foreign questions; and the maintenance of a German colonial empire.

The internal program of the party proposed: the maintenance and strengthening of Christian cultural and educational ideals in the soul of the people; freedom of conscience and of religious exercises, with coöperation between Church and State; the protection of the religious character of the marriage relation and of the family; the suppression of immoral·art and literature; the maintenance of the "confessional public school" and of sufficient religious instruction in all schools; "a free career for the advancement of the efficient" from all walks of life; and equality of opportunity for all women.

In economic and social affairs the party, while insisting upon the maintenance of the right of private property, championed the development of national economy in the service of social justice. It insisted upon the effective care of all the wounded as well as the support of the veterans of the world war.

In financial affairs the party advocated: the division of taxes in accordance with the ability of the citizen to pay; the prevention of the flight of capital abroad; and the prevention of the depreciation in value of the war loans.[279]

As a political measure this pronunciamento was of tremendous importance, for it served as a rallying point not only for those Catholics who opposed the excesses of the revolution, but also for other groups inter-

[279] Groeber in *Das Neue Reich*, Nr. 8.

ested in the fight for Christian ideals of life. In all the South German states, the party under its new name made rapid strides toward the recovery of its *ante bellum* position. In the Rhineland, the allied occupation aided rather than hindered the triumph of this conservative and Catholic program.[280]

As the campaign progressed the Catholic Party declared that the chief tasks of the National Assembly were to reëstablish peace and order and to provide the German people with bread and work. It favored the strictest adherence to the Fourteen Points and denounced the surrender of the Saar Valley and upper Silesia as well as the trial of the Kaiser by a foreign court. Disapproving of the November revolution as neither a necessity nor a boon to German political development, the party attacked the political activity of the soldiers' councils and all attempts to establish a socialistic republic. Although opposed to the waste, extravagance, and excesses of the revolution, the party supported the democratic republic and favored the admission of Catholic Austria to the union of German states.[281]

The first bourgeois party to organize after the revolution was the German Democratic Party, which issued on November 15 a declaration which supported the republic bust maintained that a National Assembly should decide the future form of the state. This platform also advocated: the partial socilization of industry, especially the monopolies; the partition of the state domains; the prosecution of war profiteers; the adoption of a single progressive capital tax; the legal guarantee of the rights of workmen, employees, and officials; the protection of the independent middle class; and the carrying out of an international social and political program.

Meanwhile the party council of the old Progressive People's Party had voted in favor of the formation of a greater party based upon democratic and republican foundations; and on November 16 it began negotiating with the national committee of the Democrats. Stresemann, Friedberg, and Richthofen favored a union with the progressives. Difficulties arose over the attitude of the progressives toward liberalism, and toward those leaders who from a democratic standpoint had compromised themselves during the war. As a result of the conferences, the right wing of the National Liberal Party broke away from the left wing, which then united with the Progressives to form the German Democratic Party.[282]

The complete collapse of the imperial administration and the impossibility of ever returning to the old conditions were factors which favored the growth of German democracy and caused large classes to adhere to

---

[280] Fassbender, "Revolution und Kultur."

[281] Groeber in *Das Neue Reich,* Nr. 8.

[282] Menke-Glückert, "Die November Revolution," 122.

this new party. The party leaders declared that democracy was a cultural movement, that it would destroy class differences, and that it would create equal responsibility or equal rights and equal opportunities.[283] Real democracy, in opposition to the old state which allowed men of one class to govern, was to be the rule of the efficient, chosen from all classes of the people.[284]

The party denounced: the theory of the divine right of kings and the "self will" of princes; the "squirearchy"; the legal disqualifications of large classes; the military bureaucracy; and bureaucratic militarism. The party advocated: equality of opportunity; the suppression of anti-semitism; moral standards for women; national sports; popular schools; freedom of conscience; the improvement of industry; and the improvement of public sanitation.[285]

During the campaign the Democrats attacked the parties of the left which preached the class struggle and the parties of the right which idealized the old form of government. It asserted that righteousness, not might, should guide the internal and foreign policies of the state, and that the entire nation should direct the fate of Germany.[286] Count Bernstorff declared: "Our chief aims are: the unity of the German people in internal and foreign affairs; justice in all public and private relations; economic prosperity upon a democratic and social basis as well as the prosperity of art, science, and literature." [287]

Of all the parties in opposition to the provisional government of the Social Democrats, the Independents conducted the most bitter campaign. They attributed the failure of the coalition government of November to the treason of the Majority Socialists toward the cause of socialism.[288] They demanded the immediate beginnings of socialization and the quickest possible transformation from the old class state to socialistic government. Although the left wing of the Independents sympathized with the Spartacans, the party leaders refused to indorse the "anti-parliamentarism" and terrorism of the German communists. Strikes and uprisings were denounced as injurious at the moment to the proletariat. Thus the Independent Party, although bitterly opposed to the Majority Socialists, became during the campaign a middle party between evolutionary socialism and communism. The chief strongholds of the party were Thuringia, Saxony,

---

[283] Bamberger, "Demokratie," 14. Jordan, "Die Demokratie und Deutschlands Zukunft."

[284] Goetz, "Deutsche Demokratie," 10–45.

[285] Abderhalden, "Die Hohen Aufgaben des Deutschen Demokraten und seiner Partei," 4–10.

[286] *Ibid.*

[287] *Vossische Zeitung*, March 10, 1919.

[288] Moldenhauer, "Von der Revolution zur Nationalversammlung," 8.

the Ruhr Valley, Bremen, and Berlin, and its entry into the political arena assured it of representation in the constitutional convention.

Finally the Social Democrats, who had guided the German Republic since November and saved it from Bolshevism almost a week before the election, entered the political arena with a prestige of success which attracted millions of voters who were not Socialists. Scheidemann, Ebert, and other leaders emphasized in the campaign the revolutionary program of November, 1918, rather than the Erfurt Program of 1891. Yet the Majority Socialists, who sincerely wished to carry out the political program so essential to Germany's salvation, found it difficult to free themselves from the dogmas of Marx. The party opposed all attempts to establish Bolshevism in Germany; rejected the Polish claims to German lands; and demanded that when the National Assembly was elected the workmen's and soldiers' councils should cease to function as administrative organizations. Especial emphasis was given by Socialist speakers to the socialization of production and distribution by means of a slow and protective method of procedure. Only those industries which were ready for nationalization were to be socialized; and during the entire process the principle of the indemnity of factory owners was to prevail. By avoiding the extreme socialistic and communistic demands of the Independents and Spartacans, the Majority Socialists gained the support of large groups of the bourgeoisie. By advocating a gradual and scientific socialization of the means of production, the party secured the votes of a considerable portion of the subordinate official class. Behind the Socialist Party were also the united forces of the German labor unionists, who, according to the Liberal Stresemann, knew more about politics before the war than the university graduates of Germany.[289]

THE NATIONAL ELECTION

Not since the election of the French National Assembly in 1871 had such an election campaign as this one occurred in Europe. The loss of the war and the revolution had rendered the platforms of the old imperial parties obsolete, so that they differed little from the Socialists in their avowed political principles. Hans Delbrück asserted that there was little to choose between the parties, since all denounced anarchy and championed democracy.[290] On the other hand Rudolf Eucken declared: "As a result of our political backwardness, a radical democracy and socialism threaten us with political serfdom. The chief task of the future is to

---

[289] Stresemann, "Die Politik der Deutschen Volkspartei," 6.

[290] *Preussische Jahrbücher,* January, 1919. *Cf.* Becker, "Deutschlands Zusammenbruch und Auferstehung."

develop, under the complete maintenance and deepening of internal freedom, genuine political freedom in our Fatherland."[291]

A vital factor in the election was the women's vote, since they were
now given the franchise for the first time. Here too the Socialists gained
an additional advantage, because they had for years advocated women's
suffrage and attempted the political education of their women adherents.
Among their candidates for the convention were a number of women.
The other parties, especially the Conservatives and Catholics, were quick
to appeal to the women voters. Delbrück, a former opponent of women's
suffrage, urged women to patriotic and political activity.[292] Mueller-
Meiningen said: "Each party must bring the women as quickly as possible
into political life. After the revolution enfranchised the women, we were
disappointed in their lack of interest." Other leaders recognized this
unpreparedness, and Richard Müller-Fulda, a Centrist, in combatting it
asserted "this new right is a duty". Fehrenbach, the able Catholic statesman, also expressed a hope that the influence of women would ennoble
and enrich the political life of the nation. Franz Behrens said that every
woman should vote because she was interested in the weighty questions
of the home and the family, school and education, law and charity, work
and professional activity. Finally the Majority Socialists boldly declared
that women's suffrage was the revolutionary present of socialism to the
nation.[293] The importance of this vote is shown by the fact that of the
thirty-eight million entitled to vote approximately twenty million were
women.

On January 19, a dry and clear winter-day, the national elections were
held throughout Germany. Minor disturbances occurred at Berlin, Hamburg, the Ruhr, and Cassel, but the Spartacans made no concerted efforts
to prevent the elections. Over 30,500,000 men and women voted in the
first election under the system of universal suffrage. The Majority
Socialists received 11,466,716 votes, and elected one hundred and sixty-
three deputies. Their opponents, the Independent Socialists, were completely defeated, electing but twenty-two deputies. The second largest
party was the former Catholic Centre, now the Christian People's Party,
which gained six million votes and eighty-eight seats. The Democrats
polled 5,600,000 votes, and gained seventy-five seats. The German
Nationalists gained 3,199,573 votes and forty-two seats, while the German
People's Party gained 1,240,303 votes and twenty-one seats. Of the
minor parties the German Hannoverian Party and the Bavarian Peasant
Party each secured four seats. The Schleswig-Holstein Peasants and

---

[291] Eucken, "Deutsche Freiheit."

[292] Ibid.

[293] "Frauen! Lernt Wählen!"

Farm Laborers Democracy and the Brunswick Election Union each gained one vote in the assembly.

The state elections, held at approximately the same time as the national elections, showed similar results. In the Bavarian election of January 12 the Centre or Bavarian People's Party gained fifty-nine seats; the Socialists fifty seats; the Democrats twenty-two seats; the Bavarian Peasants' Alliance seventeen seats; National Liberals five seats; and the Independents three seats.[294] In Wuerttemberg the relative gains of the parties in the election of January 12 were: Socialists, 52; Democrats, 38; Centre, 31; German Peace Party and Württemberg Citizens' Party, 11; Peasant Alliance, 10; Wine Gardeners and Small Proprietors, 4; and Independents, 4. In the state election in Baden, January 5, the Centre secured 41, the Socialists 35, the Democrats 24, and the German Nationalists 24 seats. The results of the Saxon election of February 8 were: Socialists, 42; Independents, 15; Democrats, 22; German Nationalists, 13; and German People's Party, 4 seats. The Prussian election was held on January 26. The results were: Majority Socialists, 145; Democrats, 65; Catholics, 55; German Nationalists, 48; German People's Party, 24; Independents, 24; Schleswig-Holstein Democrats, 1; Guelphs, 2; and United Hanoverian Party, 7.[295]

The national elections were a triumph for the democracy of Germany and proved that the middle class was far stronger politically than it had itself suspected. Although certain publicists sought to show that the elections proved Germany to be a republic without republicans, an analysis of the results indicates that the revolutionary parties gained an overwhelming majority. The two Socialist parties alone polled 13,298,745 votes as opposed to 14,775,174 votes of all the bourgeois parties.[296] The relative strength of these two groups in the National Assembly was 185 to 236. The election indicated therefore that the Majority Socialists did not possess a majority of the Assembly and would consequently have to unite with their previous allies, the Democrats and Catholics, to form a government. The nation, however, looked with confidence to the provisional Socialist government, upon whose shoulders now fell the burden of convoking the National Assembly in a place of comparative security and of defending it from a communist coup d'état.

On January 21 the government issued a decree convoking the National Assembly for February 6 at Weimar. Yielding to the demand of the South German States and against the protests of the Independents and Spartacans, the government planned to convene the Assembly in the

---

[294] Eisner states in "Schuld und Suehne," 17, that the Bavarian proletariat supported the Majority Socialists.

[295] Menke-Glückert, "Die November Revolution," 135.

[296] *Preussische Jahrbücher*, February, 1919, 281.

former seat of German culture. The majority parties of the Reichstag wished, owing to the internal situation, to consolidate as quickly as possible the gains of the revolution. Consequently they supported the plan of meeting in Weimar. To guard against a Spartacan attempt to disperse the National Assembly, Noske concentrated a force of loyal troops in Saxe-Weimar and adopted precautionary measures to maintain order.

The draft of a new federal constitution prepared by Professor Preuss of Berlin, now Minister of the Interior, had already profoundly affected the political situation. The chief characteristic of the proposed constitution was the enlargement of the powers of the federal government, which was, in addition to former rights, given jurisdiction over: railroads, waterways, schools, and land legislation. A bill of rights was included in the constitution, and republican constitutions were to be required of the several states. The legislative powers of the *Reich* were to be exercised by the *Reichstag* and *Staatenhaus*. Members of the House of States were to be chosen by the diets of the several states.

The most radical measure of Preuss, however, was the proposal that the National Assembly of Prussia should decide upon the division of the former kingdom into separate republics. Regarding Prussia as a menace to German unity, Preuss boldly asserted that it was neither culturally, economically, nor nationally an organic whole. If Austria were to enter the new democratic Germany, which was no longer held together by dynasties, the former Prussian monarchy must de divided. Although totally unconnected with the existing separatest movements in Prussia, the Preuss plan was a stimulus to the Hannoverian and Rhineland movements.[297]

On Thursday, February 6, in the New Theater of Weimar, the German National Assembly was formally convened by the head of the provisional government. In an address of welcome, Ebert declared that the Assembly, as the only sovereign power in Germany, had to restore order, to revive the economic life of the nation, and to turn Germany from imperialism to idealism. Their goal must be, in the words of Fichte, "a nation of law founded on equality". On February 7 the Assembly chose as its president the Socialist, Dr. David, former undersecretary of foreign affairs in the government of Prince Max. Fehrenbach was then elected first vice-president and Haussmann of the Democratic party, second vice-president.

Having duly organized and elected permanent officers, the Assembly promptly adopted a temporary constitution in order to establish a legal government which could act with authority at home and abroad. Preuss defended his project with great skill, but during the two days' debate it

---

[297] Menke-Glückert, "Die November Revolution," 138–139. Reichs-Gesetzblatt Jahrgang, 1919, Nr. 16; Nr. 33, Gesetz über die vorläufige Reichsgewalt. Vom 10, Februar, 1919.

became evident that particularism would prevent the formation of a unified republic or the redivision of historic German lands into new states.

THE PRESIDENCY OF EBERT

On February 11 the National Assembly elected, by 277 to 102 votes, Friedrich Ebert President of the German *Reich*. In a dignified speech of acceptance he said: "To protect the freedom of all Germans with the utmost exertion and devotion of which I am capable is the oath which I have sworn between the hands of the National Assembly." Thus a Heidelberg saddler, trained in the school of socialism, and a true son of the workers, became the successor of the German War Lord.

THE SCHEIDEMANN MINISTRY

With the adoption of the temporary constitution, Scheidemann had announced to the Assembly that the Council of the People's Commissioners, which had maintained the revolutionary republic, had finished its historic mission and now laid its powers, derived from the revolution, in the hands of the National Assembly. After the election of Ebert, Scheidemann commenced, as the Socialist Party leader, negotiations with the Christian People's Party and the Democratic Party for the formation of a ministry. The task was not difficult, since the old coalition of the Socialists, Centre and Liberals of the last Reichstag had been revived after the January elections. Party bureaucracy and practical politics had demanded these party alignments.[298] Scheidemann was, however, as Minister-President, not in a position to choose his ministers from among the coalition leaders, but each party with bureaucratic thoroughness nominated its representatives for the cabinet.[299] Although the German parties were profoundly affected by the revolution, their procedure here shows that party bureaucracy survived the empire.

The cabinet was as follows:

President of the Ministry............................Scheidemann, *Majority Socialist*
Finance Minister..Schiffer, *Democrat*
Minister of Foreign Affairs............................Brockdorff-Rantzau, *Democrat*
Minister of the Interior..Preuss, *Democrat*
Minister of Economics..Wissel, *Majority Socialist*
Minister of Food...Schmidt, *Majority Socialist*
Minister of Justice...Landsberg, *Majority Socialist*
Minister of Defense...Noske, *Majority Socialist*
Minister of Colonies...Bell, *Centre*
Minister of Posts..Giesberts, *Centre*

---

[298] Naumann, "Die Demokratie in der Nationalversammlung," 2–3.
[299] Feiler, "Der Ruf Nach den Raeten," 8.

Minister of the Demobilization Office............................Koeth, *Non-partisan*
Ministers without Portfolio...
........David, *Majority Socialist;* Erzberger, *Centre;* Gothein, *Democrat*

On February 13 Scheidemann announced to the Assembly the program of his ministry. In foreign affairs he would strive for an early peace, the restoration of the German colonies, the return of the prisoners of war, and German participation in the league of nations upon a basis of equality with the other powers. In his internal program, Scheidemann advocated a democratic national administration, the improvement of education, the ceration of a people's army, and the restoration of the national life.

Such were the beginnings of ministerial government under the National Assembly at a time when Germany was confronted with internal and foreign problems which threatened almost daily to overthrow the republic. Food conditions were precarious, and the industrial and commercial activities of the nation had practically collapsed. The great Prussian railway system was almost in ruins and transportation had broken down in all parts of the *Reich*. The Spartacans were still attempting to gain control of the workmen's and soldiers' councils. Of the Scheidemann ministry they wrote: "A half century of education of the German workmen to parliamentary cretinism by the social democracy expresses itself in the existence of the National Assembly. . . . This ghost of the past raises itself to strangle the organs of the proletarian revolution: the workmen's and soldiers' councils."[300] Many soldiers' councils were already clamoring for the dismissal of Noske. In the face of Spartacan disturbances, wild strikes, and political riots, internal order could scarcely be said to exist. Seven hundred thousand German prisoners were still in France as hostages in the hands of the Entente. As the latter had increased their demands upon Germany since the armistice, the final terms of peace were looked upon as certain to overthrow the ministry of Scheidemann.

[300] *Rote Fahne,* February 6, 1919.

VII.

REVOLUTIONARY PROBLEMS

Economic Reorganization

Although in February, 1919, the majority of the nation looked with confidence to the National Assembly as a panacea to the national ills, it soon became apparent that neither the ministry of Scheidemann nor any majority of the National Assembly could bring about the reorganization of Germany. The economic consequences of the world war, combined with the political and social effects of the November revolution, had reduced Germany to a condition bordering upon ruin and anarchy. There was but little *Realpolitik* in the fine-sounding program which Scheidemann, as head of the coalition of Socialists, Catholics, and Democrats, had announced to the representatives of German democracy. Toward the close of winter, the danger of national starvation, heightened by the maintenance of the allied blockade, created a serious problem. Meanwhile the industrial life of the nation, threatened by strikes and riots, gave evidences of a coming general collapse. Wide classes of Germans, confronted with a hopeless international situation and insoluble internal problems, turned to Bolshevism as a philosophy of despair. In addition the revolution had created a new Germany. New issues had arisen with the revolution, and demanded readjustment with old conditions. Society was in a ferment and could be saved only by the regenerative influences of a strong and far-sighted government, supported by the overwhelming majority of the nation.

Of the internal problems none were more serious than those created by the general collapse of German economic life. This condition in one of the foremost industrial states of the world was the direct result of the economic war waged for four years by the Allies, combined with the fatuous economic policies of the last three imperial ministries.

During the war the Entente systematically destroyed the economic position of Germany in world commerce and industry. The blockade deprived her in a large measure of essential imports from European states as well as from America and the Far East. By the seizure of the German cables the Entente deprived the central powers of their principal means of communication with non-European countries. The forced liquidation of German firms in enemy countries, the confiscation of German patent-rights, and the blacklisting of German firms in neutral countries, were other potent measures taken by the Entente against Germany. The Allies planned by their blockade to cut Germany off from her imported supplies of food and raw materials, and thus to break her powers of resistance. The moral effect of these allied policies was heightened by a campaign of propaganda which was waged against Germany in every neutral country of the world. Germany rendered effective aid to this plan to gain the support of the neutrals by her policy of "frightfulness" in Belgium, France, and on the high seas. Finally the recommencement of unrestricted submarine warfare in February, 1917, led to the entry of America into the war, and to the economic and military collapse of the German empire.

Without the raw materials and machinery seized in the occupied territories, Germany would have gone to pieces earlier. Before the war more than half of all German industries had worked for foreign markets. During the struggle these industries were in a large measure converted to war uses. Finally the Hindenburg program, although it was a military necessity, brought about the ruin of Germany. Schiffer said of it: "Economically it was a program of desperation. Economically it created such a terrible evil that we still have to bear the results of it." [301]

When the conflict ended, the great bulk of the German war industries collapsed. This failure of production in almost all important branches of industry created over four million unemployed workers. To add to the general confusion caused by the military defeat, the revolution, and the industrial crisis, the rapid demobilization of the imperial armies returned millions of German workers to their homes. These men found in many instances their former positions occupied by others, or the factories where they had worked before the war closed for want of raw materials. In those industries in which industrial conditions were favorable, the workmen, confronted with the increased cost of living, and encouraged by political agitators, initiated wild strikes either to secure increased wages or to bring about the immediate socialization of industry. As early as November 26, 1918, the German Demobilization Office declared: "Above all, everyone must work; otherwise we will go to pieces. . . . Each strike can immediately precipitate the catastrophe." [302]

Barth said of the crisis: "The greatest problem for our future is, next to the questions of how we can raise production and how we can restore the lowered energies of workmen ruined by four years of unregulated army life, the question where we can place the great number of unemployed who cannot go back into the industries." [303]

Equal to the crisis in industry was the financial situation of the state after the war. In October, 1918, the empire had almost exhausted its

---

[301] *Nationalversammlung*, 8 Sitzung, February 15, 1919, 93.

[302] Tafel, "Arbeitszwang und Arbeitslust."

[303] Barth, "Arbeitslosigkeit und Arbeitsnot," 28.

financial resources and had piled up loan credits to the amount of one hundred and forty billion marks. The effective war costs without regard to interest charges had reached the sum of one hundred and sixty-one billions. Year after year the cost of war had increased, mounting from 23 billions in 1915 to 48.5 billions in 1918. During the last year of the war the daily cost was 135 millions, and in November, 1918, the German government expended 4,100,000,000 marks. Even after the revolution the expenditures did not materially decrease. In January, 1919, army and government expenses amounted to 3,500,000,000 marks.

The fundamental cause of Germany's financial ruin in November, 1918, was her war finance, which had been originally organized upon the basis of a short war. In addition to this false method of financing the struggle, enormous sums were wasted in the manufacture of war material. Corrupt elements were in control of certain branches of war industries, while many government bureaus proved inefficient. Prices rose steadily during this period. Speculation in industrial stocks and profiteering could not be curbed. Finally the Hindenburg program destroyed the moral and financial foundations of the empire.

Nevertheless the government could not cancel, after November, 1918, its orders with the munition factories, since such a procedure would have ruined the factories, the owners, and the millions of men employed by them. As these industries did not, however, manufacture finished products, their work was unproductive and a total loss to the government. The demobilization of the army, including the cost of clothing, rationing, and transporting eight million men, was a tremendous expense to the republic. The increases in soldiers' pay added nine hundred millions to the national expenses. After the war an average sum of about fifty million marks was spent monthly by the state in the support of the unemployed. Another source of the deficit was the expenditures for war welfare work. Including the support of the textile and shoe industries, and the care of invalids, this item amounted by January 31, 1919, to one billion, seven hundred million marks. For family support during the war an additional 1,998,000,000 marks were expended. Finally the new political machinery of the revolution, the workmen's and soldiers' councils, was a tremendous expense to the nation, states, and communes.

One of the first acts of the coalition ministry was an attempt to organize the nation's finances upon a sound basis. War-time extravagance was to be replaced by rigid economy. The vast army-stores were to be sold at a profit to the state of three billions. The Finance Minister announced in the National Assembly that the government would neither annul the war loans nor confiscate bank values and private property. Although the necessity for further taxation was apparent, he announced that the new schedules would be drawn up in agreement with the several states, as well as with due regard to the general economic and social conditions. Every effort was to be made to prevent the flight of capital abroad.

An example of the financial situation of the republic is found in the amount of paper money in circulation on January 31, 1919. In July, 1914, the circulation of *Reichsbank* notes amounted to two billions, and in January, 1919, to twenty-three and a half billions. The total of *Reichskassenscheine* had increased from 139 millions in 1914 to 352 millions in 1919; the private bank notes from 115 millions to 218 millions. In addition there were ten billion *Darlehenskassenscheine* in circulation, making a total of 34.5 billions. The German cities and town had also issued emergency war currency to the value of one billion marks.[304]

This enormous war debt of the empire, as well as the costs of the revolution, and the certain prospect of an unbearable war indemnity, made national bankruptcy imminent. On all sides revolutionary taxation was demanded. The seizure of war profits, a capital tax, an income tax, and an inheritance tax were considered necessary measures.[305] But the worst feature of the financial situation was the prospective war indemnity, which seemed to foreshadow inevitable national bankruptcy.[306]

FOOD

Of all the revolutionary problems, that of food had rendered the lot of the German working classes desperate. The war, the allied blockade, the Ukraine fiasco, and the imperial rationing system had reduced the nation to the verge of starvation. Although the government of Prince Max had sought to alleviate the food situation, it became worse after the armistice. The revolution, with its resulting crises in administration, transportation, and business, had brought the German people to a condition of desperation.

In November, 1918, the revolutionary government was forced to inform the workers that the supplies of fats would last only a few weeks, the supplies of flour three months, and the supplies of potatoes five months. Early in December the food ministry reported that a considerable part of the potato crop which had remained in the ground, had been destroyed by the early frosts. This situation was due largely to the revolutionary unrest, and to the epidemic of influenza which had reduced the number of available agricultural laborers. The return of the allied prisoners of war had also deprived the nation of workers who had helped to harvest previous war crops. Even the existing potato supplies could not be distributed because of the transportation crisis. Consequently only the large centres had a few weeks' supply on hand in December, 1918. Confronted with

---

[304] *Nationalversammlung,* 8 Sitzung, 90–99.

[305] Keil, "Die Rettung aus dem finanziellen Elend," 3–22.

[306] Manes, "Staatsbankrotte."

the same difficulty in the grain supplies, the government announced that after February 7, 1919, the daily ration of flour would be reduced to 80 grams per person, or one-third of the existing ration. Until April 1 the ration of milk fat and margarine products was to be maintained at 3.3 grams per person. To maintain the meat ration of 100 grams per week the government contemplated importing meat. This analysis is sufficient to show that although the ration system of the government was effective during the war, it collapsed immediately after the revolution, leaving the nation face to face with starvation and Bolshevism.

By the terms of Article 26 of the Armistice Convention it is stated that the Allies and the United States contemplated the provisioning of Germany during the period of the armistice. Nothing was done up to December 13, when at the time of the extension of the armistice to January 17, 1919, the German delegates were informed that twenty-one million tons of German shipping must be surrendered to the Allies before food would be provided for Germany. The delay in furnishing food created the belief among large classes of Germans that the Allies wished to drive Germany into a condition of anarchy. Erzberger, while admitting on December 27 in Berlin that Germany was prepared to pay for the destruction of property in Belgium and France, asked the Allies for a preliminary peace and an opportunity to secure the necessary shipments of food.

Article 8 of the Armistice Convention of January 16, 1919, provided for the surrender of the German ships to the Allies in order to insure the arrival of food supplies at the Hanseatic ports. "To assure the supply of food for Germany and for the rest of Europe, the German government will take all necessary measures to place the whole German commercial fleet, during the period of the armistice, under the control and under the flags of the allied powers and the United States, assisted by a German delegate." [307] At Treves the Allies also informed the Germans that the delivery of the fleet was a condition precedent to the delivery of supplies, and that the German ships were to put to sea not later than February 12, 1919.

The allied plan did not meet with favor in Germany. The government was opposed to giving up the remainder of the merchant marine, which was so essential to the rehabilitation of German commerce and industry. Several subsequent conferences were held, and on February 6 the Germans and Allies at Spa came to an agreement which ultimately lead to the Brussels Convention.

On March 13 the allied and German delegates met at Brussels under the presidency of Admiral Sir Rosslyn Wemyss. Herbert Hoover, Director General of Relief, represented the Supreme Economic Council of the

[307] *American Relief Administration Bulletin*, No. 19, July 25, 1919.

Allies. Herr von Braun was chairman of the German delegation. Here in the capital of former occupied and oppressed Belgium, the German delegates once more agreed to abide by the terms of the armistice and the subsequent extensions. Admiral Wemyss then read to them the text of the memorandum of the Supreme Economic Council containing the conditions of the Allies for furnishing food to Germany.

By the terms of this proposal, food was to be supplied to Germany as soon as her merchant fleet had put to sea, and the necessary financial measures had been taken. Secondly, Germany was given the right to purchase monthly until September, 1919: three hundred thousand tons of breadstuffs or their equivalent, and 70,000 tons of fats, including pork products, vegetable oils, and condensed milk. Third, Germany was required to pay for these supplies by exports, sales of cargoes in neutral territories, credits in neutral states, outright sales of foreign securities and properties, hire of ships and advances against the use of foreign securities. In addition gold could be used as collateral for loans. Fourth, Germany was permitted to export commodities to neutrals, but the proceeds of all sales were to be converted into payment for foodstuffs. Finally the Allies, in order to increase the German exports available for payments, ordered "that no part of these consignments should be distributed to unemployed persons who by their own fault or choice fail to obtain work."

In the subcommittee on food, the Allies declared that no restrictions would be placed on the importations of fish caught in European waters, nor upon vegetables imported from neutrals. Separate regulations were made by the Allies for provisioning the left bank of the Rhine, while the Germans guaranteed shipments through Germany to Czecho-Slovakia and Austria, provided that German shipments arrived beforehand. The Allies also agreed to facilitate German communications with foreign countries for trade purposes as herein provided, and appointed a standing commission to meet at Rotterdam in order to discuss with the Germans the commercial details of the food traffic established by this agreement.

The Brussels Convention was a belated attempt of the German government to improve the terrible food situation produced by the economic and military collapse. The single fact that child mortality trebled in the three months following the armistice indicates the gravity of the crisis. While the shortsighted policy of the Germans resulted in the delaying of food supplies for three months, the allied and associated powers failed to pursue a wise economic policy toward a defeated nation from which they were forced to demand an unprecedented war indemnity. The Allies, emerging from a war unparalleled in history, were not in a mood to make the slightest concession to Germany. Public opinion in France, England, and Belgium rather supported a policy of revenge. The American Congress had specifically prohibited the use of the one hundred million-dollar fund for relief work in enemy states. Yet one of the principal objects of European relief was to prevent the rise and spread of anarchy, and on the other hand to encourage the establishment of stable governments.

During the period of the armistice France evinced but little interest in the problem of relief for her old enemy. She was determined to make it impossible for Germany again to attack and invade her territory. France was even ready to subordinate her hope for German reparations to assurances of national safety. As a result of the war six hundred thousand French homes had been destroyed. Thousands of peasants were living in caves. Throughout the invaded departments many factories had been levelled to the ground. The fertile soil of large agricultural areas had been laid waste. Over the roads from the battle front there had passed since 1914 two millions of crippled men. Under the sod lay one million five hundred thousand Frenchmen.

Just as public opinion among the Allies opposed any economic concessions or the lifting of the blockade, so German public opinion denounced the barbarous continuation of the economic war, and opposed the surrender of the merchant fleet as the price for food.[308] When the government finally ordered the ships to put to sea, strikes and riots broke out among the sailors at Hamburg, Bremen, Stettin, and other ports.[309] From the date of the Brussels Convention, however, the financial, tonnage, and food agreements were loyally carried out by both the Allies and the Germans.

On March 22 Germany made the first deposit of 50 million gold marks at Rotterdam, and the first German merchant ships reached allied ports.[310] Three days later the first American food ship, the *West Carnifax*, reached Hamburg with 6,627 tons of wheat flour, which was, according to the *Berliner Tageblatt*, "of faultless quality and snow white". This provisioning of Germany by the Allies had begun almost simultaneously with the collapse of the second Spartacan rebellion.[311] For the remainder of the month, 28,616 tons of foodstuffs were sent to Germany.[312] While the allied powers furnished considerable supplies to German relief, the bulk of it was shipped by the American Relief Administration. From the beginning of the Brussels agreement until July 31, 1919, America delivered for German Relief:

---

[308] *Vossische Zeitung*, March 13, 1919.

[309] *Berlin Press Review*, March 21, 1919.

[310] *A. R. A. Bulletins*, Nos. 5, 19.

[311] *Berlin Press Review*, March 26, 1919; *A. R. A. Bulletin*, No. 3.

[312] *A. R. A. Special Statistical Bulletin*, No. 4, Table 17.

Foodstuffs.[312]	Amount in metric tons of 1000 kilos each, or 2204.6 lbs.
Wheat flour	250,223
Cereal flour	58,853
Grain	164,632
Rice	29,926
Peas and Beans	37,748
Pork	24,700
Lard	24,010
Milk	11,060
Miscellaneous	433

In addition Great Britain delivered 179,571 tons of fats and cereals valued at 8,200,000 pounds sterling, and France delivered 25,456 tons valued at $18,281,700.[314] All of these foodstuffs were paid for by Germany in gold marks: 440 millions being deposited in Rotterdam and 290 millions in Brussels. This gold, valued at $173,448,000, was sold by the American government.[315]

Not only were the German ports used by the Allies for German relief, but they also became the bases from which food was trans-shipped to Czecho-Slovakia, Austria, and Poland. On February 11 an American Relief Mission was established at Danzig, and within a week the first cargoes of flour destined for the relief of Poland were being loaded on trains for Warsaw. Although the utilization of Danzig by the Allies was strictly within the terms of Article 16 of the Armistice, this traffic with Poland soon created endless difficulties. The Polish-German frontier war, the question of Haller's army, and the general problem of Danzig and the corridor of the Vistula caused German local officials to obstruct the Polish relief. Indeed the Polish-German difficulties were characterized by pettiness upon both sides. The Germans arrested leading Poles in Silesia, and the Poles retaliated against the Germans in Posen. In transporting supplies from Danzig and interchanging coal and potatoes, the Germans often hindered the work for trivial reasons or accused the Poles of confiscating railroad equipment. On the other hand the Poles delayed barges going to Warsaw and subjected the crews to indignities. All the frontier railway lines were closed, except one for transporting Haller's army; one for exchanging coal and potatoes between Posen and Upper Silesia; and one to Danzig. For military reasons the Poles closed the main line from Berlin

---

[312] A. R. A. Special Statistical Bulletin, No. 4: Total A. R. A. Deliveries for German Relief.

[314] A. R. A. Bulletin, No. 19, Nos. 6, 18.

[315] A. R. A. Bulletins, Nos. 6, 18.

to Poland via Bentschen. As a frontier war was carried on between Germans and Poles within the old province of Posen, the above-mentioned conditions are comprehensible.

The action of the German military authorities in prohibiting the transportation of cotton from Danzig to Warsaw is an illustration of the temper of East Elbe Germany. In June the American Relief Administration supplied Poland with cotton to rehabilitate the textile industry and to fight typhus. Germany demanded ten per cent of this cotton as a transportation charge, and held up the shipments. General von Bülow, commander of the Danzig district, prohibited the shipments on the additional ground that the Poles were planning to use the cotton for manufacturing war material. The Berlin government was either powerless or unwilling to order the cotton shipped, and it was not until the German Armistice Commission gave renewed orders to the East Prussian militarists that the cotton was transported to Warsaw. A week later the Berlin government ordered the German authorities to release the cotton. This incident was a violation of Paragraph 16 of the terms of the armistice; an indication of the old military spirit; and an illustration of the difficulties with which the central government of Berlin was confronted.[316]

"It is significant that soon after the first food ship arrived, the political situation made a decided change and since that time has steadily improved."[317] While the beneficent effects of the allied economic policy toward Germany have certainly been exaggerated, the menace of Bolshevism and the danger of the spread of anarchy from Germany to the Allies were present as long as Germany remained unfed. Not only had the armistice stated by implication that Germany should have food, but Germany had to be supplied with food in order to maintain a stable government capable of concluding peace. Apart from all humanitarian reasons, it was necessary that Germany should return to production in order to pay the damages inflicted upon Belgium, France and Great Britain. Summing up the answer to the question of why we are feeding Germany, Herbert Hoover wrote in March, 1919: "From the point of view of an economist I would say that it is because there are seventy millions of people who must either produce or die, that their production is essential to the world's future, and that they can not produce unless they are fed."[318]

BOLSHEVISM

Through the portals of Brest-Litovsk the Russian revolution had hurled into Germany almost as potent a force in the overthrow of the Hohen-

---

[316] *A. R. A. Bulletin*, No. 15, June 27, 1919. On June 11, 1919, the first shipload of cotton from the United States since 1914 arrived at Hamburg, *Berlin Press Review*, June 12, 1919.

[317] *A. R. A. Bulletin*, No. 19.

[318] *A. R. A. Bulletin*, No. 3, April 1, 1919.

zollern empire as were the armies of the Entente. After the November revolution, the German attitude toward Bolshevism continued to be one of the persistent problems which concerned both the government and the masses of the nation. In the German liberation of 1919 these influences are everywhere reflected. The activities of clubs, societies, and official and unofficial organs of public opinion also carried the problem into the realm of practical politics. In a campaign of propaganda, which was often distinct from Spartacan and Independent agitation, Bolshevism attempted to win over the German people to the cause of the soviets.

It was the Imperial Chancellor, von Bethmann-Hollweg, who permitted Lenine and thirty of his comrades to cross Germany on their way to Russia. The German empire is responsible therefore for the creation of that government with which it signed the peace of Brest-Litovsk. "Whoever sets fire to his neighbor's house, dare not complain when afterward sparks fly over on his own roof."[319] Whether or not a portion of the documents published by the American Committee on Public Information are genuine or clever forgeries, the fact is undisputed that the German General Staff as well as the civil government aided the Bolsheviki against the Kerensky government. Despite the denials of Scheidemann and the German government, wide circles in Germany still believe these documents to be genuine.[320]

To Freytagh-Loringhoven's accusation of arson against the imperial government may be added that of stupidity. After the peace with Russia, thousands of German prisoners, who had been trained as proselytes of Bolshevism, returned to Germany. Aided by the army of discontented industrial workers and the shirkers at the front, these war-weary soldiers from Russia began that Bolshevist agitation which undermined the discipline of the German army and became one of the fundamental causes of the revolution. On November 18, 1917, Scheidemann said that the Bolsheviki and the German Social Democrats had the same political goal: the ending of the world war.[321] Finally in April, 1918, Joffe entered the Russian embassy at Berlin as ambassador of the soviets. From then on he became the head of that propaganda which aimed at the overthrow of imperial Germany and the ending of the war by sabotage, strikes, and rebellions in accordance with the plan advocated by Radek at the Kienthal Conference of 1916.[322] Thus the first thrust of Bolshevism was planned to inflict a mortal wound upon the German empire.[323]

[319] Von Freytagh-Loringhoven, Axel Frh., "Geschichte und Wesen des Bolschewismus," 30.

[320] "Die Deutsch-Bolschewistische Verschwoerung": Preface to the translation.

[321] Frenzel, "Die Bolschewiki und Wir," 41.

[322] Fenner, "Die Despoten der Sowjetrepublik."

[323] Von Altrock, "Deutschlands Niederbruch," 36–41.

Long before the November Revolution, the German proletariat had been profoundly influenced by the success of the Bolsheviki. The Russian revolution had for the first time in European history established the rule of a Socialist party over a great power. This triumph had been achieved by the use of dictatorial methods. Lenine formally denounced the democratic programs of the two German Socialist Parties and attempted to reëstablish "the true teachings of Marx concerning the state."[324] Kautsky for the Independents rejected, however, the methods and policies of Lenine, although he recognized Bolshevism to be the most radical and determined conception of the socialistic demands. Otto Braun, a Social Democratic leader, attacked the arbitrary methods of Bolshevism, and declared that it was neither socialism nor democracy, but really insurrectionism and anarchy.[325] Lassalle had prophesied that the freeing of the proletariat would occur amid universal cries of love and fraternity. German critics now pointed out that this prophecy had not been fulfilled, at least in the Russian revolution.

Bolshevism was, however, in the eyes of the German proletariat, a remarkable political and social system, which had at least the prestige of temporary success. All were aware that this Russian communism had developed from Marxian thought and teaching, and that its fundamental conception was the socialization of the means of production through the dictatorship of the proletariat. As in the modern capitalistic state, even universal suffrage is prostituted by the gold and the corrupt press of the upper classes, Bolshevism asserted that the working classes must assume a dictatorship over the nation in order to carry out the work of socialization. Not only does this dictatorship suppress the capitalist class and its supporters, but it also uses force to put down crime and the lawlessness of the masses.

The Bolshevist principles of government are established in the constitution of the soviets. This creates a national system of political as well as economic councils, which are pinnacled in the All-Russian Central Council and the Supreme Council for Political Economy. As each Russian commune, district, province, and government is governed by a council, the soviet system is built up like a pyramid. Executive and legislative powers are united in the councils, and all members have definite administrative duties. The government represents moreover the working classes and not the entire people; and the principle is enforced that only those who do useful work are entitled to rule the state. Bolshevism established therefore a despotism of the proletariat in Russia.[326]

---

[324] Kautsky, "Die Diktatur des Proletariats."

[325] Frenzel, "Die Bolschewiki und Wir," 40.

[326] Eltzbacher, op. cit., 20–31. Gisbert, "Die Ideologie des Bolschewismus" in the Preussische Jahrbücher, April, 1919.

After the November revolution, a pamphlet war broke out in Germany between the supporters of Soviet Russia and their opponents.[327] Societies which were formed for the study of Bolshevist propaganda published accounts of the organization and methods of the soviets.[328] Especially emphasized was the oppression of the lower middle class.[329] Other pamphlets, as for example those published by the Press Counsellor of the German Legation in Latvia and Esthonia, gave in detail the atrocities of the Bolshevists in the Baltic States.[330] Another group attacked Radek and Trotzki as the renegade Jews, Sobelsohn and Bronstein, and naïvely declared Lenine to be incomprehensible, because he was a real Russian of the Simbirsk noble family called Uljanow.[331] Thus anti-Semitic propagandists joined in the crusade against Bolshevism as a convenient way of continuing their agitation.

On the other hand the writings of Lenine, Trotzki, and Radek were translated and eagerly read in Germany. Lenine's *State and Revolution*, an analysis of the Bolshevist conception of the state and the dictatorship of the proletariat, had a wide circulation among the German masses.[332] As the result of the spread of this propaganda literature, Bolshevism came to be regarded as a fundamental cause of the German revolution, and perhaps its final goal.[333] The German revolution appeared to prove the correctness of the theory that from Russia would go forth the triumphant idea of the world revolution.[334] Under the banner of Bolshevism, Germany was to become the organizer of a new world which would accept everywhere the proletarian rule.[335] The German agents of Lenine and Trotzki reiterated the dictum of their masters: "The proletariat must rule the world."[336] This appealed strangely enough to a nation whose Junkers and bourgeoisie had pursued *Weltpolitik* with such fatal consequences. The left wing of the Independents voiced the wishes of several million Germans when it demanded, upon the meeting of the National Assembly, the resumption of diplomatic relations with Russia.

---

[327] "Führer Durch die Bolschewistische und Antibolschewistische Literatur."

[328] Revolutions. Flugschriften des Generalsekretariats zum Studium und zur Bekämpfung des Bolschewismus; Revolutions Streitfragen; Vereinigung zur Be kämpfung des Bolschewismus; Beitraege zu den Problemen der Zeit.

[329] Sochaczewer, "Bürgertum und Bolschewismus."

[330] Köhrer, "Das Wahre Gesicht des Bolschewismus."

[331] Fenner, "Die Despoten der Sowjetrepublik."

[332] Lenin, "Staat und Revolution," Berlin, 1919.

[333] Kautzsch, "Vom Imperialismus zum Bolschewismus," 113. Von Schilling, "Der Imperialismus der Bolschewiki."

[334] Oehme, "Mein Ziel ist die Weltrevolution," 5.

[335] Pratap, "Deutschlands Zukunft unter den Grossen Nationen."

[336] Harald, "Wer war Spartakus," contains a questionable account of the work of Korsakoff, one of Trotzki's agents.

Finally Bolshevism was accepted by wide classes of Germans who rejected both the doctrines of the Independents and the Spartacans. This was due to the fact that the only escape from the peace terms of the Entente seemed to be in the acceptance of Bolshevism. German conversion to the soviet system would be the fatal spark to the communist fires in Italy, France and England; and once the doctrines of Lenine were accepted by the western powers, Alsace-Lorraine and the left bank of the Rhine would return to Germany. Many Germans proposed, however, that the Fatherland should merely transplant Bolshevism to France and England, and not accept the doctrines of Soviet Russia.[337]

Due primarily to the high standard of Germany's economic development, the Russian version of Marx was not accepted by the majority of the nation.[338] For every pamphlet favoring Bolshevism, two at least appeared denouncing it. Conservatives, Liberals, Catholics, and Democrats united against Bolshevism, while the two Socialist parties assumed a varying but critical attitude. Popular writers of these parties asserted that Bolshevism endangered the peace of the world and that it was a menace to the Entente as well as to the defeated central powers. Stadtler in "Revolutionary Controversies" said that the only possible salvation for Europe would be an alteration of the peace policy of the Allies, since a policy of force toward Germany would plunge humanity into the abyss.[339] Mette exclaimed in the *Preussische Jahrbücher* that the fate of the world was in the hands of the Entente; and that either the western powers must unite with Germany in a real constructive league of nations or else destroy their civilizations in a new war and Bolshevist terror.[340] Germany must also be allowed and encouraged by the Entente to raise a new and formidable army in order to combat the rise and spread of Asiatic Bolshevism.[341]

At the very moment when many Germans were frankly asking for the support of the western powers against Bolshevist expansion, the inspired press of the government was assuring the Entente that, if an unbearable peace were dictated to the Fatherland, it would be forced to unite with Russia. Finally Hans Delbrück summed up this doctrine in the menace: "If the Entente threatens to impose terms of peace upon us, which will destroy us economically as well as nationally, there is only one answer for us to give: 'Come on! you shall at least plunge with us into the abyss.' "[342]

[337] Eltzbacher, *op. cit.*

[338] Hirschberg, "Bolschewismus."

[339] Stadtler, "Der Bolschewismus und Seine Überwindung"; "Der Einzige Weg zum Weltfrieden."

[340] *Preussische Jahrbücher,* March, 1919.

[341] Antropow, "Asiatischer Bolschewismus." Schiemann, "Die Asiatisierung Europas."

[342] *Preussische Jahrbücher,* April, 1919.

Meanwhile Trotzki was assuring the Russian people that the hope of European civilization lay in communism. "For my report it will suffice, when I say, that in so far as the fate of the Russian revolution depends upon the world situation, this fate is united with that of the European revolution. If the revolution does not break out in Europe, if the European working class shall prove itself incapable of rising against capitalism at the final ending of this war, if this monstrous assumption should become a reality, then that would mean the doom of European culture. The failure of communism means that Europe relapses into barbarism."[343]

---

[343] Trotzki, "Arbeit Disciplin und Ordnung Werden die Sozialistische Sowjet-Republik Retten."

VIII.

CONSOLIDATION OF THE REPUBLIC

THE MARCH REBELLION

The murder of Karl Liebknecht and Rosa Luxemburg after the disastrous failure of the January revolt of the Spartacans did not, however, end the Spartacan propaganda in Germany. Although the death of the two great communist leaders was a terrible blow to the movement, the Spartacan league continued the struggle with the help of the Russian soviet leaders, who even promised to send a Bolshevist army to East Prussia. Munich, Duesseldorf, Duisburg, the Ruhr, Brunswick, Wilhelmshaven, and Bremen contained strong groups of communists. When their boycotting of the elections failed, the Spartacans determined to disperse the National Assembly by a concentration of red guards. Their sporadic advance on Weimar, February 8, nevertheless failed. The overthrow of the National Assembly and the reversal of the elections of January could not be accomplished by a handful of unorganized communists.

In order to assure the success of the communist movement, the leaders now began active preparations for a second revolution, which had for its goal the overthrow of the Assembly and the establishment of the dictatorship of the proletariat. Recognizing but one sovereignty, the sovereignty of the revolution, the Spartacans declared that the power of capitalism had falsified the elections returns, and that this fact alone gave them an ethical right to proclaim the second revolution. Spartacan speakers exclaimed in the words of the historian Mommsen: "For history there are no high treason paragraphs." [344]

The internal condition of Germany, moreover, rapidly altered the situation in favor of Spartacism. The danger of national starvation was imminent, the industrial life had collapsed, wild strikes and widespread agitation created economic unrest, the National Assembly failed to bring order out of chaos, and the reports from Paris indicated that the final terms of peace would be almost unbearable. Faced by these dangers, large classes of Germans turned to the Spartacans and Independents for salvation. [345] Intellectuals, such as Hans Delbrueck, openly threatened the Entente with Bolshevism. Lenine, who had planned to make Germany the first link in his chain of world revolution, had his agents in Berlin working with the

---

[344] Feiler, "Der Ruf Nach den Raeten," 11–12. Froelich, "Der Weg zum Sozialismus," 3–5.

[345] Stadtler, "Ist Spartakus Besiegt?"

Spartacans. Trotzski's slogan, "The failure of communism means that Europe relapses into barbarism," was placarded on the walls of the capital, while Lenine's dogma, "The Bolshevist theory is a consistent carrying-out of Marxism and strives to reëstablish the true teachings of Marx concerning the state," won many converts for the Spartacans among the workers. Alarmed at this propaganda, the German Finance Minister, Schiffer, exclaimed in the National Assembly: "The Russian ruble circulates in Germany not because of economic but because of political reasons." Thus the second German revolution was to receive thorough Bolshevist support, and to lead to that social revolution which Kautsky had predicted as a natural consequence of the world war.

By the end of the winter the coalition government of Majority Socialists, Catholics, and Democrats found it increasingly difficult to maintain order in Germany. The National Assembly was unable to agree upon an economic policy which would restore the nation's industrial life. The Independents, enraged by their recent political defeats and by the betrayal of their cause at the hands of the Majority Socialists, now encouraged "direct action." The Spartacans determined therefore to strike once more for the dictatorship of the proletariat, and to avenge the murder of their former leaders. They were encouraged by publicists, such as Arthur Feiler, who asserted: "When the government suppresses a rebellion with free corps, martial law, and severity, it does not suppress the Spartacan leaders who bob up again." [346] Aided by the Bolshevist agents and by Russian gold, they planned a revolution for the first week of March, 1919. While their leaders secretly conspired with the troops of the Berlin garrison, the Independent and Spartacan newspapers openly attacked the government. The *Rote Fahne* of March fifth announced:

"The hour has come again. The dead arise once more. Again the downtrodden ride through the land. The followers of Ebert and Scheidemann believed that they had ridden *you* down in a more effective manner than that crazed Hohenzollern in the elections of January, 1907. . . . That which Hindenburg and Ludendorff committed in Belgium, Northern France, Poland, and Finland amid the curses of an entire world and to the disgrace of present and future generations, namely the thousandfold murders of a foreign proletariat, that is repeated today by Noske against German workmen. The Socialist government of Ebert and Scheidemann has become the general hangman of the German proletariat. They lie in wait for the opportunity to establish order. Wherever the proletariat raise their standards, there Noske sends his mercenaries. Berlin, Bremen, Wilhlemshaven, Cuxhaven, Rhineland-Westphalia, Gotha, Erfurt, Halle, Duesseldorf: those are the bloody stations of the crusade of Noske against the German proletariat." [347]

---

[346] Feiler, "Der Ruf Nach den Raeten," 4.

[347] Noske, "Von Kiel bis Kapp," 101–102.

For the first time too, the Spartacans dominated the Berlin workmen's councils and had the support of the soldiers' councils. On the morning of March fourth a complete assembly of all the councils met in the *Gewerkschaftshaus* and voted for a general strike. This proletarian assembly represented theoretically one thousand five hundred workmen's councils of a thousand members each, and was, therefore, a formidable revolutionary body. The strike was voted with an opposition of only one hundred and twenty-five votes and was the first great political decision ever taken by the Berlin proletariat. That it was the prelude to revolution was the unanimous conviction of both the bourgeoisie and the Socialists.[348] The fact that the Unions Commission of Berlin and vicinity supported the general assembly of the workmen's and soldiers' councils in the strike question, shows the seriousness of the situation.[349] Proletarian leaders boasted that the general strike would be followed by "direct action" which would establish socialism in place of the parliamentarism of the Social Democracy.[350]

The demands of the strikers, according to the official bulletin of the strike committee, were: recognition of the workmen's and soldiers' councils; immediate enforcement of the Hamburg Points concerning military authority; release of all political prisoners, especially Ledebour; abolition of military justice; immediate formation of a revolutionary workmen's army; dissolution of all recruited free corps; immediate resumption of political and economic relations with the Soviet Government of Russia; and recognition of the economic rights of the workmen's councils.[351]

On the day set the Spartacans again raised the red flag of Bolshevism on the Alexander Square in Berlin. Active preparations for the uprising had been made by the Red Soldiers' Alliance, which had drawn up on February 15 a secret plan for seizing the principal government buildings and newspaper offices of the city.[352] During the night of March 3 groups of Spartacans attacked and captured thirty-two police stations in the eastern sections of Berlin. The fighting was especially severe at the Lichtenberg Station. Bands of criminals took advantage of the revolutionary disorder to rob and plunder the shops and warehouses in these districts. The executive committee of the Berlin workmen which was directing the political strike denounced this *lichtscheue Gesindel* as "the hyenas of the revolution." The Spartacan attack on the government forces began with the seizure of the Police Presidency by the Marine Division, the Republican Guards, and bands from the criminal classes. Within a few hours of the commencement

---

[348] Däumig, "Das Raetesystem."

[349] *Vorwaerts* and *Berliner Tageblatt*, March 8, 1919.

[350] Noske, "Von Kiel bis Kapp," 105.

[351] Roche, "Organisierte Direkte Aktion."

[352] *Berliner Tageblatt*, March 15, 1919.

of the attack, 30,000 armed Spartacans had seized control of the eastern suburbs of Berlin. The police headquarters were defended by a cadre, 200 strong, of the active One Hundred Seventy-fourth Lorraine Infantry Regiment, and by two companies of the Augusta Regiment. Possessed of mine throwers and machine guns, this small force was able to defend the government stronghold, which was located in the heart of the rebellious district.

During the night of March 3 the Minister of National Defense Noske proclaimed martial law in Berlin and ordered the government troops which were stationed at Potsdam and other suburbs to march into the capital. As a precautionary measure the artillery depot at Spandau, which contained quantities of machine guns, was occupied by the Luettwitz Corps, and the unreliable pioneer battalion of Spandau was disarmed. By March 4 the government offices in Berlin had been reinforced by the arrival of loyal troops.

The Spartacan forces after attacking the Police Presidency attempted to advance their lines into the center of the city, and for a time they seemed on the point of success. Spartacan patrols and bands of criminals broke into the *Tiergarten,* and even penetrated the western sections of Berlin, where they terrorized the inhabitants. Heavy fighting continued for a week between loyal government troops and the Spartacans. Machine guns, airplanes, and artillery were freely used on both sides. Noske, however, was fully prepared for the uprising, and the government troops were equal to the emergency.

To inflame the people against the communists, Noske falsely accused them of a general massacre of prisoners at the Lichtenberg Police Station, and therefore ordered them to be exterminated.[353] Noske's military proclamation of March 9 declared: "Every person who is found fighting with arms in his hands against government troops will be executed at once." In a four days' battle, the Spartacans were driven back from the line Prenzlauer Allee, Alexander Square, Jannowitz Bridge, Silesian Railway Station to the suburb of Lichtenberg. There the communist bands were defeated and dispersed. The People's Marine Division, which had been a thorn in the side of the government since November, 1918, was driven from its headquarters in the Marine House and later broken up. Many depots of the Republican *Soldatenwehr,* which had joined the Spartacans, were disarmed, and this force was reduced to 6,500 men.[354]

As early as March 7 the Unions Commission of Berlin called off the general strike, ostensibly because the government accepted certain of their

---

[353] *Berliner Zeitung am Mittag,* March 9, 1919, and *Vorwaerts,* March 10, 1919, reported the details of this massacre.

[354] *Nationalversammlung,* 27 Sitzung: Report of Noske, March 13, 1919.

demands, and because the strike had endangered food control as well as the health of the city! In reality the leaders abandoned an unequal revolutionary struggle with a government which was ably supported by a remnant of the old imperial army as well as by volunteers from the middle class. The disappointment of the Independent Socialists over the failure of the strike and uprising was expressed in violent attacks on the Minister of National Defense, Noske.

The Guard Cavalry Rifle Division, the Free Corps Huelsen, and the German Rifle Division were the forces which by March 14 were able to bring the armed resistance of the Spartacans to an end.[355] Over one thousand two hundred persons had been killed during the fighting, and property valued in millions had been destroyed. The Spartacans committed many atrocities against the government troops during the course of the uprising, while the latter retaliated against their enemies.[356] Lieutenant Marloh, at the head of a detachment of Noske's forces, brutally murdered twenty-nine men of the People's Marine Division.[357] After the fighting stopped, the eastern sections of the capital were thoroughly searched for rebels and arms. Hundreds of machine guns and thousands of rifles and side arms, together with ammunition supplies, were found in these quarters. As a result of the demobilization of the German army and the break-up of discipline, the Berlin proletariat was better armed than the populace of any European capital in previous revolutionary uprisings. The failure of the March rebellion was due to a lack of leaders, discipline, and coördination of plans.[358]

After Noske had suppressed the general strike and put down the rebellion with an iron hand, the political leaders of the Spartacans and Independents made desperate efforts to disclaim all responsibility for the miserable failure of the uprising. An inspired article in the Independent newspaper, *Freiheit,* explained the rebellion as the result of military rivalries between the Reinhardt Troops and the Republican Guards and the People's Marine Division.[359] The Central Committee of the Communist Party of Germany issued a circular which denied that Spartacus had taken part in the unsuccessful rebellion. It gave the following causes for the March uprising: "The armed conflicts were carried on by the People's Marine Division and detachments of the Republican Guards. Although these are proletarian organizations, they are not closely affiliated with our party. On the con-

[355] *Berliner Tageblatt,* March 13, 1919. *Vossische Zeitung,* March 18, 1919.
[356] Herzfelde, Schutzhaft Erlebnisse vom 7 bis 20 Maerz, 1919, bei den Berliner Ordnungstruppen.
[357] Noske, "Von Kiel bis Kapp," 110.
[358] Georg Schoeplin, Governor of Berlin, in *Berliner Tageblatt,* April 2, 1919.
[359] Freiheit, March 11, 1919.

trary, they were the troops who, during the January rebellion, either attacked our forces in the rear or at least remained neutral during the fighting. Not only that, but now they are fighting for another goal than the one toward which the Spartacans are striving. We are struggling for socialism against capitalism and its representatives; they are fighting for their military posts against their mercenary masters with whom they are discontented. All these facts divide us from them. We are therefore able to console ourselves with the statement: There is no political union between these fighters and ourselves." [360]

THE NEW ARMY

At the outbreak of the world war German militarism exclaimed: "If God in His Grace should give us victory, then 'Woe to the conquered.' " [361] At its close these same militarists led home a defeated and disintegrating army amid allied shouts of *"Vae victis."* The demobilization of the German armies in the winter of 1918-1919 marked the end of that Prussian military system which had assured internal peace to Germany since 1866 and had finally aroused the fear and hostility of an entire world. During this period of demobilization the defeated imperial forces were still further demoralized by the political activities of revolutionary soldiers' councils and by the collapse of the authority of the regular officers. The revolution had made it impossible to maintain the old system of universal military service or to utilize the 1920 class for garrison duty. On the other hand the original revolutionary project for forming a red army had been everywhere abandoned. The need for a new national army, organized upon a different basis, became, therefore, apparent to the provisional government.

On December 12 the Council of the People's Commissioners issued a decree for the formation of a Volunteer People's Army. Among the radical provisions of this decree were: election of the officers by the men; restriction of volunteers to men twenty-four years of age with service at the front; and maintenance of this force independent of the regular army organization.[362] This military reorganization did not, however, result in the formation of any important volunteer units.[363] The Minister of War, Scheuch, who had supervised the work of demobilizing the old army since November 11, resigned on December 15. Although he had approved of the appointment of Deputy Goehre as Adjutant of the Minister of War, Scheuch in his letter of resignation protested against the hatreds, suspicions, indignities, and insults which were constantly hurled against the

[360] Noske, "Von Kiel bis Kapp," 110.

[361] *Militär-Wochenblatt*, August 4, 1914.

[362] Kriegs-Gesetze-Verordnungen und-Bekanntmachungen 6. Band, 177. This series contains the important military decrees.

[363] Noske, "Von Kiel bis Kapp," 113.

war ministry and the officer class in general. He correctly stated that peace, freedom, and order could not be maintained in the new state without the aid of these veteran officers and their disciplined men. Finally he recognized the necessity for a complete reorganization of the military forces of the state.[364]

A decree of the government, issued on January 19, reëstablished the military power of the army and paved the way for the reorganization by the Minister of War of those forces which had defeated the Spartacans in January. Between this period and the March rebellion the demobilization of the old army was completed to a point where only administrative officers, training schools, hospitals, and sections dealing with enemy or returning German prisoners were left intact.[365] Exceptions to these generalizations were the command of Hindenburg on the Polish front and the frontier guards in the Rhineland. It was the *Reichswehr*, the new army, which gained the March victory over the Spartacans, and so from then on became a factor in the maintenance of the republic.

To designate the forces under Noske's command as reorganized is, however, to overlook the almost chaotic condition of the new army. Old war units existed side by side with new republican formations. Ersatz, volunteer, and regular forces were united in so-called divisions or corps. In certain units soldiers' councils were in control, while in others the old regular officers maintained the discipline of imperial days.[366] As a general rule the reserve officers corps, which had been called to active service during the war, had failed to hold the confidence of the troops. After the creation of the *Reichswehr*, the officers of the new army opposed the policies of the government and maintained the monarchical traditions of Prussianism. While their love of country kept many monarchical officers in the service, the majority remained either because of economic reasons or because of the desire to participate in the inevitable coup d'état.[367] Noske was able, however, to control even the monarchical cliques as long as the danger from the Spartacans and Independents was apparent.

At the close of the March rebellion the capital of Germany was defended by volunteer corps and skeleton formations of the old units, which in many cases occupied their former barracks. Practically all the active organizations maintained recruiting offices. General von Lettow-Vorbeck raised a force called Division Lettow, which soon rivaled the Reinhardt Brigade, the Lüttwitz Corps, and the Huelsen Free Corps. In addition the Berlin dis-

---

[364] *Deutscher Geschichtskalender*, 173. Maercker, "Vom Kaiserheer zur Reichswehr" is a well written account of the reorganization of the German army.

[365] *Berlin Press Review*, June 6, 1919.

[366] Boelcke, "Deutschlands Neue Wehrmacht," 5–14.

[367] *Preussische Jahrbücher*, August, 1919.

trict contained the Guard Cavalry Rifle Division, the German Defense Division, the Land Rifle Corps, and the Potsdam Free Corps.[368]

While the old army was being demobilized and the evils of the imperial military system were being eradicated, frantic efforts were made to organize security police, home guards, reserve units, volunteer corps, and a national guard.   To the Entente demands that the army must be reduced to one hundred thousand men, Germany replied with the assertion that a much larger force of organized militia was needed in order to maintain order and to repel invasions.[369]   The officer class still clung to the system of universal military service.   Indeed the Socialist government did not hesitate, during the Polish troubles, to enforce the old imperial universal military service law in the eastern provinces in order to raise fresh troops.[370]   America was cited as the classic example of unpreparedness in 1917, and the organ of the German Officers' Alliance asserted: "A peace-trained American army, despite the valor of the one which did fight in the autumn of 1918, would have been irresistible for our tired troops." [371]   Militarism, as Kautsky boldly asserted, was raising its head again and was gaining support too, because of the Spartacan excesses.[372]   Various excuses and reasons were given for a strong Germany military policy.   The Junker leader, von Kardorff, blandly declared that the fourteen points of Wilson would enable Germany to maintain a strong army.[373]

With the exceptions of the veteran forces on the Rhenish and Polish fronts, the German troops in the various garrison towns of the interior were similar in character to the revolutionary forces of Berlin.   Neither the Prussian ministry of war, nor the ministries of the other federal states possessed complete confidence in their troops.   The rebellious influences of Spartacism and Independent Socialism were a constant menace to discipline and order.   Yet these scattered military forces represented the last line of defense for a new democratic republic, which was subjected to a constant attack by radical Socialists and Communists.

Since the organization of the *Reichswehr* by the decree of March 6, 1919, there has been an almost constant interchange of notes between the allied powers and Germany concerning the reduction of the new army, the delivery of arms and material, and the suppression of the various German police forces.   By the terms of the Treaty of Versailles, the German army was limited to one hundred thousand men, including four thousand officers.

[368] *Vorwaerts,* March 27, 1919; *Berlin Press Review,* April 16, 1919.

[369] Mueller-Brandenburg, "Die Armee des Neuen Staates," 19.

[370] Noske, "Von Kiel bis Kapp," 113.

[371] *D. O. B. Schriften,* 19.

[372] *Berliner Tageblatt,* March 29, 1919.

[373] *Vorwaerts,* March 27, 1919.

The great general staff and universal military service were abolished—a fitting tribute to their military efficiency. Finally the treaty provided that all military clauses affecting Germany must be executed by April 10, 1920.

According to the German Minister of National Defense, the strength of the German army at the conclusion of peace was four hundred thousand officers and men. About half of these forces were stationed in the Baltic States and on the southern and eastern frontiers of Germany. After the ratification of the peace treaty, President Ebert ordered both the Reischwehr and the forces under the command of General Headquarters at Kolberg to be gradually reduced. As late as March 18, 1919, Field Marshal von Hindenburg and General Groener had informed Minister Noske: "The army has confidence in the government, limited confidence in the ministry of war, and unlimited confidence only in the Minister of National Defense." [374] This is sufficient proof of the existence of a military spirit which hoped to maintain the army at a greater strength than that provided for by the treaty of peace. Noske was unable, however, to secure any important concessions from the Entente, and he therefore attempted to carry out gradually the reduction of the army. The problem was still further complicated by the existence of police forces, such as *Zeitfreiwilligen, Sicherheitspolizei,* and *Einwohnerwehren,* which were regarded by the Entente as disguised military reserves for the active German army. The Prussian militarists were accused of attempting to imitate that policy which Prussia had pursued so successfully after the Treaty of Tilsit.

According to reliable allied information, the strength of these German forces on February 1, 1920, was as follows:

THE ACTIVE ARMY

Cadres and detachments of former imperial army units.... 90,000
Detachments on guard at the camps for Russian prisoners of war ... 40,000
Reichswehr, or new army comprising 30 brigades........... 300,000

Total.................. 430,000

THE POLICE FORCES

Zeitfreiwilligen, or emergency volunteers................ 150,000
Sicherheitspolizei, or security police.................. 120,000
Einwohnerwehren, or civic guards...................... 100,000
Orgesch, or Bavarian home guards...................... 30,000

Total.................. 400,000

[374] Noske, "Von Kiel bis Kapp," 168–169.

Germany attempted to secure permission from the allied conference at San Remo to maintain the strength of the *Reichswehr* at 200,000 men. This was refused. By a decision of the Allies on April 27, Germany was allowed to maintain an army of 200,000 men until July 10, 1920, when her forces were to be reduced to 100,000, as stipulated by the Treaty of Versailles. Meanwhile a German decree of March 6, 1920, established a new table of organization for an army of transition which was to supplant the *Reichswehr*. This *Uebergangswehr* was to have the same number of units as the future army in its final form, namely, twenty mixed brigades, three cavalry divisions, and special and sanitary troops. At the Spa conference of July 7, 1920, between the Germans and the Allies, General von Seekt, speaking for Germany, asked for a delay of fifteen months in order to reduce the army from two hundred thousand to one hundred thousand men. This request resulted in fresh negotiations and the granting of further delays to Germany. It was finally agreed that by January 1, 1921, the German army should be reduced to 100,000 men, and that it should then be organized in accordance with the provisions of the Treaty of Versailles.

The same difficulties were experienced by the Allies in reducing the German police forces. The technical and emergency volunteers, civic guards, and volunteer corps were gradually disbanded or reduced in strength during the year 1920. On the other hand the security police increased in numbers as the other organizations were broken up. The Berlin government was also unable to reduce the strength of the Bavarian civic guards. At the allied conference of Boulogne on June 22, 1920, Germany was ordered to reduce gradually the strength of the security police and to increase the ordinary police forces, which existed before the war, from ninety-two thousand to one hundred fifty thousand men. It was further ordered that the total strength of both organizaions should not at any time exceed 150,000 men.

Although the new German army has been finally reduced to the table of organization provided by the Treaty of Versailles, it reflects nevertheless the best work of those German military leaders, such as General von Seekt, who have since the November revolution devoted all their energies to the military reorganization of the Fatherland. As a result, the present German ministry of war is perhaps better organized than the war ministries of France, England, and Italy. It incorporates in the details of its organization many of the important lessons of administration and instruction which were learned during the world war.

This new military organization is also regarded as a force which would bring about the moral regeneration of the Fatherland. At the close of the revolution the *Reichswehr* was composed almost entirely of regulars, who had served in or belonged to the imperial army. Supporting this force were the majority of the seven million veterans who had participated in the war. The cadres were therefore ready to marshal the national army of the future. The former leaders and writers of the imperial army proclaimed their belief in future wars and announced to Germany: "Eiserne Zeiten werden wiederkommen."

MINOR COMMUNIST UPRISINGS

Although twice defeated in the winter and spring of 1919, the Spartacans did not abandon faith in the method of "direct action". After their second failure in Berlin, they planned a series of sharp attacks upon the government in the industrial centers of the nation. Their schemes were aided by the Independents, who in various parts of Germany favored the establishment of the dictatorship of the proletariat. Almost simultaneously with the March uprising in Berlin, disturbances occurred in Koenigsberg, Breslau, Upper Silesia, Hamburg, Emden, the Rhineland, Westphalia, and Thuringia. These minor uprisings were almost all checked either by political concessions to the soldiers' councils of the rebellious districts or by granting the economic demands of the striking workmen.[375] They illustrate, however, the serious situation of the German republic during the week ending March 12, 1919.

The establishment by Bela Kun of the soviet system at Budapest, and the subsequent formation of a Bolshevist Hungary, created a profound impression throughout Germany. The government adroitly attempted at this juncture to consolidate German public opinion against the allied peace demands, which now included the surrender of the merchant fleet and the landing of Haller's army at Danzig. This firmer tone of the Socialist-Catholic-Democratic government was echoed by the monarchists, militarists, and bureaucrats, who protested violently in Berlin against the allied proposals concerning Danzig. In the streets of the capital, Citizen Ludendorff was given an ovation, while over a half million Germans sent greetings to their former Emperor. Many Germans believed that with the spread of Bolshevism into Hungary, democratic western Europe would be engulfed, while Germany, protected by her Junkers and bureaucrats, would escape from the red flood.

To the German Communists the Bolshevist revolution in Hungary was merely a sign of their approaching triumph, toward which events appeared to be moving rapidly in Germany. Paid Spartacan agitators had supported the seamen's riots in Hamburg and other German ports. The argument that the Allies planned to starve Germany into submission was used with as great success by the communists as it was by the monarchists.[376] Allied

---

[375] *A. R. A. Bulletin*, Confidential, No. 1.

[376] *A. R. A. Bulletin*, Confidential, No. 2.

agents reported in March from various districts that the danger of a Bolshevist Germany was a real one.[377]

On April 7 soldiers of a guard regiment at Magdeburg arrested Minister of Justice Landsberg and General von Kleist, commander of the Fourth Corps, because of the imprisonment of certain Independent leaders by the government. A general strike was then organized April 8 at Magdeburg; the warehouses of the American Red Cross were partially looted; and order was not restored until the city was occupied by Noske's government troops. During these disturbances Spartacan aviators had dropped propaganda leaflets over Magdeburg.[378]

In the Ruhr district the miners and industrial workers proclaimed a general strike. Here again the Spartacans were behind what appeared upon the surface to have been an economic rather than a political movement. The decrease in production in the Ruhr reduced the monthly output of coal to 100,000 tons. Two hundred and twenty-one mines were shut down and about 372,000 miners joined the strikers. At Essen the Krupp workmen, railway men, electrical workers, and others had joined the movement. So serious did the situation appear that the Congress of the Workmen's and Soldiers' Councils in session in Berlin urged the Ruhr strikers to return to work, while the government was counseled by the Congress to grant the just demands of the miners.[379]

As the Ruhr situation was attracting the attention of the Allies, Berlin adopted an energetic policy toward these strikers. Martial law was proclaimed at Essen and throughout the whole Ruhr district. Announcing the arrival of food shipments from the Allies, the government stated that, acting under instructions from the allies, it would give nothing to those who continued to strike. From then on the revolutionary movement declined, although general conditions had been favorable to a successful rising of the Rhineland proletariat. Nevertheless the Ruhr district was destined to become the stronghold of Spartacism.

In other parts of western Germany strikes and revolutionary movements broke out. Mannheim, Karlsruhe, Duesseldorf, and Frankfort were the scenes of strikes or uprisings.[380] At Wolfenbüttel a republic of councils was organized and did not disband until attacked by government troops. While the Allies and Germany were discussing the Danzig question, a strike occurred in that city on April 11. The presence in the city of the Bolshevist

[377] *Ibid.*, No. 1.

[378] *Berlin Press Review,* April 7, 10, 11; *A. R. A. Bulletin,* Confidential, No. 3. Maercker, *op. cit.,* 180–192.

[379] *A. R. A. Bulletin,* Confidential, No. 4; *Berlin Press Review,* April 7, 11, 13.

[380] *A. R. A. Bulletin,* Confidential, Nos. 3, 4.

emissary, Schleisstein, and three hundred Russians indicated the political character of the strike.[381]

Meanwhile Spartacans and Independents were planning a general strike in Berlin for the second week in April. Their movement was well advertised, and the just economic grievances of the Berlin workers were accentuated in a determined effort to secure Socialist support. The government organ, *Vorwaerts,* attacked the plan as ruinous for the workers, who would thus prevent the arrival and distribution of the purchased foodstuffs. The Executive Committee of the Social Democratic Party of Greater Berlin also issued a proclamation to the workers against striking at this time.[382] While these attempts were being made to quiet the Berlin proletariat, the department-store clerks, the metal workers, and the bank employees of Berlin created another menace by starting new strikes. Bauer, Minister of Labor, attempted with partial success to mediate between the employers and these employees.[383]

During this period Berlin was almost in a state of siege. Military forces guarded the *Wilhelmstrasse* and the principal government buildings. On April 9 the Spartacans and strikers planned to use a parade of wounded veterans for an attack upon the government. Noske, however, stopped all traffic into the inner city and closed off the government quarter with barbed wire entanglements.[384]

Early in April the revolutionary party, supported by labor, assumed control of the capital of Brunswick and proclaimed a general strike. The radicals demanded: proclamation of a council republic; an alliance with Hungary, Russia, and Bavaria; abolition of militarism and capitalism throughout the world; overthrow of the Ebert government and dissolution of the National Assembly.[385] Whereupon the city officials, physicians, and pharmacists started a counter strike. Telephone, telegraph, and post offices were promptly closed, and the railroads stopped all traffic. The revolutionists, supported by a people's marine division, were, however, able to maintain their soviet government. Noske, who had previously put down the Magdeburg Communists, now ordered General Maerker to occupy Brunswick, and on April 20 the Majority Socialist government of that state resumed office. To maintain democracy in this hotbed of communism, a volunteer corps was formed.[386] Meanwhile the Saxon Spartacans, together with disgruntled veterans and war-wounded, had murdered the Saxon Min-

[381] *Berlin Press Review.* April 11, 1919.

[382] *Berlin Press Review,* April 9, 1919.

[383] *Berlin Press Review,* April 16, 1919.

[384] *Berlin Press Review,* April 10, 1919.

[385] Noske, "Von Kiel bis Kapp," 128–129. Maercker, *op. cit.,* 193–220.

[386] *Berlin Press Review,* April 9–20, 1919.

ister of War, Neuring, on April 12.[387]   Strikes were already ordered in the
Saxon coal regions, while at Leipsic the Independents had actually favored
the establishment of a republic of councils.   The Spartacans too had planned
a general revolt of the Russian prisoners in Saxon prison camps, and hoped
to form a red guard from the numerous Bolshevists among these prisoners.   By proclaiming martial law at Dresden, the Socialist government was
able to maintain itself, and the murderers of Neuring were promptly dis-
avowed by even the Communists.   The Independents, however, warned
the government not to send volunteer troops to Dresden.[388]   Above all, the
Dresden Communists had acted before their comrades in Leipsic were fully
organized, and their premature rising ruined the plans for a general Communist rebellion.   Once more Noske sent Maerker's little army against the
Communists and Independents, and Leipsic was pacified.[389]

In April the second Congress of the Workmen's and Soldiers' Councils
of Germany met in Berlin.   Four terrible months had elapsed since the first
proletarian congress had summoned the National Assembly, and the Spartacans and Independents hoped that the second congress would denounce the
coalition government and establish a soviet republic.[390]   The Majority Socialists, however, had controlled the elections to this congress, and meant
for it to discuss only the questions of shop councils and the socialization of
industry.   During the course of its meetings the congress nevertheless discussed questions beyond its competence, such as: the peace terms, the state
of siege, the new army, and the Polish problem.[391]

Voicing the Independent viewpoint, Richard Mueller declared: "The
National Assembly has completely failed, and on that account the people
are enraged."   Däumig asserted that the radicalized masses must establish
the soviet system.[392]   On the other hand the Majority Socialists denounced
the Independents for supporting the Communist uprisings and accused them
of complicity in the March plunderings in Berlin.

Concerning the military policy of Germany, unanimity of opinion did
not prevail.   The German soldiers' councils favored the complete demobilization of the old imperial army and the establishment of the Swiss system
of military service.   Many Socialist delegates vigorously assailed the new
militarism.   Dr. Steuber-Kassell, a reserve lieutenant, said: "Does Noske
believe that with the aid of the old generals he can remove politics from

[387] *Berlin Press Review*, April 13–14.
[388] *Freiheit*, April 13, 1919. Maercker, *op. cit.*, 233–260.
[389] *Berlin Press Review*, May 12, 1919.
[390] *Freiheit*, April 8, 1919.
[391] *Berliner Tageblatt*, April 12, 1919.
[392] *Freiheit*, April 13, 1919.

the army? There are no unpolitical soldiers." [393]   After adopting general
resolutions concerning the problems of the moment, this congress adjourned.
Its meeting had been without important results, and it was apparent that no
revolutionary group could count upon the workmen's and soldiers' councils
for support.

THE MUNICH COMMUNE

Communism, which had failed in its efforts to establish soviet republics in North Germany, was able in April, 1919, to succeed temporarily in
Bavaria.   Here the results of the January state election had convinced the
leaders of the councils and the radicals that the deliverance of the proletariat could not be expected from a democratic republic which was largely
influenced by the reactionaries and the bourgeoisie.   Kurt Eisner, the head
of the revolutionary government, therefore remained in office after the
convocation of the Bavarian Assembly, although the Independent Socialist
Party was barely represented in the constitutional convention.   Realizing,
however, that his position was untenable, he was about to give up his office
when he was murdered by Count Arco on February 21, 1919.   On the same
day his Majority Socialist colleague, Auer, was murdered by a member of
the Executive Committee of the Workmen's and Soldiers' Councils.   Martial law was proclaimed on February 22 in Munich; the Munich newspaper
offices were closed for ten days; the assembly was placed under a revolutionary guard; and the councils assumed for the moment the control of the
provisional government.   Nevertheless a new ministry was soon organized
under the presidency of Hoffmann, a leader of the Majority Socialists.
This government was under the control of the extremists, and was forced,
for example, to undertake under the direction of Dr. Neurath the immediate
socialization of the Bavarian newspaper publishing companies.[394]

Despite these concessions by the government, the opposition of the Independents and Socialists increased.   Russian agitators appeared on the scene,
and by April the seizure of power by the advocates of a government of
workmen's and soldiers' councils was imminent.   The government of Hoffmann was helpless to prevent the catastrophe.[395]   On April 6 the Central
Council of Bavaria proclaimed to the people: "The decision has been made.
Bavaria is a republic of councils.   The working people are masters of their
fate.   The revolutionary proletariat and peasantry of Bavaria as well as
our brother soldiers are united without party distinctions, and determined
that henceforth all exploitation and oppression shall cease in Bavaria.   The
Landtag is dissolved.   The councils have appointed confidential men to
govern as commissioners of the people.   The press is socialized.   A red

[393] Berliner Tageblatt, April 11, 1919.
[394] Cf. Schmitt, "Die Zeit der Zweiten Revolution in Bayern."
[395] Noske, "Von Kiel bis Kapp," 134–136.

army is in process of formation. We decline to coöperate with the contemptible government of Scheidemann." [396]   Munich thus passed into the hands of the Communists, and the movement began spreading northward. Hoffmann, head of the republican government, fled from the capital. Ingolstadt, Ansbach, Amberg, and Regensburg were among the first Bavarian towns to set up soviets in imitation of Munich. A council republic of North Bavaria was formed with its center at Nuremberg.

The Communists began their rule in Munich by proclaiming a national holiday and commencing a campaign of propaganda.[397]   A manifesto of Erich Muehsam, published on April 8, declared that the new government would work without regard to the interests of the bourgeoisie and the capitalists; that a union would be formed with Soviet Russia and Hungary; and that henceforth the united proletariat had but one common enemy : reaction, capitalism, oppression, and special privilege.[398]   Dr. Tipp, who directed the foreign affairs of the Bavarian Republic of Councils, solemnly announced to the other commissioners of the people : "I have declared war on Württemberg and Switzerland because these dogs have not at once loaned me sixty locomotives. I am certain that we will conquer them. As an additional aid to victory, I have asked the Pope, with whom I am well acquainted, for his blessing." [399]   All publications directed against the dictatorship were prohibited, and a revolutionary tribunal was appointed to try the enemies of communism. To guard against the counter revolution, the Bolshevist Commandant, Egelhofer, ordered on April 14 the surrender of all weapons within twelve hours, under pain of death. A program of action for the immediate success of the revolution called for the seizure of all food in the city and the arming of all proletarian males. Supported by troops from the Second and Third Bavarian Regiments and other detachments of the Munich garrison, this red army soon became a reality. Every effort was made to strengthen this force, since the Communists realized that unless they could control the agricultural districts of Bavaria, their experiment in government would fail. On Monday, April 14, Dr. Levine was proclaimed head of the Communist government.[400]   On the same day it was overthrown by the garrison, but restored on April 15. In order to provide funds for the army, Maenner, the Commissioner of Finance, ordered all safe deposit boxes in the city to be opened and the currency seized. Elaborate military plans were made to defend the Communist territory of Bavaria from the gathering forces of Hoffmann and Noske.

---

[396] *Berlin Press Review,* April 8, 1919.

[397] For a general account of the communist regime see Gerstl, "Die Muenchener Raete-Republik."

[398] *Ibid.*

[399] Noske, "Von Kiel bis Kapp," 136.

[400] *Berlin Press Review,* April 16, 1919.

The Communist Commandant of Munich, Egelhofer, issued on April 16 in the official *"Communications of the Executive Committee of the Workmen's and Soldier's Councils"* the following proclamation: "Proletarians of all lands unite! You will and must conquer! Therefore discipline yourselves! Choose for yourselves able leaders! Obey them implicitly but remove them immediately from office if they fail in battle! Form companies and battalions! Assemble daily at the designated places in your factories for military training. These places should serve in case of danger as your rallying points, where you can receive immediate commands and instructions. Practice close order drill daily and be able to march in military formation. March through the city in close formation as a demonstration of your martial strength. Keep your arms and ammunition and do not let them be taken from you. Discipline and proletarian order will alone save the revolution and the proletarian republic of councils. Long live the proleletariat and the revolutionary soldiers."

Upon the proclamation of the Bolshevist rule in Munich, Hoffmann, the Minister-President of Bavaria, had retired with his cabinet to Nuremberg, which he proclaimed the seat of the government of the free state of Bavaria. Unsettled conditions in that city forced him, however, to remove his government to Bamberg. The remaining South German States—Baden, Württemberg, and Hesse—recognized the Bamberg government, while the Scheidemann ministry had from the start seen the necessity of suppressing the Bavarian Communists. Only the danger of arousing Bavarian susceptibilities had prevented Noske from advancing at once to the Danube with Prussian troops.

After a conference at Weimar between Hoffman, his War Minister, Schneppenhorst, and Noske, Prussian regiments were marched into Bavaria. Württemberg troops under General Haase also advanced from the western border and gradually Munich was surrounded by government forces. The towns of northern Bavaria, as well as Augsburg, were reoccupied and the local soviets suppressed.[401] The Munich Communists fought desperately against the advancing government forces. Kempten, Rosenheim, and Partenkirchen were the scenes of heavy fighting. Many Russian prisoners in the camp at Puchheim joined the Communists.[402] The Bolshevist terrorists were unable, however, to withstand Noske's Prussian troops, and on the night of May 1 Munich was at last occupied by government forces, commanded by Lieutenant General von Oven.

The brief reign of terror in Munich had been a miserable failure, although Russian methods were slavishly imitated. One of the last acts of the Communists was to execute a number of hostages at the Luitpold Gymna-

[401] *Berlin Press Review*, April 10, 12, 14, 19, 22, 1919.
[402] *Berlin Press Review*, April 20–27, 1919.

sium. Among those murdered were Professor S. Berger, Countess Hilla von Westharp, and a Prince von Thurn und Taxis.[403] Many of the foreign intriguers who had aided in establishing the proletarian dictatorship fled over the border. The overwhelming majority of the Bavarian people supported the Hoffmann government, which at once set to work to restore order in the capital.

In the face of these repeated failures, the Spartacan propaganda continued in Germany. Professor Eltzbacher wrote in the *Tägliche Rundschau:* "Germany should immediately become communistic, burn all Entente bridges, and join forces with the Russian revolution, which will purge and purify the world." [404] A typical narrow-minded bourgeois asserted that Spartacus was bound to rule since the masses understood his doctrines as implying the right to plunder the propertied class.[405] In reality the German workman was indifferent to the reasons and programs of the radicals, but he was profoundly affected by the constant reiteration of the Spartacan and Independent slogan: "We alone can save Germany, which has been betrayed and ruined by the Social Democrats and the bourgeoisie."

German Communist risings had occurred in the Rhineland, Westphalia, the Hanseatic Republics, Thuringia, Saxony, and several industrial centers of eastern Prussia and Bavaria. Except in Berlin and Munich they had failed to threaten seriously the coalition government. At the end of spring, 1919, the national interest was diverted from internal affairs to the drama of Versailles. Political Germany became absorbed in the great question of the conclusion of peace.

---

[403] *Berlin Press Review*, May 4–5, 1919.

[404] *A. R. A. Bulletin,* Confidential, No. 3.

[405] Gustav, "Das Programm für eine bürgerliche Gegenrevolution."

IX.

THE ACCEPTANCE OF THE TREATY OF PEACE.

THE GERMAN ATTITUDE TOWARD PEACE

The goal of the German armies under Hindenburg and Ludendorff had been: "The victory of our banners, the welfare of our Fatherland, a peace worthy of the sacrifices which our people had made."[406] These able leaders at least entertained no delusions concerning the peace terms which the allied and associated powers would impose upon a defeated Germany. Indeed the higher officers of the German army were fully aware of the magnitude of their military defeat and of their escape by the signing of the armistice from a débâcle which would have made Napoleon's disastrous retreat from Moscow seem insignificant. Having themselves partially approved of the Pan-German plans of conquest, the German officers naturally expected that allied militarists would insist upon the partition of Germany. Consequently pessimism and despair pervaded those who in 1914 had exultingly shouted *"Vae Victis!"* It is true that military propagandists raised the cry of the treason of the country toward the army; but this camouflage deceived no one but uninformed civilians.[407]

On the other hand German public opinion in the winter of 1918–1919 gave unmistakable evidences of a lack of national understanding of the real military and political situation resulting from the German defeat. The press and government carefully concealed from the people the fact that Germany had accepted as a peace basis the fourteen points of President Wilson *with the reservations demanded by France and England.* Consequently the civilian population expected a peace of justice based upon a debatable interpretation of the fourteen points, which soon became in the eyes of the masses the symbol of Germany's national recovery. Thousands asserted that the German nation, undefeated on the battlefield, had broken off the unequal struggle with a world of enemies in order to secure those equitable terms of peace, which America had generously offered. The average German publicist was profoundly ignorant of the widening gulf, which had separated Germany since 1914 from the rest of the civilized world, and he was also unaware of the great moral, political, and economic problems, which the Entente, during the course of the world conflict, had attempted to solve. On New Year Day, 1919, the Lusitania Medal was still publicly displayed in the Wilhelmstrasse, almost within the shadow of the former American Embassy.

---

[406] Hindenburg, "Aus Meinem Leben," 78.
[407] Noske, "Von Kiel bis Kapp," I.

Even after the revolution there was not an adequate realization by the Germans of the problem of their war responsibility and war guilt, which was of course the determining factor in allied psychology. Pan-Germans boldly asserted that Germany was not guilty of having provoked the world war. Dietrich Schaefer of Berlin placed the blame for the conflict upon Germany's enemies.[408] The revelations of Kurt Eisner, however, stirred the German world profoundly, and were followed by an announcement of Kautsky's study of the documents in the Berlin Foreign Office. Professor W. Foerster was among the first German intellectuals to take a definite stand on the question of Germany's guilt.[409] Dr. Alfred Fried, a pacifist, in his work, "Auf hartem Grund," asserted that Germany planned the world war, and that even after the revolution nothing was done to break with this old military tradition, which had ruined the nation.

The German peace agitation was therefore founded upon an almost total misconception of the seriousness of the international situation. Neither the internal nor the foreign policy of the Scheidemann ministry gave evidences of the necessity of solving such problems as: militarism, war guilt, or Germany's relation to Poland and Russia. A general confusion prevailed at Berlin concerning the actual conditions under which France and England had agreed to make peace. Count Max Montgelas and Count Bernstorff both denounced any peace proposals which should not be strictly in accordance with the fourteen points.[410] Kautsky looked to Wilson's foreign policy as the only hope which the millions of Germans had of escaping from a foreign yoke.[411] Meanwhile despatches from Paris indicated that the final terms of peace would be almost unbearable.

THE QUESTION OF GERMAN-AUSTRIA

During the period of the armistice German public opinion was profoundly concerned with the expected allied proposals for peace. The questions of the war-guilty, cessions of territory, reparations, military occupation, and future reorganization were freely debated. Among these many problems, the solution of which were vital to the nation, none was more widely discussed than the question of German Austria. As early as November, 1918, the National Assembly of Austria had voted in favor of an eventual union with Germany. The partisans of the union of Austria and Germany raised the question in both lands. The election decree of the German provisional government, issued November 30, 1918, provided, in case of a union of the two states, for the admission to the German National

[408] "Die Schuld am Kriege."

[409] *Preussische Jahrbücher,* October, 1919, 117.

[410] *Berliner Tageblatt,* March 30, 1919.

[411] Kautsky, "Die Wurzeln der Politik Wilsons."

Assembly of all members of the Austrian parliament who had been elected by universal suffrage.[412]   From the extreme left to the extreme right, and irrespective of their former attitudes toward the Great German question, all German political parties welcomed the admittance of Austria as a federal state of the *Reich*.   Government, press, and publicists advanced the principle of self determination as governing this case.   At the moment of the break-up of Austria-Hungary, the majority of German Austrians favored the plan of joining Germany.   To Austrian publicists there seemed but three possible policies: the formation of a federal state composed of former members of the Austrian Empire; the formation of a customs union with Czecho-Slovakia, Poland and Jugo-Slavia; or union with Germany.[413]   A small minority offered vigorous opposition to the union of Austria with Germany, and demanded that the red, white, and red colors of the Babenberg dukes should, from October 31, 1918, on, wave over a free and independent Austria.[414]

The union of Austria with Germany would have brought about the realization of the Great German policies of 1813 and 1848.   It would have compensated the *Reich* for the loss of Alsace-Lorraine and the German Polish lands, and would have united all branches of the German nation in one federal state.   Germany's desire to solve this problem, which had existed since 1740, was sincere, and her statesmen of all parties believed that the revolution at least would lead to the union of all Germans in one commonwealth.

The two able Austrian statesmen, President Seitz and Chancellor Renner, who directed the policies of the Danube Republic, were, however, more cautious in their attitude toward unification.   Certain Austrian leaders believed that a general agitation for union with Germany would result in the granting by the Entente of more favorable terms for Austria.   All parties were agreed, however, that Austria could not exist as a separate state if the proposed peace terms of the Allies were carried out.

The German-Austrian Minister in Berlin, Dr. Ludo Hartmann, declared in April, 1919, that a peace conference could not permanently separate the two nations, and that history would destroy the artificial diplomatic picture which was being painted at Paris.   "The decision," he added, "is near at hand.   Until then, however, every German must raise his voice in favor of that commandment of justice and of necessity which is called Greater Germany."[415]

---

[412] Triepel, "Grossdeutsch oder Kleindeutsch."

[413] Rosenfeld, "Wilson und Oesterreich."

[414] Succovaty, "Zwei Fragen über Deutschösterreichs Zukunft."

[415] Verdross, "Deutsch Oesterreich in Gross-Deutschland."

PEACE PLANS AND NEGOTIATIONS

Not only did the foreign policy of the Republic envisage the union with Austria, but it also looked forward to the restoration of the lost colonies. Dr. Solf was the champion of Germany's right to recover her colonies, and in a series of political pamphlets he defended the former imperial colonial policy and advocated the restoration of at least a portion of the former African and Pacific possessions of Germany. The German Socialists and Catholics also favored the maintenance of a German colonial empire.[416] Germans themselves had been before 1914 the greatest critics of the imperial colonial system. During the war and the period of the armistice Germany was accused of infamous crimes in the conduct of its colonial governments. Although the Germans made many blunders, both in Africa and in the Far East, the results of their colonization policies compare favorably with those of the principal European powers. Germany was not to lose her colonies because of her failure as a colonizing power, but for economic, political, and naval reasons, which the allied and associated powers could not ignore.

Above all, Germany hoped that the League of Nations would enable her to escape from the natural consequences of her defeat in the world war. The Prussia of Frederick the Great had produced strangely enough the immortal work of Kant on peace, and the Prussia of 1918 developed with incredible rapidity a group of pacifist organizations which as early as December 8, 1918, met in Berlin and pledged the new republic to the League of Nations and a peace of justice. Schücking, Helene Stoecker, and Elisabeth Rotten appealed to the conscience of the world for a just peace.[417]

Eduard Bernstein then published an able work on the peace question, while Minister Erzberger had as early as September, 1918, issued a scholarly work on the problem of the League of Nations. His carefully prepared bibliography of German works on the subject illustrates the interest taken even in imperial Germany in the project of a league.[418] The sudden enthusiasm after the armistice for the league of nations was largely of course the result of a national effort to secure favorable terms of peace. Notes of warning were sounded too. Publicists declared that the league would very probably become a Trust of the Victors, which would endeavor to rule the world.[419] Prince Maximilian von Baden stated on February 3,

---

[416] Solf, "Germany's Right To Recover Her Colonies." Solf, "Kolonialpolitik, Sozialdemokratie und Kolonien."

[417] Schücking, "Durch zum Rechtsfrieden." Schücking, "Internationale Rechtsgarantien."

[418] Erzberger, "Der Voelkerbund."

[419] Kuttner in "Das Neue Reich," Nr. 2.

1919, that either the Entente would establish a world rule, or it would develop a new universal political tendency in the league of nations.[420]

Although Germany had negotiated with the victorious powers concerning armistice extensions, food, Haller's army, and other problems, it was not until April, 1919, that the formal invitation was extended to the nation to send delegates to a peace conference at Versailles. By that time German public opinion had become pessimistic of a final settlement, while the allied discussions, telegraphed to Germany week after week, convinced the conservative and liberal classes that nothing would be too extravagant or fantastic for the Allies to demand from the Fatherland.

The first exchange of diplomatic notes resulted in an awkward *démarche* by Germany, and the American break with Italy warned the nation that Wilson was having difficulties in carrying through his modified program. Although the National Assembly passed a resolution urging the government to refuse to sign a peace detrimental to the German people, the Foreign Office was well aware of the nature of the terms of the Allies, and was preparing data in an effort to secure their modification at Versailles.[421]

As the time approached for the German Minister of Foreign Affairs, Count Brockdorff-Rantzau, to depart for Paris, members of the National Assembly, such as the Centrist Pfeiffer as well as former annexionists, made veiled threats of a future war of revenge in case the peace terms were unsatisfactory.[422] The Independents at once took up the gauntlet of the coalition parties, denounced the criminal idea of a war of revenge, and advocated the signing of peace even if Wilson failed to carry through his program. Here are the beginnings of that internal political strife over peace, which was destined to hamper the German delegation in its negotiations and to prevent the carrying out of that policy of passive resistance upon which the cabinet of Scheidemann had staked its existence.

Kautsky not only criticized the personnel of the German peace delegation, especially Landsberg, but he also accused the government of creating a jingoistic public opinion, which was opposed to signing peace. Harden wrote: "The men now in power refuse to publish the incriminating documents, hoping that the Hohenzollerns upon their return will keep their places for them, or at least bestow pensions on them."

---

[420] *Preussische Jahrbücher,* March, 1919.

[421] *Materialien Betreffend die Waffenstillstandsverhandlungen,* Teil VIII. *A. R. A. Bulletin,* Confidential, No. 4. The authentic delegation propaganda which Germany endeavored to present at the Peace Conference included over sixty-seven titles. In 1919 the German Foreign Office also reissued certain war propaganda works which were still of value in setting forth Germany's position.

[422] *A. R. A. Bulletin,* Confidential, No. 4.

The author of *J'accuse* opposed the plan of a plebiscite on the allied peace terms, and declared that the present government must assume the responsibility for their acceptance or rejection by Germany. Bernstein criticized the socialistic and pseudo-democratic press for persisting in the methods of the old régime. Breitscheid wrote that the terms of peace would be severe, since Germany had been defeated in a war which her leaders frivolously perpetrated, ruthlessly conducted, and recklessly prolonged until the complete catastrophe. Considering the past of politicians like Scheidemann, David, Landsberg and Erzberger, he added that the Entente could not trust Germany.[423]

REACTION TO THE CONDITIONS OF PEACE

On May 8 the terms of peace of the allied and associated powers were received in Berlin. Scarcely had the German press disseminated the principal allied demands than a wave of protest arose from the entire nation. Had the Allies destroyed Prussia, reëstablished the kingdoms of Westphalia and Hannover, and restored the confederation of 1815, they could not have added to the crushing effect of the peace terms upon the German people. The first act of the Berlin government was to publish proclamations to the nation and East Prussia attacking the hard terms, while thousands of the people of the capital gathered before the headquarters of the American Military Mission. For hours these mobs shouted: "Where are our fourteen points? Where is Wilson's peace? Where is your peace of justice?"[424]

Württemberg, Baden, and other States issued proclamations attacking the treaty. All political parties except the Independents rejected the allied proposals, and appealed to their followers for support. The directorate of the Majority Socialists issued a proclamation to the Socialists of all lands stating that: the proposed terms make the German workers slaves of foreign capitalists for years; that they are a death sentence and a mockery of the fourteen points; and that as they contain the seeds of new wars they will not establish permanent peace. "Proletarians of all lands," concluded the appeal, "unite your strength in order to prevent a peace of force."[425] The German Democratic Party voted at once that it would not sign the treaty.[426]

From all Germany protests were forwarded to the capital. National mourning was proclaimed for a week. Protest meetings were held in the principal cities, while in Silesia and West Prussia the population was in a state of desperation.

---

[423] *A. R. A. Bulletin*, Confidential, No. 6.
[424] *Berliner Tageblatt*, May 9, 1919.
[425] *Vorwaerts*, May 10, 1919.
[426] *Berlin Press Review*, May 11, 1919.

The National Assembly, which had hitherto feared to meet in the capital, was convened on Monday, May 12, in special session in the New Aula of the University of Berlin. Amid the applause of all parties except the Independent Socialists, Scheidemann announced: "The treaty is, according to the conception of the national government, unacceptable." Haase replied that, although the treaty violated the principle of the self determination of nations and contained unbearable economic demands, the German nation demanded peace. He added: "The blame for this catastrophe rests with the German and Hapsburg militarists, who, in the imperialistic overheated atmosphere of the summer of 1914, kindled the flames of the world war. All those also bear the blame who supported the war policy of the former government, who prolonged the war, and who even after the armistice have prevented all traces of the old régime from being swept away. . . . The world revolution will everywhere bring about the freeing of the proletariat, and thus the emancipation of humanity. It will also bring about the revision of the treaty of peace which is now forced upon us."

The spokesmen of all the other German political parties denounced the peace terms of the allied and associated powers and refused to accept them. Hermann Mueller (Breslau), Social Democrat, said in part: "We must make up our minds that this peace is nothing more than the continuation of the war with other means. It is truly a genuine product of a half year's secret diplomacy. Who in the entire world will believe that a new era of international law will begin with this peace? What has become of all those ideals under which the associated governments conducted their crusade against Kaiserism and Militarism?" Groeber declared in the name of the Centre Party that the treaty violated the fourteen points of Wilson, that it was not a peace of justice and that it destroyed politically, economically, and culturally one of the great nations of the world. Haussmann, Democrat, exclaimed: "If our army and our workmen had known on the fifth and the ninth of November that the peace would look like this, the army would not have laid down its arms and all would have held out until the end." Count von Posadowsky-Wehner, Nationalist leader and statesman, declared without a word of apology for the treaties of Brest-Litovsk and Bucharest: "In the history of diplomatic records there is a notorious treaty, the so-called Methuen Agreement which England concluded with Portugal, and this infamous treaty which completely destroyed the Portuguese industry was regarded heretofore as the classic example of brutal power and perfidy. . . . If these peace terms are forced upon us, they will become dragons' teeth, sown by our enemies in German soil, and from these dragons armed warriors will arise in the future who will restore to us our freedom."[427] Dr. Stresemann, the leader of the German People's

---

[427] *Berliner Tageblatt*, May 13, reported that Posadowsky-Wehner cited the Missouri Compromise as the classic example of an infamous treaty.

Party, said: "We are defeated, but whether or not we will be despised and will add to all our other losses that of our honor, depends alone upon ourselves." Professor Count zu Dohna of Koenigsberg, the author in 1917 of "Participation of the Representatives of the Nation in the Conclusion of Peace," declared that the treaty was treason, a breach of pledges, and the rape of a defenseless state. Finally Fehrenbach, destined as a future premier to accept this treaty, exclaimed: "The German people, the most peaceful folk in the world, had no part in this war. It only had a desire for a modest place in the sun. It did not wish to oppress any other people and only claimed for itself that which it did not begrudge to others. . . . The blame for the causes of the war rests on the shoulders of our enemies. . . . *Memores estote, inimici, exoriare aliguis ossibus nostris ultos.* . . . However, the German women in the future will also bear children, and these children, who will grow up in bondage, will be able to double their fists, to break their slave chains and to absterge the disgrace which rests upon Germany."[428]

Not only was this meeting of the National Assembly the most dramatic in its career, but it was a formal commitment of the government to the policy of rejecting the allied proposals unless thoroughly revised. The moderate tone of the party leaders then became more violent in the national forum. Reactionary and liberal opinion urged extreme measures, including rejection at the cost of enemy occupation. "Let the Entente march in and occupy Germany," became the slogan of wide classes of Germans. President Wilson was called a hypocrite, an assassin, an Indian.

German statesmen and publicists united in denouncing the treaty. Friederich Stampfer, editor of the *Vorwaerts*, said that only a treaty involving a new world principle could be signed by Germany. Lichnowsky urged its rejection. Erzberger called it a demoniacal piece of work. Fehrenbach uttered veiled threats against it. Prince Maximilian opposed acceptance of the terms. Stresemann urged national revenge for this additional humiliation. Protests against specific provisions of the treaty were made. Groeber of the Centre Party correctly declared that the financial conditions were the worst feature of the treaty.[429] Noske protested against the delivery to the Entente of 140,000 milch cows, and the reduction of the German army.[430] Before a great assemblage in the Koenigsplatz, Berlin, Miss May Beveridge, who claimed to be a full-blooded American woman, said: "Only a just peace is possible; any other peace is a dishonor to all mankind. If the men at Versailles cannot bring about this peace, I must appeal to the masses of the proletariat to bring

[428] *Nationalversammlung,* 39 Sitzung, Montag den 12 Mai, 1919, 1081–1111.

[429] *Berliner Tageblatt,* May 13, 1919.

[430] *Berlin Press Review,* May 15, 18. 1919.

about peace, freedom, and fraternity."[431] Colonel Emerson, an expatriated American, denounced the treaty and asserted that Germany had the right of self determination. Finally President Ebert issued through the American press representatives in Berlin a direct appeal to America, as follows: "The political demonstration which I herewith direct through you to the American public signifies the moral declaration of war by the New Germany on the entire remaining system of old international politics."

From the eighth of May to the conclusion of peace the Berlin populace demonstrated almost daily before the American Military Mission Headquarters on the *Pariser Platz*. Neither the French nor the British missions were disturbed by the Berlin masses, but the American mission, owing to the spontaneous feeling of the people as well as to the work of government agitators, was continuously molested by various groups of demonstrators. There is no doubt that Pan-Germans incited the Berlin masses against the Americans.[432] The chief of police of Berlin finally cautioned the citizens against any form of demonstration before the allied missions. It was not, however, until May thirtieth that the government showed its hand when Noske, who had allowed the illegal demonstrations against peace to take place, prohibited them for the future and ordered a strict watch kept over all meetings indoors.[433]

As early as May twenty-first the Independent Socialist Party held a great mass meeting in favor of peace in the *Lustgarten*. Adolf Hoffmann, Wurm, and Haase addressed the radical proletariat. To the masses Haase shouted: "For the future the treaty means nothing more than a scrap of paper."[434] The *Freiheit* wrote: "Compared with Brest-Litovsk, the terms are rather moderate." "A gradual growth of moderate opinion in France and England," said Kautsky, "will eventually rectify the unjust peace terms."[435]

The Independents insisted that the political parties which had supported Germany's war policy should also conclude peace after a dispassionate examination of the allied terms. When the military authorities seemed to favor an armed rising against the Entente, the Independents denounced the plan of the General Staff as a preparation for the counter revolution. A bitter press controversy sprang up between the Majority Socialists and the Independents over the question of rejecting the peace terms. Throughout Germany the Independents supported their leaders. They pointed out that if the treaty were not signed, a new hunger blockade

---

[431] *Berlin Press Review*, May 16, 1919. *Berliner Zeitung am Mittag*, May 13, 1919.
[432] *Vorwaerts, Berliner Tageblatt*, and *Berlin Press Review* for May 14, 1919.
[433] *Berlin Press Review*, May 31, 1919.
[434] *Berlin Press Review*, May 21, 1919.
[435] *A. R. A. Bulletin*, Confidential, No. 7.

would be proclaimed, that the importation of raw materials and the restoration of the economic life would be rendered impossible, that more territory would be occupied by the Allies, and that the German prisoners would be kept indefinitely in France. The Berlin Congress of Councils favored signing the peace. Bernstein wrote: "The nation must make an objective study of the allied terms of peace. These demands, although they hit Germany hard, do not lack real justification. Germany must make reparation for much devastation, confiscation, and destruction. Her objections must be untainted with nationalism."[436]

Not only the Independents objected to the jingo policy of the government, but wide circles of the bourgeoisie also favored signing the peace. In *Die Welt am Montag*, von Gerlach denounced the plan of passive resistance. Count Reventlow also warned the nation against a policy of desperation, and declared that a national Bolshevist uprising was inadvisable because of the military and naval strength of the Allies. The German cabinet, which had committed itself to the policy of rejection, now feared the movement of non-acceptance was beyond its control and therefore proposed the plan of a national referendum. The coalition parties supported the plan, which Bernstein himself said was feasible. In the *Vorwaerts*, Stampfer proposed a national referendum if a refusal to sign was agreed upon by the government. The *Koelnische Zeitung* on the other hand condemned the policy of the referendum, and stated that the government must assume the responsibility. Harden also asserted that the government must conclude peace with the Entente, but he hoped for a revision of the articles concerning: the Saar valley; the admission of Germany to the League of Nations; and German coöperation in the all-powerful reparations commission.[437]

During the critical period following the receipt of the allied peace terms, the government and the three Socialist parties were in close touch with Russia. An armed Bolshevist rising was one of the possibilities of escape from the terms of Versailles, which was carefully studied by Germany. In the National Assembly threats of universal revolution were uttered, and the peace committee voted to resume friendly relations with Soviet Russia.[438]

For their part, the soviet leaders prepared to join hands with a Bolshevist Germany which would defy the Entente.[439] Chicherin, commissary for foreign affairs, issued a proclamation condemning the treaty and expressing Russia's sympathy with the enslaved German proletariat. The

---

[436] *A. R. A. Bulletin*, Confidential, No. 8.

[437] *A. R. A. Bulletin*, Confidential, No. 9.

[438] *A. R. A. Bulletin*, Confidential, No. 7.

[439] Erhart, "Dieser Friede Wird Kein Brest-Litovsk."

Isvestia called the treaty the most cruel one ever dictated by imperialistic rapacity and hatred.[440]   These Bolshevist advances were, however, unsuccessful, since the heart of the German scheme for escape was passive and not active resistance to the Entente.

Within a few days after the German courier reached Berlin with the copy of the allied proposals for peace, the press department of the German Admiralty had phototyped and distributed thousands of reproductions of the full text to German officials. The German Union for a League of Nations also reproduced the text. Germany was thus flooded with full information concerning the allied demands. It was this wide publicity and the general despair of official, business, and intellectual classes which accounted for the momentary acceptance of the policy of passive resistance by the nation. Delbrueck wrote in May in the *Preussische Jahrbuecher*: "Purposeless is every appeal to humanity, but also every reference to the vitality of our nation. We are disarmed, starved, dead, sick, and powerless; besides we are fighting among ourselves and strike when we should work. A peace which takes away territory inhabited by Germans, which makes Germans the serfs of the victors, a peace which annexes German Alsatians and deprives Germany of colonies, would not be permanent even if Germany would sign it, because it is unnatural. The government which signed a peace of force would be overthrown by the revolutionary elements, and Bolshevism would be established in Germany."[441]

While advocating non-acceptance of the treaty, the cabinet, the peace committee of the National Assembly, and the peace delegation worked with extreme rapidity and efficiency in preparing the counter proposals which were to be made to the Entente. After a conference at Spa between Brockdorff-Rantzau and Scheidemann, Dernburg, and Erzberger, the German counter proposals were submitted to the Allies on May 28, and immediately afterward published in Germany. Public opinion regarded these as the utmost limit of concessions, but the press, with few exceptions, supported them. The *Deutsche Tageszeitung* attacked the financial concessions, while the *Taegliche Rundschau* held the counter proposals to be as unacceptable as the original demands of the Entente. The *Frankfurter Zeitung* stated that the federal government and the several states had agreed upon a common attitude in case peace was not signed. The *Vorwaerts* advocated the rejection of the treaty unless the original terms were modified.[442]

The government now fully realized that the attitude of the Independents was ruining their peace policy. Consequently they naïvely sought to

[440] *A. R. A. Bulletin*, Confidential, No. 8.
[441] *Preussische Jahrbücher*, May, 1919.
[442] *A. R. A. Bulletin*, Confidential, No. 10.

influence allied and neutral opinion by using the Wolff Telegraph Bureau for propaganda purposes. The Allies were, notwithstanding, well aware of the plans of the Independents and of the real internal situation. Although Haase had asserted in May that the Independents would not take over the government, sign the treaty, and then be chased away by Noske's guards, he announced nevertheless in June that if the Allies advanced into Germany the Independents would form a government and sign the treaty.[443] The Independents now demanded the publication of all official documents on German war guilt and the trial of the guilty persons by a German court.[444] The *Freiheit* stated that a refusal to sign the peace terms would mean the dismemberment, dissolution, and devastation of Germany.

Meanwhile the campaign for the rejection of the treaty continued in Germany.[445] Although the radical press accused the reactionaries of welcoming an Entente invasion, the principal newspapers of the country urged a policy of passive resistance. In the *Tageblatt*, Minister Dernburg urged the rejection of the treaty. In the *Frankfurter Zeitung*, Professor Quidde advocated a policy of passive resistance, declaring that Germany should sign nothing, pay nothing, deliver nothing, and declare a general strike. Finally Count Reventlow, in the *Tageszeitung*, proposed the rejection of the treaty.

It was the policy of the government to suppress all agitation for the acceptance of the terms of the Allies, but the Independent campaign made this an impossibility. Ebert informed the nation, through the *Deutsche Allgemeine Zeitung*, that peace could only be signed by the National Assembly and the House of States, and that both bodies supported the government's policy of rejecting the original allied terms. Brockdorff-Rantzau said that unless the terms were modified, they should be refused, making it incumbent on the Allies to govern Germany.[446]

It was not until June 17 that the final demands of the Allies were known throughout Germany. Certain important modifications of the original proposals were made, but the mantle note with which these were presented to the German peace delegation left no doubt in German minds concerning the temper of the allied and associated powers. Summing up all the charges which the Allies had brought against imperial Germany since 1914, this mantle note was a moral declaration of war against a civilization which had condoned the Belgian atrocities, the aerial bombardment of open cities; and unrestricted submarine warfare.

---

[443] *Freiheit*, June 16, 1919.

[444] *A. R. A. Bulletin*, Confidential, No. 10.

[445] Helfferich, "Die Friedensbedingungen," is an important study of the conditions of peace which influenced public opinion.

[446] *A. R. A. Bulletin*, Confidential, No. 11; *A. R. A. Bulletin*, No. 16.

The effective answer of the Allies to the German plan of passive resistance was made in the decision to reëstablish the blockade in case Germany refused to accept the terms of peace. At the seventeenth of May meeting of the Supreme Economic Council there was a complete discussion of all measures which should be undertaken if it became necessary to reimpose the blockade upon Germany. .At the same time the American Relief Administration continued the shipment of food to Hamburg, although it was uncertain whether or not Germany would sign the peace treaty. "For four years the German authorities officially stated that the blockade was a failure and that the food supply of the German people was satisfactory."[447] During the peace negotiations the German government suddenly maintained that the allied blockade had caused the death of eight hundred thousand German civilians. Although this official report was obviously an exaggeration and did not take into account the character of war work, the scarcity of fuel, the lack of sufficient clothing, and the reduction of the medical profession, there is no doubt that in the spring of 1919 Germany would have been starved to death by a new allied blockade.

ACCEPTANCE OF THE ALLIED ULTIMATUM

The climax of the peace drama occurred not in the Gallery of Mirrors at Versailles but in the Theater of Weimar. Brockdorff-Rantzau returned to Weimar from Paris with the final demands of the Entente, and the Scheidemann cabinet, which had staked its existence upon the securing of fundamental concessions from the Allies, was now face to face with the failure of its peace policy. A conference of the majority parties indorsed the chauvinistic stand of the cabinet, but it could not escape from the fact that the German people demanded peace. Negotiations by the cabinet with the parties were commenced, but an acceptable peace formula could not be agreed upon. In Berlin, three reactionary papers, *Kreuz Zeitung*, *Lokal Anzeiger*, and *Taegliche Rundchau*, and the Socialist *Vorwaerts* and Democratic *Tageblatt* all united in demanding the rejection of the treaty. On the other hand the *Vossische Zeitung* declared: "Signing means at least that the realm can be kept together ; rejection means disintegration and terror without end. This is not the time for placing hopes in the miracle of foreign help."

The Independent Socialist Party led the fight in the assembly for the acceptance of the allied terms. Opposed vigorously by the Democrats, German Nationalists, and the Liberals, they were, however, able to weaken the opposition of Majority Socialists and Centrists to peace. By accusing the conservatives of planning a counter revolution, they gained additional

---

[447] Dr. Alonzo E. Taylor, "A New Sample of German Psychology" in *A. R. A. Bulletin*, No. 10.

proletarian support.   Shortly after one o'clock on the morning of June 20 the Scheidemann cabinet resigned.[448]

The strength of the opposition, as had been apparent for some time, shattered the policy of rejection which Scheidemann in a spirit of adventure had advocated to the last.   Neither the extreme right nor the extreme left were in a position to take over the government, and a new ministry was formed without the Democrats by the Socialists and Catholics.   Thus the two political parties which in the old days used to be called the enemies of the empire, assumed control of Germany.[449]   The program of the new cabinet remained the same as that of the Scheidemann government.   The appointments to office in the ministry were:

Minister President:	Bauer
Foreign Affairs	Hermann Müller
Interior	Dr. David
Finance	Erzberger
Treasury	Dr. Mayer
Economics	Wissell
Food	Schmidt
National Defense	Noske
Posts	Giesberts
Communications and Colonies	Dr. Bell[450]

The work of the government and National Assembly at Weimar was concealed by an enormous amount of camouflage which deceived the German people concerning the serious situation into which the Scheidemann cabinet had plunged the country.   At no period had the cabinet been able to command the undivided support of even the three coalition parties.   At Weimar, the South German States had counselled acceptance of the terms of peace, while the Rhine territories, face to face with invasion or continued occupation, denounced the policy of passive resistance.   The ministers of food and of economics both rendered reports advocating the signing of peace and the majority of the commanding generals urged the acceptance of the terms of the Entente.[451]

On the afternoon of Sunday, June twenty-second, the new Minister-President, Bauer, announced to the National Assembly: "In the name of the government of the *Reich*, I declare therefore that, in consideration of all existing circumstances and on the condition of ratification by the National Assembly, we will sign the treaty of peace. . . . We will

[448] *A. R. A. Bulletin*, Confidential, No. 13; *Berliner Tageblatt*, June 26, 1919.

[449] *Preussische Jahrbücher*, August, 1919, 298.

[450] *Nationalversammlung*, 40 Sitzung. Sonntag den 22 Juni, 1919.

[451] Scheidemann, "Der Zusammenbruch," 243–251, contains that minister's defense of his policy, as well as Erzberger's memorandum in favor of signing the treaty.

authorize the signing of the treaty in the following form: The government of the German Republic is ready to sign the treaty of peace without nevertheless recognizing thereby that the German people were the authors of the war and without assuming any responsibility according to Articles 227 to 230 of the treaty of peace." The motion of Schulz-Groeber: "The National Assembly is in accord with the signing of the treaty of peace," was then debated by the party leaders. It finally carried by a vote of 237 to 138, with five deputies not voting. A resolution of confidence in the government was then adopted by a vote of 235 to 89, with 69 deputies not voting.

Thereupon the Bauer government sent a note to the Entente offering to sign the treaty of peace with reservations concerning German responsibility for the war and the surrender of those accused of violations of the rules of land and naval warfare. This offer was promptly rejected by the Allies, who stated that the treaty must be accepted in its entirety or rejected. General Maercker now called upon Noske to proclaim himself Dictator of Germany and reject the treaty. The National Assembly was, however, again convened on Monday afternoon, June 23, and at last the government proposed the unconditional acceptance of the treaty. Bauer said in part: "Only a period of four short hours separates us now from the recommencement of hostilities. We could not be responsible for a new war even if we had arms. We are defenseless." A motion authorizing the government to sign the treaty was then carried by a rising vote, which the President announced to be the large majority of the Assembly. The great German peace offensive was over and there remained only the formalities of notification, signing, and ratification. A proclamation to the German army stated: "In the hour of deepest misfortune for the Fatherland, the German National Assembly thanks the German military forces for their self-sacrificing defense of their country."[452]

The mantle note with the final terms of the Allies had repeated all the accusations made against the Germans since the outbreak of the war, but the people, whom it forced into submission, were not the warlike Teutons of the national rising of 1914, but a war-weary and half-starved nation, which was torn by conflicting class struggles and state interests. Internal unity had become practically non-existent. While the South German States threatened the national government with a separate peace, the idea of the Rhine Confederation appeared again in German history. Georg Bernhard, von Gerlach, Harden, Bernstein, and the Independents led the attack which forced the government and majority parties to accept the peace terms of the Allies.[453]

---

[452] *Nationalversammlung*, 41 Sitzung, 1139–1142. Maercker, *op. cit.*, 289.
[453] *Preussische Jahrbücher*, July 19, 142.

The oppressive conditions of the peace imposed upon the German Republic in 1919 are unparalleled in European history. They are in a large measure the cause of that unrest in Central Europe which followed the armistice. Their revision is demanded not only by the necessity of maintaining normal economic and political conditions in Central Europe, but also by the dictates of humanity. The verdict of the allied world that Germany should make restorations, reparations, and guarantees for the damage done to France and Belgium, is just. Nevertheless the peace treaty goes far beyond this and practically enslaves the German people. Summing up the German view Hermann Oncken writes: "The peace of Versailles has for the German nation only one single content: oppression, pillage, death." [454]

---

[454] *Preussische Jahrbücher,* March, 1920, 359. Oncken's "Weltgeschichte und Versailler Friede" is an able and extensive discussion of the consequences of the peace.

X.

THE ADOPTION OF THE REPUBLICAN CONSTITUTION

THE PROVISIONAL CONSTITUTION

The constitutional history of the German revolution is that of the transition from imperial to republican government. Revolutionary as are the changes in the new constitution, it altered neither the social relations of the people, nor the federal character of the *Reich*. As the most recent interpretation of republican government by a great people, the underlying philosophy of the constitution of 1919 is, however, of interest to the democracies of the world.

The agitation for constitutional reform antedated the revolution, and was a result of the democratic movement in Germany, which, in the course of the struggle with the western democracies, gained the support of the majority of the armies and the people of the empire. When Prince Maximilian attempted to found a liberal empire in October, 1918, he made constitutional reform one of his fundamental policies. His last official act was to announce the Kaiser's abdication and the convening of a constitutional convention. A decree of the revolutionary council of the people's commissioners, which was issued on November 12, 1918, informed the German people that elections would soon be held for a constitutional assembly. In the face of the universal demand for a constitutional convention, the Independent Socialist leaders in the provisional revolutionary government were forced to abandon their policy of postponing the reorganization of the fundamental laws of Germany.

On November 30, 1918, the Council of the People's Commissioners issued a decree announcing the date of the elections as February 16, 1919, and establishing the electoral regulations for the same. The decree was countersigned by Dr. Preuss, Secretary of State for the Interior, who was already preparing the draft of a provisional constitution. Among the important provisions of this electoral law were the following:

"The members of the constitutional German convention will be elected in universal, direct, and secret elections, according to the principles of proportional representation.

"Entitled to vote are all German men and women who on election day are twenty years of age, i. e., born before January 19, 1899. . . . Soldiers are entitled to vote and take part in political meetings. . . . One deputy is to be elected for approximately every one hundred fifty thousand inhabitants in each electoral district. Registration lists are to be drawn up in each district and the right to vote exercised only in the district where the citizen is registered." [455]

At the third session of the National Assembly on Feburary 8 Dr. Preuss in presenting the draft of a provisional constitution said: " 'We shall create a constitution for Germany, for the entire people. The calling and the authorization for this creative work are found in the sovereignty of the nation. Germany will be one: one realm, ruled by the will of its people with the coöperation of all of its parts; it also lies with this assembly as a part of its mission to bring about this coöperation of the state governments. Although doubts exist about many questions, there is no doubt about the demand for national unity; it is the demand of the entire nation. It wishes unity, it will have unity.' With these words Heinrich von Gagern once greeted the first constitutional national convention of the German people in Saint Paul's Church at Frankfort. . . . At that time the work of the Frankfort National Assembly was wrecked largely by the resistance of the dynastic powers in Germany. Any such resistance has been effaced today by the revolution." After explaining the important provisions of the provisional constitution, Dr. Preuss asked the assembly to adopt the act in order to create a power which could act with legal authority at home and abroad.

In the first great constitutional debate which occurred on February 10, the leaders of the majority parties supported this provisional measure. Dr. von Pregar, the Bavarian Minister, declared in the name of the governments of Bavaria, Württemberg, and Baden that this act was not to be regarded as a final settlement of the question of state rights. Dr. von Delbrück, as the spokesman of the German Nationalists, declared: "We believe that the credit of the future government with the hostile foreign states would be considerably increased if this act is not only quickly but also if possible unanimously adopted." The Independents attempted to amend the measure. They attacked the provision which maintained secret diplomacy and objected to the absence from the text of the words "revolution" and "republic". They even attempted to bestow upon the Central Council of the Workmen's and Soldier's Councils the right to review the work of the National Assembly. Especially bitter were the Independent attacks on Article 4 of the Act, which provided that the territorial integrity of the several states could not be altered save with their consent. After a protracted debate the provisional constitution was finally adopted by the great majority of the Assembly, which then unanimously authorized the President of the Assembly, Dr. Eduard David, to sign the new fundamental law of the republic. [456]

---

[455] Von Volkmann und Boettger, "Revolutions—Bibliothek, Band II: Die Wahlordnung des Rates der Volksbeauftragten."

[456] *Nationalversammlung*, 4 Sitzung. Montag den 10 Februar, 1919, 17–36.

The important provisions of the temporary constitution were: The National Assembly should draw up the permanent constitution and other urgent laws for the *Reich,* which should require, however, the consent of a Committee of the States. This committee should consist of representatives of those German state governments which possess democratic constitutions. Each state should have one representative, and the larger states one for every million inhabitants. Thus Prussia should have nineteen votes out of a total of fifty-eight. In case of a conflict between the National Assembly and the Committee of the States, the Provisional President of the *Reich* should have power to refer the question to a vote of the people. The President should be elected by the Assembly and should hold office until his successor should be chosen under the provisions of the permanent constitution. He should be the chief executive of the nation and should appoint a ministry, responsible to the Assembly, which should conduct the national government. The provisional government of the council of the people's commissioners was thus superceded by a cabinet government, which enjoyed the confidence of the majority parties of the constitutional convention.[457]

CONSTITUTIONAL PROBLEMS

After the adoption of the provisional national constitution, the several states of Germany drew up fundamental laws, which established democratic frames of government. In many states the form of government, with the exception of the monarchical powers, was little altered by the revolution, and all the states maintained their former administrative systems. Even after the flight of the dynasties and the revolution, the differences between states and the conflicting theories of state rights continued to influence the political situation. As in 1848, the German states in 1919 prevented the political unification of the German people. Only in Prussia was there a strong movement toward disunity.

The attempt to divide the former Prussian kingdom is of tremendous importance to the constitutional history of the German revolution. Had it succeeded the democratic Germany of the future would have developed without the conservative traditions of the Prussia of Bismarck and Moltke. After the November revolution a considerable body of Rhenish Prussian Catholics, and a stronger group of particularists in the Rhineland, wished to destroy that Prussian unity which had been welded by the Hohenzollerns in the fires of two centuries of warfare. This movement was everywhere aided by the French army of occupation.[458] *"Los von Berlin"* became a

---

[457] *Ibid.*

[458] Schulte, "Frankreich und das linke Rheinufer," is an excellent study of French plans of expansion and contains, p. 356, a prophetic summary of French imperialistic aims. General Mangin, Commander-in-Chief of the French Army of Occupation, planned in 1919 a revolution to establish a Rhineland Republic. In the proclamations issued, Dr. Dorten of Wiesbaden was announced as the President of the Rhineland Republic. This movement, however, was a failure.

popular cry from the Belgian border to the Elbe. Bismarck had believed that only the Hohenzollern dynasty held such different cities as Cologne and Koenigsberg in one state, and many Germans now thought that religious, political, and economic differences would result in the division of Bismarck's kingdom of blood and iron.[459] The astonishing fact was, however, that the majority of the people in every Prussian province were determined to maintain the unity of the Prussian state. Was it not Prussian efficiency which had caused the political, cultural, and economic development of the *Reich?* Was it not Prussianism, with its power of organization, which had alarmed all the powers of Europe and created that national army which, for the first time since the days of Napoleon, had sought to master the European continent? The revolutionists who planned to partition Prussia were blind to the patriotism of conservatives, liberals, and even the Prussian democrats and socialists.

Notwithstanding these facts, the question of the partition of Prussia was agitated for months before it became apparent that the old militaristic state would retain its former boundaries. Delbrück asserted that the internal necessity for the continuation of Prussia did not exist, although he recognized that the people were opposed to the absorption of Prussia in a unified state.[460] Jacobi acknowledged the necessity of destroying the Prussian hegemony in Germany, yet he favored the maintenance of a federal state. Oddly enough, he admitted the truth of an allied accusation against Germany in stating: "Until 1918, the empire was indeed fundamentally nothing more than an extended Prussia." [461] Professor Binding also declared that while the competition between the *Reich* and Prussia must cease, the federal state should be the goal of the constitution makers.[462] The result of this agitation, which was carried on by thousands of Prussian leaders, was that all hopes of dividing Prussia failed. Prussia remained with her old Bismarckian internal boundaries.[463]

It required a half year's work by the National Assembly before the draft of the permanent constitution was completed. Committees of the convention, the committee of the states, the political parties, and the national government all discussed the innumerable projects and compromises. In general a Democratic-Social Democratic line of development was followed by the constitution makers. In order to preserve internal peace important concessions were made to the Catholics in the school and religious questions. The preamble of the constitution reads: "The German People,

---

[459] Rachfahl, "Preussen und Deutschland," 43.

[460] *Preussische Jahrbücher,* January, 1919, 131–135.

[461] Jacobi, "Einheitsstaat oder Bundesstaat," 36.

[462] Binding, "Die Staatsrechtliche Verwandlung des Deutschen Reichs."

[463] Huebner, "Was Verlangt Deutschlands Zukunft v. d. Neuen Reichsverfassung?"

united in all their parts, and inspired by the will, to renew and strengthen their *Reich* in freedom and justice, to maintain peace at home and abroad and to promote social progress, have adopted this constitution." The First Principal Part of the constitution deals with the following subjects: the National Government and States; the Reichstag; the National President and National Government; the National Council; National Legislation; National Administration; and Administration of Justice. The Second Principal Part, entitled Fundamental Rights and Duties of Germans, contains: The Rights of the Individual; Community Life; Religion and Religious Societies; Education and Schools; Economic Life; and Transitional and Final Provisions.

THE ECONOMIC COUNCIL SYSTEM

Throughout the document the influences of the former imperial constitution are visible. Indeed many of the provisions are copied in a general way from the great constitutional work of Bismarck, and several articles are taken bodily from it. However, the new constitution introduces several new and important provisions to the science of government. Of special interest are those articles which pave the way for economic development, regulate business, and establish the economic council system. "The *Reich* may by law," according to Article 156 of the Constitution, "without detriment to the right of compensation and with a proper application of the regulations relating to the right of expropriation, transfer to public ownership private business enterprises which are adapted for socialization." By creating a *Reichswirtschaftsrat,* or National Economic Council, beside the future Reichstag, the constitution laid the foundation for revolutionary changes in the national economic life. The possibility of the future socialization of the means of production and distribution was thus legally assured to the German people. Article 165 reads as follows:

Workmen and employees are qualified to coöperate on equal terms with their employers in the regulation of wages and conditions of work as well as in the entire economic development of the forces of production. The organizations of both groups and the agreements between them will be recognized.

The workmen and the employees receive for the protection of their social and economic interests legal representation in the workmen's shop councils, in the district workmen's councils organized for each economic area, and in a National Workmen's Council.

The district workmen's councils and the National Workmen's Council meet together with the representatives of the employers and with other interested groups of the people in district economic councils and in a National Economic Council for the purpose of performing all required economic tasks and coöperating in the execution of the laws of socialization. The district economic councils and the National Economic Council are to be so organized that all important vocational groups are represented therein according to their social and economic importance.

Drafts of laws of fundamental importance relating to social and economic politics before introduction shall be submitted by the National Government to the National Economic Council for an expert opinion. The National Economic Council has itself the right to propose such measures for enactment into law. If the National Government does not approve them, it shall nevertheless introduce them into the Reichstag, together with a statement of its own position. The National Economic Council may have its bill presented by one of its own members to the Reichstag.

Control and administrative functions within assigned areas may be delegated to the workmen's councils and to the economic councils.

The regulation of the organization and functions of the workmen's councils and the economic councils as well as their relation to other autonomous social bodies, is exclusively a right of the *Reich*.

The establishment of a National Economic Council of three hundred twenty-six members is an attempt to do away with the conflict between socialism and privilege. It is also a splendid example of a statesmanlike effort to take German politics out of business. The result of this movement has been the creation of a conservatism which sprang from the ultra revolutionary demands of 1918. The National Economic Council will undoubtedly play an important part in the rehabilitation of German industry and commerce.

Results of the Compromises

As a convention of intelligent patriots capable of reorganizing a shattered state, the Weimar Assembly compares very favorably with the French National Assembly which met at Bordeaux in 1871. During the half year's work of the German constitutional convention, the nation recognized however in its dilatory policies the methods of the former Reichstag debating society, and became therefore almost indifferent to the great constitutional compromises. Many Germans thought that the prompt adoption of the temporary constitution was an indication of the practical ability and statesmanship of the National Assembly. The patriots assembled at Weimar evinced, however, an uncontrollable desire to debate extraneous issues rather than to complete the political, economic, and social reorganization of the Fatherland. At an hour when every constructive piece of statesmanship would have contributed to the national recovery, this Assembly consumed months of valuable time debating such questions as: the family and marriage; titles of nobility and orders; the law of bastard children; capital punishment; and the artistic appearance of postage stamps.[464] A great debate took place over the question of the national flag. Finally the colors of the Jena University Burschenschaft of 1815, the later black, red, and gold flag of 1848, were chosen as the standard of the republic.

After violent debates and in the face of the opposition of Conservatives, Liberals, and Independent Socialists, the constitution was adopted on July

[464] Delbrück in *Preussische Jahrbücher*, August, 1919, 295.

31, 1919, by a vote of 262 to 75. Bauer, President of the National Ministry, then announced on behalf of the government: "Ladies and gentlemen! As a result of your vote the Constitution of the German Republic has become the supreme law of the land. It is the true birth certificate of the free state which from now on will establish the form of our national existence. A new era begins; may it also be a better one. Today we set foot once more upon firm ground after an almost five-year march through the sea of blood and hate and privation. We take hold together irrespective of our party or our view of life, and together we must begin a new national existence. Not even in this solemn hour will I attempt to conceal the disunion of our people. The experiences of war and peace have divided us; we are grouped in hostile political parties. . . . We could not, however, separate even if we wished, since the treaty of peace, like an unbreakable chain, has bound us together." [465]

If the National Assembly had adjourned after the ratification of the peace treaty on August 9, and the national elections had then taken place, German political life would have escaped from the upheavals of 1920. Uncompleted, however, was the task of restoring to a semblance of order the financial and economic life of the nation. Therefore the National Assembly did not adjourn but attempted an impossible program of reform. In spite of its failures, however, it gave to the German Nation: peace and a republican constitution. While its debates reveal much wasted effort, lack of practical political sense, and indifference to the national ills, its leaders were after all men of high ideals and patriotism. Dr. Preuss, the father of the political reorganization of Germany, aptly stated: "The organization of law, political freedom, and social justice have been the leading thoughts of the Weimar Constitution."

[465] *Nationalversammlung,* 71 Sitzung, 2193.

AFTER THE REVOLUTION

The National Assembly remained in session for over a year subsequent to the conclusion of peace. Over its constitutional work, great as it was, hung the baleful shadow of the Peace of Versailles. As a contribution to modern political theory, the new republican frame of government contained but one great constructive achievement: the anchoring of the industrial council idea in the constitution. Thus the Spartacans and Independents were encouraged to continue their revolutionary attacks upon the democratic republic. On the other hand the conservatives and liberals, who continually denounced the November revolution, did not cease their anti-democratic agitation, which had as its goal the restoration of the monarchial principles of government. Hands were not wanting to raise the red banner of January and the black, white, and red of the former empire against the black, red, and gold of the republic.

The economic collapse, universal social unrest, and national indignation over the terms of peace, favored the development of a counter revolution. Possessing able leaders and propagandists among the bureaucrats, army officers, and agrarians, as well as efficient organs of public opinion, large party funds, and a devoted following, the monarchists prepared quietly but effectively to overthrow the republic. Helfferich's attack on Finance Minister Erzberger had exposed the questionable practices of that official and consequently discredited the government. There was also widespread discontent with the National Assembly and the Prussian Assembly for their failure to finish their appointed work and adjourn. Many army officers and conservatives sincerely believed that the welfare of the Fatherland demanded the overthrow of the coalition governmnt of Socialists, Catholics, and Democrats. Noske, Minister of National Defense, was totally unaware of the conspiracy formed by his immediate subordinates. The Kapp rebellion of the spring of 1920 was the first determined effort of the German militarists and royalists to recover control of the Fatherland. Their success would have placed Germany in the control of reactionaries; prevented any attempt at the rational socialization of industries; and marked the beginning of an era of political *revanche*. They failed because their rising was premature, but at every crisis in the future history of the republic the man on horseback with the imperial banner will be present.

Aided by a general strike and the loyalty of the nation at large, the Ebert government put down the Kapp rebellion in five days. Unfortunately for Germany the attempt of the monarchists was followed by a communist rising in various German cities. That the government had been negligent in dealing with reactionary plots was beyond a doubt. The rebellion of the communists and the sending of troops into the neutral zone led to renewed allied pressure against Germany and to those excesses of French imperialism culminating in the occupation of Frankfort. The formation of a new German ministry under Hermann Mueller resulted in fresh negotiations with the Allies, the suppression of the communists and the election of the first Reichstag of the republic.

The second national election since the revolution was held in June without serious disorder. The Majority Socialists elected one hundred and ten deputies, a loss of fifty-five seats. The Centre elected eighty-eight deputies, losing but two seats. The Democrats, the third party of the Mueller coalition, were decisively defeated, by a loss of thirty seats, which reduced their strength to forty-five. The German People's Party, the old National Liberals, elected sixty-one deputies, a gain of thirty-nine, while the German Nationalists, the former conservatives, elected sixty-five, a gain of twenty-three seats. The largest increase was made by the Independent Socialists, who elected eighty members to the Reichstag, a gain of fifty-eight seats. The Communists secured but two seats, and all other minor parties nine seats.

The election was a triumph for the German extremists. The great gains of the German Nationalists and the German People's Party show that the conservative and liberal elements are still powerful factors in Germany. Their successes indicate that the barometer of the reaction is rising in Germany, and they thus become a possible danger to the peace of Europe. On the other hand the rise of the Independent Socialist Party indicates the vital force of Marxian socialism and the discontent of a considerable body of the German working classes with the failure of the government to carry out the revolutionary program of socialization. The very growth of the Independents by the adhesion of the extremists foreshadowed, however, their coming dissolution. Originally a party opposed to the democratic and war policies of the Majority Socialists, it found itself in the hour of triumph lacking a definite policy toward Russian Bolshevism, and handicapped by the feud of 1917 with the Majority Socialists.

Although the Majority Socialists remained the largest party in the Reichstag, they refused to form a coalition government without the support of the Independents. The latter declined, however, the invitation to join forces with the bourgeoisie. Under the leadership of Constantin Fehrenbach, a Catholic statesman, a coalition of Centre, People's Party, and Democrats was then formed. With the creation of this ministry, the nation entered upon an era of republican parliamentary government. The great experiment in democratic self-government by the German people had begun, and it remained to be seen whether this nation, which had often boasted of its *kultur,* had been able to arrive at that plane of political development which the western European and Anglo-Saxon democracies had reached in the nineteenth century.

Obviously it needed only able leaders and a dramatic incident to unite the German communists under the banner of sovietism and make them a real menace to German democracy. That contingency occurred in the summer of 1920 when the Bolshevist invasion of Poland seemed to presage the triumph of Lenine and Trotzki. From the Rhine province to East Prussia all ranks of German communists welcomed the advance of the soviet armies toward the German borders as a fulfillment of the Russian promise to aid in the formation of a German soviet system. To the transit by the Allies of war material through Germany to Poland, they raised vigorous objections. Strikes, demonstrations, and uprisings indicated that the German Socialists and even sections of the bourgeoisie favored a policy of benevolent neutrality toward the soviets. The workmen's organization for the control of railway men menaced the coalition government of Fehrenbach with revolt if it did not accede to their demands. So serious became the menace of the proletariat toward the bourgeois government that conservative elements began uniting for defense in the coming struggle. Many Germans regarded the Bavarian *Einwohnerwehr,* popularly called *Orgesch,* as the only German force capable of preventing the triumph of Bolshevism.

There is a striking resemblance between the Russia of 1917 with its provisional government struggling with the soviet of workmen and soldiers' councils and the Germany of 1920 combatting the forces of communism. There is also an analogy between the readiness of the Russian Socialists of 1917 to surrender to the soviet demands and the recent capitulation of the majority of the Independent Socialists to the German communists.

Nothing reveals the strength of German communism after the revolution so clearly as the party congress of the Independents at Halle. Before it convened Soviet Russia delivered the ultimatum that Independent German Socialism must accept the twenty-one theses of Lenine embodied in the platform of the Second Congress of the Third Internationale. The result was a violent struggle within the Independent party. Dittmann, Kautsky, and other leaders refused to join the Bolshevists·and were followed by many Independent groups in industrial centres. At Coblenz the American military authorities wisely refused to allow the Independents to join the Third Internationale under the Moscow conditions. Däumig and Hoffman, however, supported the Bolshevists. Lenine then denounced in the *Rote Fahne* his opponent, Dittmann, stating: "It is quite natural that Kautsky, Dittmann, and Crispien are dissatisfied with Bolshevism; in fact it would be regreftul if Bolshevism gave satisfaction to such people. It is only natural that such bourgeois democrats—they do not differ from our Mensheviki—are very often to be found in the bourgeois camp during the decisive struggle between proletariat and bourgeoisie. The executions seemed to have aroused Dittman's special indignation. It is only a matter of course that revolutionary workers execute Mensheviks which fact naturally can not please Dittmann."

Again the Russian Bolshevists pleaded with the Spartacans to proclaim the terror as the only method of spreading the world revolution. Trotzki wrote to his German sympathizers: "We will take the sword in hand; we will arm the others." In the final session in August, 1920, of the Third Internationale, Sinovieff exclaimed: "I am convinced that the second congress of the third internationale will be the predecessor of the international congress of Soviet Republics."

The result of this Bolshevist propaganda was that the Independent party definitely split into a democratic and communist group. This latter group immediately affiliated with the successors of the Spartacans and the small communist labor party. After two years of struggle with the organized forces of German Social Democracy, the Communists at last secured control of a party organization and party machinery. The Spartacan movement of Liebknecht and Luxemburg in the last days of the empire had become the Communist Party of German in the second year of the republic. It aimed at the establishment of the soviet system in alliance with Bolshevist Russia and held before the German masses the prospect of escaping from the international obligations of the Treaty of Versailles by means of the world revolution. Opposed to communism, however, were the loosely-organized forces of German democracy and the well-trained groups of conservatives and monarchists. Their combined strength was sufficient to remove, after two years of insurrections, this danger to the German *Reich*.

Meanwhile the republic attempted to carry out as far as possible the provisions of the Treaty of Versailles, although it made constant efforts to bring about the revision of that treaty by the allied powers. Two years after the revolution the German Foreign Minister Simons said: "It is not a policy of revenge or prejudice which can save Germany, but a policy of right." The German financial policies failed however to satisfy the demands of France, and the question of reparations remained the chief difficulty between the *Reich* and the allied powers.

A great civilized nation of sixty millions living in the heart of Europe and freed from the menace of militarism, is certain notwithstanding the indebtedness for reparations to recover from the effects of the world war and to assume a new and better place among the leading states of the world.   Meinecke in his work, "After the Revolution," states: "The most important task is to realize at last the aspirations of German idealists and Prussian reformers of a century ago and to cause even the lowest strata of society to be permeated by that civil virtue which flows from the moral liberty of the individual." [466]

[466] Meinecke, "Nach der Revolution," 8.

BIBLIOGRAPHY

[All of the following authorities are to be found in the Hoover War Library of Stanford University.]

ABDERHALDEN, EMIL: Die hohen Aufgaben des deutschen Demokraten und seiner Partei. Halle an der Saale, 1919. Pp. 23.

AHNERT, KURT: Die Entwicklung der deutschen Revolution und das Kriegsende. Nürnberg, 1918. Pp. 240.

ALTROCK, GENERALLEUTNANT VON: Deutschlands Niederbruch. Berlin, 1919. Pp. 55.

American Relief Administration. Bulletin Nos. 1–22, March 17, 1919–August 15, 1919.

——— Special Statistical Bulletin Nos. 1–4, May 27, 1919–August 12, 1919.

——— Weekly Summary of Political Situation. Confidential, Nos. 1–14, March 12, 1919–July 1, 1919.

ANTROPOW, A.: Der Asiatische Bolschewismus-das Ende Deutschlands und Europas. Berlin, 1919. Pp. 10.

AUSWÄRTIGES AMT: Nachrichten-Abteilung Wochenberichte der Auslands lektorate. 1917–1918.

BALCK, W. GENERALLEUTNANT: Entwickelung der Taktik im Weltkriege. Berlin, 1920. Pp. 336.

BAMBERGER, MAX: Demokratie. Marburg, 1919. Pp. 22.

BARTH, ERWIN, Arbeitslosigkeit und Arbeitsnot. Berlin, 1919. Pp. 40.

BAUER, OBERST: Der grosse Krieg in Feld und Heimat. Tuebingen, 1921. Pp. 323.

——— Konnten wir den Krieg vermeiden, gewinnen, abbrechen? Berlin, 1919. Pp. 70.

BAUMGARTEN, OTTO: Die Schuld am deutschen Zusammenbruch. Tübingen, 1919. Pp. 36.

BECKER, OTTO: Deutschlands Zusammenbruch und Auferstehung. Berlin, 1921. Pp. 120.

Bekanntmachungen über den Ernteverkehr nebst den anderweitigen Gesetzen und Verordnungen wirtschaftlicher Natur aus den Jahren, 1915–1918. Berlin.

BERGER, MARTIN: Die Ursachen des Zusammenbruches des Deutschtums in Elsass-Lothringen. Freiburg im Breisgau, 1919. Pp. 35.

BERGSTRÄSSER, PROFESSOR DR. LUDWIG: Geschichte der politischen Parteien. Mannheim, 1921. Pp. 148.

Bericht über den Ersten Parteitag der deutschen Volkspartie. Berlin, 1919. Pp. 115.

Berliner Tageblatt. Berlin, 1914–1921.

Berliner Zeitung am Mittag. Berlin, March–August, 1919.

BERNSTEIN, EDUARD: Die deutsche Revolution. Berlin, 1921. Pp. 198.

BERNSTORFF, GRAF JOHANN-HEINRICH: Deutschland und Amerika. Berlin, 1920. Pp. 414.

Bibliothek der Kommunistischen Internationale I. Hamburg, 1920. Pp. 379.

BINDER, HEINRICH: Die Schuld des Kaisers. München, 1918. Pp. 47.
────── Was Wir als Kriegsberichterstatter nicht sagen durften. München, 1919. Pp. 63.

BINDING, KARL: Die Staatsrechtliche Verwandlung des Deutschen Reiches. Leipzig. Pp. 50.

BÖLCKE, WILHELM: Deutschlands neue Wehrmacht. Berlin, 1919. Pp. 36.

BRAUN, FRIEDRICH EDLEN: Kann Deutschland durch Hunger Besiegt werden? München, 1915. Pp. 75.

BROENNER, W. DR. HAUPTMANN A D.: Die Revolutionstage in Danzig. Danzig, 1918. Pp. 27.

BUCHNER, EBERHARD: Revolutionsdokumente I. Berlin, 1921. Pp. 400.

COHEN-REUSS, MAX: Der Aufbau Deutschlands und der Rätegedanke. Berlin, 1919. Pp. 19.

COHN, CARL: Die Zukunft unserer Wirtschaft und das Ausland. Hamburg, 1919. Pp. 11.

DÄUMIG, ERNST: Das Rätesystem. Berlin. Pp. 37.

DAVID, EDUARD: Führen wir einen Eroberungskrieg? Berlin, 1915. Pp. 20.

Deutsch-Bolschewistische Verschwörung. Berlin. Pp. 16.

Deutscher Geschichtskalender. Die Deutsche Revolution. Heft 1. Pp. 151. Heft 2. Die weitere Entwicklung der Revolution. Leipzig, 1919.

D. O. B. Schriften (Schriften d. Deutschen Offizier-Bundes) Zeit u. Streitfragen I Heft. Oldenburg, 1919.

Deutscher Reichs-und Staatsanzeiger. Berlin, 1918.

Deutsche Tageszeitung. Berlin, March–August, 1919.

Deutsche Vaterlands-Partei. Deutsche Ziele Reden bei der ersten öffentlichen Partei-Kundgebung. (24 Sept. 1917.) Berlin, 1917.

EGELHAAF, GOTTLOB: Deutsche Betrachtungen über den Weltkrieg. Leipzig. Pp. 32.
────── Historisch-politische Jahresbericht für 1918. Stuttgart, 1919. Pp. 222.

EISNER, KURT: Schuld und Sühne. Berlin, 1919. Pp. 31.

ELTZBACHER, PAUL: Der Bolschewismus und die deutsche Zukunft. Jena, 1919. Pp. 48.

ERHART, LUDWIG: Dieser Friede wird kein Brest-Litowsk! Berlin, 1919. Pp. 15.

ERZBERGER, M. REICHSFINANZMINISTER A D.: Erlebnisse im Weltkrieg. Stuttgart, 1920. Pp. 428.
────── Der Völkerbund. Berlin, 1918. Pp. 196.

EUCKEN, RUDOLF: Was Bleibt unser Halt? Leipzig, 1919. Pp. 29.
────── Deutsche Freiheit. Leipzig, 1919. Pp. 36.

FASSBENDER, MARTIN: Revolution und Kultur. Berlin, 1919. Pp. 29.

FEILER, ARTHUR: Der Ruf nach den Räten. Frankfurt am Main, 1919. Pp. 34.

FENNER, HEINZ: Die Despoten der Sowjetrepublik. Berlin, 1919. Pp. 18.

FOERSTER, PROF. FR. WILHELM: Zur Beurteilung der deutschen Kriegsführung. Berlin, 1919. Pp. 21.

FORSTNER, FREIHERR VON: Die Marine-Meuterei. Berlin. Pp. 31.

FOSS, M.: Enthüllungen über den Zusammenbruch. Halle an der Saale. 1919. Pp. 103.

Frankfurter Zeitung. Frankfurt am Main. 1914–1919.

Frauen! Lernt wählen! Eine Sammlung von Losungsworten bedeutender deutscher Männer und Frauen zum Wahlrecht der deutschen Frauen. Leipzig. Pp. 62.

Freiheit. Berlin, 1919.

FRENZEL, HEINRICH: Die Bolschewiki und wir! Berlin, 1918. Pp. 63.

FREYTAGH-LORINGHOVEN, AXEL FRHR. VON: Geschichte und Wesen des Bolschewismus. Breslau, 1918. Pp. 41.

FREYTAG-LORINGHOVEN, FRHR. VON: Heerfuehrung im Weltkiege. Vol. I. Berlin, 1920. Pp. 200.
——— Politik und Kriegführung. Berlin, 1918. Pp. 252.
——— Was Danken wir unserem Offizierkorps? Berlin, 1919. Pp. 93.

FRIEDLÄNDER, PROF. DR.: Wilhelm II, Eine Politische-Psychologische Studie. Halle an der Saale, 1919. Pp. 56.

FRÖLICH, PAUL: Der Weg zum Sozialismus. Hamburg, 1919. Pp. 32.

Führer durch die Bolschewistische und Antibolschewistische Literatur. Berlin, 1919. Pp. 24.

Germanicus. Zum 9, November! Ein politisches Bilderbuch. Leipzig, 1921. Pp. 79.

GERSTL, STADTRAT MAX: Die Münchener Raete-Republik. München, 1919. Pp. 135.

GEYER, KURT: Sozialismus und Rätesystem. Leipzig, 1919. Pp. 32.

GIESECKE, DR. JUR. KARL: Im Kampf an der inneren Front. Leipzig, 1918. Pp. 68.

GOETZ, WALTER: Deutsche Demokratie. Leipzig. Pp. 66.

GOLTZ, GENERAL GRAF R. VON DER: Meine Sendung in Finnland und im Baltikum. Leipzig, 1920. Pp. 312.

GOTHEIN, GEORG: Warum verloren wir den Krieg? Stuttgart, 1919. Pp. 94.

GROSSMANN, FRITZ: Was sind wir unser Kaiser Schuldig? Hannover, 1918. Pp. 24.

GUMBEL, E. J.: Vier Jahre Lüge. Berlin, 1919. Pp. 32.

GUSTAV, MORITZ: Das Programm für eine bürgerliche Gegenrevolution. Leipzig, 1919. Pp. 40.

HAASE, HUGO: Reichstagsreden gegen die deutsche Kriegspolitik. Berlin. Pp. 206.

HAGENAU, PETER: Ein wort für Wilhelm II. Berlin, 1919. Pp. 16.

Handbuch Deutscher Zeitungen 1917 Bearbeitet im Kriegspressamt von Rittmeister a. D. Oskar Michel. Pp. 440.

HARALD, LEO: Wer war Spartakus? Heroldsrufe im Dienste der Zeit Nr. 3. Stuttgart, 1919. Pp. 8.

HARZ, CARL: Die Revolution als Lehrerin und Erlöserin. Altona-Ottensen, 1919. Pp. 82.

HEINEMANN, BRUNO: Ziele und Gefahren der Sozialisierung. Berlin, 1919. Pp. 23.

HELFERRICH, KARL: Die Friedensbedingungen. Berlin, 1919. Pp. 50.
——— Der Weltkrieg. III Band. Berlin, 1919. Pp. 658.

HERTLING, KARL GRAF VON (RITTMEISTER): Ein Jahr in der Reichskanzlei. Freiburg, 1919. Pp. 192.

HERZFELDE, WIELAND: Schutzhaft Erlebnisse vom 7 bis 20 März bei den Berliner Ordnungstruppen. Berlin, 1919. Pp. 16.

HEUSS, THEODOR: Deutschlands Zukunft. Stuttgart, 1919. Pp. 23.

HEYDE, LUDWIG: Abriss der Sozialpolitik. Leipzig, 1920. Pp. 168.

HILDEBRAND, KARL; HEINE, WOLFGANG: Zwei Reden. Stuttgart, 1919. Pp. 44.

HINDENBURG, GENERALFELDMARSCHALL VON: Aus meinem Leben. Leipzig, 1920. Pp. 406.

HIRSCHBERG, MAX: Bolschewismus. München, 1919. Pp. 107.

HOENSBROECH, PAUL GRAF VON: Wilhelms II Abdankung und Flucht. Berlin, 1919. Pp. 64.
——— Zurück zur Monarchie! Berlin, 1919. Pp. 56.

HOFF, FERDINAND: Am Abgrund vorüber! Berlin, 1919. Pp. 361.

HOFFMANN, R. F.: Sozialismus oder Kapitalismus. Halle an der Saale, 1919. Pp. 15.

HOPPE, WILLY: Elsass-Lothringen. Berlin. Pp. 32.

HÜBNER, RUDOLF: Was verlangt Deutschlands Zukunft von der neuen Reichsverfassung? Halle an der Saale, 1919. Pp. 24.

IMMANUEL, OBERST: Siege und Niederlagen im Weltkriege. Berlin, 1919. Pp. 274.

JACOBI, ERWIN: Einheitsstaat oder Bundestaat. Leipzig, 1919. Pp. 39.

JANSSON, WILHELM: Arbeiterinteressen und Kriegsergebnis. Berlin, 1915. Pp. 167.

JORDAN, HERMANN: Die Demokratie und Deutschlands Zukunft. Berlin, 1918. Pp. 80.

KANTOROWICZ, PROF. DR. HERMANN: Der Offiziershass im Deutschen Heer. Freiburg, 1919. Pp. 50.

KAUTSKY, KARL: Die Diktatur des Proletariats. Wien, 1918. Pp. 63.
——— Sozialdemokratische Bemerkungen zur Uebergangswirtschaft. Leipzig, 1918. Pp. 166.

—— Die Wurzeln der Politik Wilsons. Berlin, 1919. Pp. 40.

—— Der Internationalität und der Krieg. Berlin, 1915. Pp. 40.

KAUTZSCH, WERNER: Vom Imperialismus zum Bolschewismus. Berlin, 1919. Pp. 188.

KEIL, WILHELM: Die Rettung aus dem finanziellen Elend. Berlin, 1919. Pp. 22.

KLEINSCHROD, DR. FRANZ: Die Geisteskrankheit Kaiser Wilhelms II? Wörishofen, 1919. Pp. 31.

KÖHRER, ERICH: Das wahre Gesicht des Bolschewismus. Berlin. Pp. 20.

KRIEGER, BOGDAN: Die Wahrheit über die angebliche Abdankung und Flucht des Kaisers. Berlin, 1919. Pp. 13.

Kriegs-Gesetze—Verordnungen und Bekanntmachungen, Saemtliche. 6 Baende. Berlin, 1919.

KUHL, H. VON, GENERAL DER INFANTERIE: Der deutsche Generalstab in Vorbereitung und Durchführung des Weltkrieges. Berlin, 1920. Pp. 218.

KUMPMANN, KARL: Die Bedeutung der Revolution. Tübingen, 1919. Pp. 66.

—— Die neuere Entwicklung der sozialen Fragen. Tübingen, 1919. Pp. 66.

Kritik des Weltkrieges. Von einem Generalstaebler, Leipzig, 1920. Pp. 150.

KUTTNER, ERICH: Die Deutsche Revolution. Berlin, 1918. Pp. 16.

—— Von Kiel bis Berlin. Berlin, 1918. Pp. 30.

LAMBACH, WALTHER: Ursachen des Zusammenbruchs. Hamburg. Pp. 112.

LAMPRECHT, KARL: Der Kaiser. Versuch einer Charakteristik Zweiter Abdruck. Berlin, 1916. Pp. 136.

LAUBE, MAX: Das wahre Gesicht der Parteien. Berlin, 1919. Pp. 30.

LAUFENBERG, DR. HEINRICH: Die Hamburger Revolution. Hamburg, 1919. Pp. 32.

LEDERER, EMIL: Einige Gedanken zur Soziologie der Revolutionen. Leipzig, 1918. Pp. 40.

LEGIEN, CARL: Warum müssen die Gewerkschaftsfunktionaere sich mehr am inneren Parteileben beteiligen. Berlin, 1915. Pp. 20.

LEHMANN-RUSSBÜLDT, OTTO: Warum erfolgte der Zusammenbruch an der Westfront? Berlin, 1919. Pp. 28.

LEIDIG, E.: Liberalismus und Demokratie. Berlin, 1919. Pp. 14.

LENIN: Staat und Revolution. Berlin, 1919. Pp. 102.

LENSCH, PAUL: Die deutsche Sozialdemokratie in ihrer grossen Krisis. Hamburg, 1916. Pp. 31.

—— Die deutsche Sozialdemokratie und der Weltkrieg. Berlin, 1915. Pp. 64.

—— Am Ausgang der Deutschen Sozialdemokratie. Berlin, 1919. Pp. 38.

LENTULUS: Wer war Spartakus? Stuttgart, 1919. Pp. 8.

LERCH, GENERALMAJOR VON: Kritische Betrachtungen über die letzten Kaempfe an der deutschen Westfront. Wien, 1919. Pp. 11.

LIEBIG, PROF. DR. HANS FRHR. V.: Der Betrug am deutschen Volke. München, 1919. Pp. 228.

LOEBELL, ARTUR VON: Aus Deutschlands Ruinen. Berlin, 1919. Pp. 31.

LUDENDORFF, ERICH: Das Friedens-und Waffenstillstandsangebot. Berlin, 1919. Pp. 80.

────── Meine Kriegserinnerungen 1914–1918. Berlin, 1920. Pp. 628.

────── Urkunden der Obersten Heeresleitung über ihre Tätigkeit 1916–1918. Berlin, 1920. Pp. 713.

MAERCKER, GENERALMAJOR: Vom Kaiserheer zur Reichswehr. Leipzig, 1921. Pp. 220.

MANES, ALFRED: Staatsbankrotte. Berlin, 1919. Pp. 275.

Materialien, betreffend die Waffenstillstandsverhandlungen, Teil VIII. Die Deutsche Waffenstillstandskommission. Charlottenburg, 1920. Pp. 370.

MEINECKE, FRIEDRICH: Nach der Revolution. München, 1919. Pp. 144.

MENKE-GLÜCKERT, E.: Die November Revolution 1918. Leipzig, 1919. Pp. 147.

Militär-Wochenblatt. 1914–1919. Berlin.

MÖCKEL, KARL: Das deutsche Bürgertum und die Revolution. Leipzig. Pp. 72.

MOLDENHAUER, PAUL: Von der Revolution zur Nationalversammlung. Bonn, 1919. Pp. 20.

MOSER, OTTO VON, GENERALLEUTNANT: Kurzer Strategischer Überblick über den Weltkrieg 1914–1918. Berlin, 1921. Pp. 74.

MÜHSAM, DR. KURT: Wie wir belogen wurden. München, 1918. Pp. 189.

MÜLLER, KARL VON, KAPITÄN ZUR SEE: Das betörte deutsche Volk. Berlin, 1919. Pp. 12.

MÜLLER, OSCAR: Warum mussten wir nach Versailles? Berlin, 1919. Pp. 72.

MÜLLER-BRANDENBURG: Die Armee des neuen Staates. Berlin, 1919. Pp. 19.

Nationalversammlung. (Verhandlungen der) Nos. 1–103. Februar–Oktober, 1919.

NAUMANN, FRIEDRICH: Die Demokratie in der Nationversammlung. Berlin, 1919. Pp. 16.

────── Demokratie als Staatsgrundlage. Berlin, 1919. Pp. 16.

────── Mitteleuropa. Berlin, 1915. Pp. 299.

Neue Reich, Das. Nos. 1, 2. Berlin, 1919.

NEURATH, OTTO: Die Sozialisierung Sachsens. Chemnitz, 1919. Pp. 103.

NICOLAI, W. OBERSTLEUTNANT: Nachrichtendienst Presse und Volksstimmung im Weltkrieg. Berlin, 1920. Pp. 200.

NOSKE, GUSTAV: Von Kiel bis Kapp. Berlin, 1920. Pp. 211.

Nowak, Karl Friedrich : Der Sturz der Mittelmaechte. München, 1921.
——— Der Weg zur Katastrophe. Berlin, 1919. Pp. 299.

Oehme, Walter : Mein Ziel ist die Weltrevolution. Berlin, 1919. Pp. 32.

Oncken, Hermann : Das Alte und das neue Mitteleuropa. Gotha, 1917. Pp. 150.
———Weltgeschichte und Versailler Friede. Frankfurt a M., 1921. Pp. 27.

Persius, L. : "Wie es kam." Berlin. Pp. 15.

Pesch, Heinrich : Neubau der Gesellschaft. Frieburg im Breisgau, 1919. Pp. 24.
——— Sozialisierung. Freiburg im Breisgau, 1919. Pp. 32.

Posters, German War and Revolutionary. Nos. 1–2300. 1914–1919.

Pratap, Mahendra : Deutschlands Zukunft unter den Grossen Nationen. Berlin, 1919. Pp. 20.

Preussische Jahrbücher. Berlin. Januar, 1919–März, 1921.

Rachfahl, Feliz : Preussen und Deutschland. Tübingen, 1919. Pp. 46.

Radek, Karl : In den Reihen der Deutschen Revolution 1909–1919. München, 1921. Pp. 463.
——— Rosa Luxemburg, Karl Liebknecht, Leo Jogiches. Hamburg, 1921. Pp. 48.

Rathenau, Walther : Der Kaiser. Berlin, 1919. Pp. 60.
——— Kritik der dreifachen Revolution. Berlin, 1919. Pp. 125.
——— Nach der Flut. Berlin, 1919. Pp. 72.

Revolutions-Bibliothek Nr. 3. Das Programm der Kommunistischen Partei Deutschlands (Spartakusbund).

Reichs-Gesetzblatt Jahrgang 1919, Nr. 1–Nr. 153. Berlin, 1919.

Roche, Karl : Organisierte direkte Aktion. Berlin. Pp. 12.

Rosenfeld, Heinrich : Wilson und Österreich. Wien, 1919. Pp. 140.

Rückführung des Westheeres, Die. Berlin, 1919. Pp. 32.

Rump, Johann Diedrich : Paul Reichsgraf von Hoensbroech als Gefolgsmann der Hohenzollern. Leipzig, 1919. Pp. 110.

Runkel, Ferdinand : Die deutsche revolution. Leipzig, 1919. Pp. 232.

Schaefer, Dietrich : Der Krieg 1914–1919. 3 Bände. Leipzig, 1920.
——— Die Schuld am Kriege. Oldenburg, 1919. Pp. 59.

Scheer, Admiral : Deutschlands Hochseeflotte im Weltkrieg. Berlin, 1919. Pp. 524.

Scheidemann, Philipp : Der Zusammenbruch. Berlin, 1921. Pp. 250.
——— Es lebe der Frieden! Berlin, 1916. Pp. 32.

Schiemann, Paul : Die Asiatisierung Europas. Berlin, 1919. Pp. 19.

Schlachten und Gefechte des Grossen Krieges 1914–1918, Die. Quellenwerk nach den amtlichen Bezeichnungen . . . vom Grossen Generalstab. Berlin, 1919. Pp. 560.

Schilling, Caesar von : Der Imperialismus der Bolschewiki. Berlin, 1919. Pp. 13.

SCHMITT, DR. FRANZ AUGUST: Die Zeit der zweiten Revolution in Bayern. München, 1919. Pp. 71.

SCHÜCKING, WALTHER: Internationale Rechsgarantien. Hamburg, 1919. Pp. 134.

SCHÜCKING, WALTHER; STÖCKER, HELENE; ROTTEN, ELISABETH: Durch zum Rechtsfrieden. Berlin, 1919. Pp. 20.

SCHULTE, ALOYS: Frankreich und das linke Rheinufer. Stuttgart, 1918. Pp. 364.

SCHWARTE, M. GENERALLEUTNANT Z. D.: Die Militaerischen Lehren des Grossen Krieges. Berlin, 1920. Pp. 489.

SOCHACZEWER, HANS: Bürgertum und Bolschewismus. Berlin, 1919. Pp. 16.

SOLF, W. H.: Kolonialpolitik. Berlin, 1919. Pp. 99.

——— Germany's Right to Recover Her Colonies. Berlin, 1919. Pp. 43.

Sozialdemokratie und nationale Verteidigung. Berlin, 1916. Pp. 30.

SPICKERNAGEL, DR. WILHELM: Ludendorff. Berlin, 1919. Pp. 142.

STADTLER, E.: Der Bolschewismus und seine Ueberwindung. Berlin, 1919. Pp. 19.

——— Der einzige Weg zum Weltfrieden. Berlin, 1919. Pp. 59.

——— Ist Spartakus besiegt? Berlin, 1919. Pp. 20.

STÄHLIN, OTTO: Hindenburg. München, 1918. Pp. 35.

STAUDINGER, FRANZ: Profitwirtschaft oder Versorgungswirtschaft. Berlin, 1919. Pp. 32.

STEGEMANN, HERMANN: Geschichte des Krieges. Vierter Band. Stuttgart, 1921.

STEIN, DR. V. GENERAL, KRIEGSMINISTER: Erlebnisse und Betrachtungen aus der Zeit des Weltkrieges. Leipzig, 1919.

STEINHAUSEN, PROF. DR. GEORG: Die Grundfehler des Krieges und der Generalstab. Gotha, 1919. Pp. 42.

——— Die Schuld der Heimat. Berlin, 1919. Pp. 79.

STEINMEYER, H.: Neudeutschland. Braunschweig, 1919. Pp. 20.

STRESEMANN, GUSTAV: Die Politik der Deutschen Volks-partei. Berlin, 1919. Pp. 26.

STROEBEL, HEINRICH: Die Sozialisierung. Berlin, 1921. Pp. 236.

SUCCOVATY, EDUARD: Zwei Fragen über Deutschösterreichs Zukunft. Graz. Pp. 31.

Taegliche Rundschau. Berlin, 1919.

TAFEL, W.: Arbeitszwang und Arbeitslust. Gotha, 1919. Pp. 40.

TESDORPF, DR. PAUL: Die Krankheit Wilhelms II. München, 1919. Pp. 31.

TIRPITZ, ALFRED VON: Erinnerungen. Leipzig, 1919. Pp. 532.

TRIEPEL, PROF. DR. HEINRICH: Grossdeutsch oder Kleindeutsch. Berlin, 1919. Pp. 30.

TROTZKI, LEO: Arbeit, Diziplin und Ordnung werden die sozialistische Sowjet Republik retten. Berlin, 1919. Pp. 23.

VALENTIN, VEIT: Deutschlands Aussenpolitik 1890–1918. Berlin, 1921. Pp. 418.

VERDROSS, ALFRED: Deutsch-Österreich in Gross-Deutschland. Stuttgart, 1919. Pp. 32.

Verhandlungen des Reichstags. 4 August, 1914–26 Oktober, 1918.

VETTER, KARL: Der Zusammenbruch der Westfront. Berlin, 1919. Pp. 25.

VOLKMANN, SIEGFRIED; BOETTGER, ERNST: Die Wahlordnung des Rates der Volksbeauftragten vom 30 November, 1918. Berlin, 1919. Pp. 73.
——— ——— Die Rechtsverordnungen des Rates der Volksbeauftragten vom 12 November, 1918. Berlin, 1919. Pp. 65.

Vorgeschichte des Waffenstillstands. Berlin, 1919. Pp. 186.

Vorwärts. Berlin, 1914–1919.

Vossische Zeitung. Berlin, 1914–1919.

Wahrheit, Die Zeitgemässe Broschüren. 15 Hefte. von T. Hauptmann und Univ-Prof. Dr. F. Hauptmann. Bonn, 1919.

War Information Library of British Ministry of Information. 1914–1918. German Collection.

WEBER, MAX: Sozialismus. Wien, 1918. Pp. 36.

Welt am Montag, Die. Berlin, 1919.

WINTZLER: Das Neue Belgien. Essen, 1918. Pp. 20.

WOLFFHEIM, FRITZ: Knechtschaft oder Weltrevolution. Hamburg. Pp. 16.

WOLZOGEN, ERNST: Harte Worte, die gesagt werden müssen. Leipzig, 1919. Pp. 24.

WRISBERG, ERNST VON, GENERALMAJOR: Heer und Heimat 1914–1918. Leipzig, 1921. Pp. 150.
——— Der Weg zur Revolution 1914–1918. Leipzig, 1921. Pp. 120.

WULFF, ERWIN: Die Persönliche Schuld Wilhelms II. Dresden, 1919. Pp. 48.

Zentralstelle für Auslandsdienst Zeitungskontrolle Amerikanische Presse. Wochenberichte, 1917.

ZIMMERMANN, BODO: Der Zusammenbruch. Berlin, 1919. Pp. 45.

ZITELMANN, ERNST: Das Schicksal Belgiens beim Friedensschluss. München, 1917. Pp. 97.

ZWEHL, HANS VON, GENERAL DER INFANTERIE A. D.: Der Dolchstoss in den Rücken des siegreichen Heeres. Berlin, 1921. Pp. 27.
——— Die Schlachten im Sommer 1918, an der Westfront. Berlin, 1921.

INDEX

Abdication of the Federal Princes, 56–57.

Abdication of the Kaiser: Effect of President Wilson's Notes, 25; Views of the Majority Parties, 42; Visit of Drews to General Headquarters, 41; Bavarian Socialist Demands, 36; Ultimatum of Majority Socialists, 41; Policy of Prince Max, 40–41; Interfractional Committee's Demand, 42; Conclusion of Conference of Field Officers, Spa, November 9, 43; Proclamation of Prince Max, November 9, 43; Effects, 44.

Agriculture, 16.

Alexander Square, 97, 127.

Alsace-Lorraine, 21.

American Relief Administration: Character of German Relief, 116–117; Foodstuffs Delivered, 117–118; Danzig Mission, February 11, 1919, 118–119; Food Shipments, 155.

Allied and Associated Powers: Sign Armistice, 27; Extend Period of Armistice, 115; Negotiations at Versailles, 147; Ultimatum, June, 1919, 155–156.

American Expeditionary Force, 8, 10.

American Military Mission, 150–151.

Amnesty, Political, 26.

Annexationists, 17, 147.

Anti-Semitism, 100.

Antwerp-Metz Line, 9.

Armistice Negotiations, 24, 25, 45.

Armistice, of November 11, 1918, 27, 74.

American Red Cross, 136.

Armistice Period: Article 16 of Armistice Convention, 118; Article 26 of Armistice Convention, 115; Article 8 of Armistice Convention, January 16, 1919, 115; Treves, 115; Spa, February 6, 1919, 115; Brussels, March 13, 1919, 115–116.

Army, Imperial: Situation at Close of 1917 Campaigns, 7; March Offensive, 8; Offensives of April, May, and June, 8; Second Battle of the Marne, 8; August 8, 9; Retreat of the Western Forces, 9; Effect of Propaganda, 10–11; Request for an Armistice, 23; The Stab in the Back, 13; Mutinies in North Germany, 34, 37–38; Mutiny of Munich Garrison, 35–36; Mutiny of Berlin Garrison, 47–50; Return of Field Armies after Armistice, 74–76; Demobilization of, 76–78; Frontier Guards in the Rhine Districts, 133; Hindenburg's Command, 133.

Army, Revolutionary: New Formations, 128; Cadres of Old Army, 128; Free Corps, 127; Marine Division, Berlin, 127; Republican Guards, Berlin, 128; Augusta Regiment, 128; 174 Lorraine Regiment, 128; Plan of Volunteer People's Army, December 12, 1918, 130; Decree of January 19, 131; Reichswehr, 131, 132; Free Corps of Lettow, Huelsen, Reinhardt, and Lüttwitz, 129, 131; Guard Cavalry Rifle Division, 132; German Defense Division, 132; Land Rifle Corps, 132; Potsdam Free Corps, 132; Strength at Conclusion of Peace, 133; Strength, February 1, 1920, 133.

Atrocities, 154.

Auer, Bavarian Socialist, 139.

August 4, 1914, 61.

August, 8, 1918, 9.

Austria, Republic of, 144–145.

Austria-Hungary, Collapse of, 26.

Austrian Peace Offensive, September, 1918, 21.

Baden, 107.

Belgium, 16, 18.

Bank Strike in Berlin, 137.

Barth, Emil, 19, 29, 46, 73, 84.

Bauer, Colonel, 9, 12.

Bauer, Gustav, 45, 156–157, 165.

Bauer, Cabinet, 156.

Bavaria: Revolutionary Movements since January, 1918, 35–37; Election of January 12, 1919, 107.

Bernstein, Eduard, 68.

Bernstorff, Count, 17, 144.

Beveridge, May, 150.

Bela Kun, 135.

Bell, Minister, 109, 156.

Berlin, Revolt of, November 9, 44–53.

Berlin Conference of November 25, 1918, 83.

Berlin Workmen's and Soldiers' Council: Meeting, November 9, 1918, 52–53; Meeting, November 10, 1918, 80–81; Proclamations, 80, 82; Meeting, November 19, 1918, 81; Conference, November 22, 1918, 82.

Bernstein, Eduard, 11, 70, 146, 157.

Bethmann-Hollweg, Chancellor von, 14, 16, 62–63.

Binding, Professor, 162.

Bismarck, 15, 38, 56, 161–162.

Bloc, Reichstag, 22.